With the author's very best wishes —
Happy reading - happy listening!

Paul Campion

FERRIER
– *A Career Recorded*

Paul Campion

With a Foreword by
Bryn Terfel

A Thames / Elkin Publication
Distribution by Elkin Music

Fully revised second edition published 2005
by Thames Publishing

Distributed by Elkin Music
Wood Green Industrial Estate, Station Road,
Salhouse, Norwich NR13 6NY
Tel: 01603 721302
Web: www.elkinmusic.co.uk

First edition published 1992 by Julia MacRae

ISBN 0 903413 71 X

Type management and design by John Saunders
john@saunderspages.co.uk

Printed and bound in England by Thanet Press Ltd, Union Crescent, Margate, Kent CT9 1NU
Web: www.thanet-press.co.uk

Contents

Foreword by
Bryn Terfel

THE NAME OF KATHLEEN FERRIER still raises strong emotions, even in those who, like me, were not born during her lifetime. More than any other singer of whom I know, Kathleen is remembered today with a telling mixture of joy and sadness; joy for the pleasure that her singing brought, and continues to bring, to many thousands of admirers, and sadness that she died at such a young age.

Her many recordings allow us still to hear Kathleen in her glorious prime and in so much of her favourite repertory. She performed and recorded some of the same music as I do now – the Lieder of Schubert, Schumann, Brahms and Mahler and songs by Britten, Quilter, Gurney, Warlock and Parry. How I would love to have been able to share the platform with her in *Messiah* and *Elijah* because, as her records prove, she sang their alto arias with incomparable radiance and warmth.

The Kathleen Ferrier Singing Awards have now reached their 50th year and that is indeed a cause for rejoicing. Many of the young singers who have taken part in the 'Ferrier' have progressed to great international success, bringing credit not only to their teachers and their own musical dedication, but also to the memory of Kathleen herself. One of the proudest moments of my life was in April 1988, when I had the honour of winning the competition at London's Wigmore Hall. It was my first big break after several years' study at the Guildhall School of Music and Drama, and I have always been truly grateful for the impetus that it gave to my young career.

The new edition of Paul Campion's discography has been published as a celebration of this auspicious 50th anniversary. Its research and writing have clearly been a labour of love and I wish the book, and the Kathleen Ferrier Awards themselves, all possible success, both this year and in the future.

April 2005

For Joshua, Samuel, Alice and William
with love

Introduction

THIS NEW EDITION of *Ferrier – A Career Recorded* is published as a celebration of the 50th anniversary of the Kathleen Ferrier Memorial Scholarship; I warmly thank the Trustees for their encouragement to me on this special occasion and the Administrator, Katie Avey, for updating Winifred Ferrier's original contribution on the history of the Scholarship.

There can be few music lovers who have the good fortune to write a book about a favourite subject – in my case the English contralto Kathleen Ferrier; even fewer are those who receive a second chance and are able to update, improve and correct the first attempt, thirteen years later.

In 1992 I was fortunate indeed in my publisher, Julia MacRae, to whom I remain immensely grateful; her enthusiasm for Ferrier was as great as mine, and she skilfully guided me through the pitfalls of writing a first book. In 2005 it is Richard Elkin of Thames Publishing who has shown similar faith and has helped me to prepare a new edition, in order to reflect the discovery of previously undocumented recordings and the issue of an extraordinarily large number of CDs, from a wide variety of companies, that have appeared over the last decade.

Much of my original introduction below remains unaltered but where necessary it has been amended to suit the changed circumstances of the intervening years.

The first Kathleen Ferrier discography was published in *The Gramophone* in February 1954. Alec Robertson and Andrew Porter reviewed Kathleen's recording career and listed her currently available records. In the issue of January 1955 Andrew Porter corrected errors that had appeared in his earlier list and added some issues which had since been released. In the biography of her sister, *The Life of Kathleen Ferrier*, Winifred Ferrier listed the works that Kathleen regularly performed and indicated which of them had been recorded; she did not include the many issues that have since been released, by both Decca and other companies, such as the Dutch performances of *The Rape of Lucretia*, *Orfeo ed Euridice*, *Kindertotenlieder* and Mahler's *Second Symphony* which had not, at that time, been discovered. These, and other broadcast performances that have been issued since the publication of Winifred's book, were included in a discography compiled by Maurice Leonard for his biography *Kathleen*, published in 1988; but even since then, yet more recordings have been found and released and it has been the discovery of these, and of some others still unpublished, that has made my research so rewarding.

After tracing a number of surviving broadcasts in the BBC Sound Archives* I realised that there might be other unpublished material, not only in the possession of broadcasting organisations for which Kathleen sang in a number of different countries, but also in private hands. So it proved, and a few unique recordings came to light; three Schubert songs accompanied by Britten; Mahler's *Third Symphony* conducted by Boult; *Bist du bei mir* in the Library of Congress in Washington; more recently two broadcast versions (1949 and 1952) of Berkeley's *Four poems of St Teresa of Avila*; *Land of Hope and Glory* from Manchester in 1951; extracts from several BBC broadcasts taken off air by K H Leech and now in the National Sound Archive, including some otherwise unrecorded songs, and part of a 1951 radio recital with Bruno Walter; two tantalisingly short extracts from the first Edinburgh Festival's *Das Lied von der Erde* and two complete versions of the same work, both claiming Vienna on 17 May 1952 as their source, have been 'discovered'. In addition, several recordings documented in this book's first edition have, since 1992, been issued commercially for the first time; these include the 1946 BBC broadcast of *The Rape of Lucretia* (not quite complete); a complete *Das Lied von der Erde* conducted by Bruno Walter in New York in 1948 and yet another conducted by Sir John Barbirolli in 1952; the world prèmiere of Britten's *Spring Symphony* from Amsterdam in July 1949, Brahms' *Alto Rhapsody* from Norway later the same year and a BBC broadcast of Bach's *Mass in B minor* recorded in London in 1951.

Other major developments in the Ferrier discography since 1992 include Dutton's superb re-mastering of Decca's original 78s of *St Matthew Passion*, Pergolesi's *Stabat Mater*, Brahms' *Alto Rhapsody* and the Glyndebourne *Orfeo ed Euridice*, restored at last to its full (but still abridged) extent; Andante's excellently re-mastered *Matthäus-Passion* from Vienna in 1950; Wisp's and Tahra's versions of the 1951 Italian recital (the former issue now apparently unobtainable); Naxos' Brahms and Schumann CD with innovative pitch adjustments by Mark Obert-Thorn; APR's joint recital with Isobel Baillie that offers all of Kathleen's 1944-45 EMI records, including her four test sides; EMI's first CD issue of the complete Dutch *Orfeo ed Euridice*; and Decca's commemorative 2003

Recordings from both the BBC Sound Archives and the National Sound Archive (NSA) may be heard, after giving due notice, at

The British Library National Sound Archive
The British Library
96 Euston Road
London NW1 2DB
Telephone: +44 (0) 20 7412 7676
Email: sound-archive@bl.uk
Website: www.bl.uk/collections/sound-archive/nsa.html

in different parts of the world remain (at the time of writing) unpublished in any form. It should be borne in mind here that, uniquely, *KF 210* refers to two different recordings (of *Das Lied von der Erde*) - see Chapter Seventeen for full details.

Apart from a **KF** number, the following information, where available, has been included for each item:

1. The surname of the composer.

2. The names of the librettist, and the translator of the libretto into the sung language.

3. The title of the item, the name of any larger work from which it comes, and the opus number.

4. The language in which the item is sung.

5. The time, date and place of the recording.

6. The matrix and take number(s) to which the **KF** number refers, with the take number used for issue underlined.

7. The accompanist, conductor, orchestra, choir and other musicians who participated in the recording. Kathleen's name is always omitted here, her presence being understood.

8. In the case of a set of 78 rpm records, the form of presentation is usually shown, with straight and automatic record numbers and coupling order, matched to the appropriate matrix and take numbers.

9. Excerpts from an item (e.g. *KF 114a* or *KF 136c*) are shown after the details of the main item.

10. Question marks indicate that there is doubt about the accuracy of the information. See the relevant text for details.

Checking in 1991, I discovered that, in one quarter year alone, Kathleen's recordings were distributed to the following countries: Australia, Belgium, Canada, Denmark, Germany, Ecuador, Taiwan, France, Greece, UK, Hong Kong, Eire, Israel, Italy, Japan, Korea, the Netherlands, Norway, Portugal, Spain, Sweden, Switzerland, South Africa and the USA; and there was one additional category - the Rest of the World. Thirteen years later the distribution of Kathleen's records has certainly increased. All these recordings were made in the space of a little over eight and a half years, between June 1944 and January 1953. No British classical singer is remembered with such admiration and affection worldwide as is Kathleen; it is our good fortune still to be able to hear her, and to understand why.

I hope that this book will be of interest to everyone who admires Kathleen Ferrier's singing. As well as enabling listeners to check immediately the details of every recording she made, it provides some biographical information, which helps to put those recordings into the larger context of her career; brief pen portraits and the dates of some of her colleagues are now also included.

The publication in 2003 by the Boydell Press of *Letters and Diaries of Kathleen Ferrier* has enabled me to quote more extensively from her surviving correspondence and diaries, which throw a fascinating light on her recorded performances, and on her friendships and professional relationships with a number of colleagues. I am deeply indebted to both Caroline Palmer and the editor Christopher Fifield for permission to quote from their most absorbing book.

During the preparation of *Ferrier – A Career Recorded*, I have tried to verify and double check every item of information; it is inevitable, however, that mistakes have crept in at some stage, and for these I take full responsibility. Any information that readers have, that may clarify, correct or enhance what I have written, will be much appreciated.

Acknowledgements

Very many people helped with my research for the first edition of this book between 1988 and 1991 and I still recall with particular gratitude the following, whose patience with me was astounding: Timothy Day, Curator of Western Art Music at the National Sound Archive, and the staff of the Listening Service; Ruth Edge of EMI Music Archives and her staff; Norma Jones of the Sound Library of the BBC Sound Archives; and John Parry of Decca International. Others whose help was invaluable in providing me with information and encouragement during my early research were: André Achtien, Ann Ayars, Arthur Bannister, Lady Berkeley, Lady Bliss, Alan Blyth (whose interest and encouragement in 1989 prompted an initial approach to my publisher, Julia MacRae), Jesper Buhl, Director of Danacord Records, Bryan Crimp, formerly of EMI, Robert Dearling of *The Guinness Book of Recorded Sound*, Christopher Dyment, Nils Eriksen, Bjørn Granlund and Marit Grimstad of Norsk Rikskringkasting, Oslo, Norway, Dr Howard Ferguson, Walter Foster, Edward Greenfield, William Griffis, Keith Hardwick of EMI, the Earl of Harewood, Roy Henderson, Harald Henrysson of the Swedish National Radio Company, Luuk Hoekstra of the Netherlands Theatre Institute, Amsterdam, J J van Herpen of Hilversum, Barry Irving of *The Gramophone*, Maurice Leonard, Michael Letchford, formerly of Decca, Derek Lewis, BBC Gramophone Librarian, Arthur Luke, Fred Maroth of Music and Arts Programs of America Inc, Edwin M Matthias of the Library of Congress, Washington DC, Don McCormick, Curator, Rodgers and Hammerstein Archives of Recorded Sound, New York Public Library, Bernice Mitchell, of Angel Records, New York, Christopher Pollard, Managing Editor of *The Gramophone*, Geoff Pollock, L Richman of

Rococo Records Ltd, Gordon Rowley, Rosy Runciman, Archivist of Glyndebourne Festival Opera, Patrick Saul, Julia Spencer, John Steane, Joan Taylor, Jon Tolansky of the Music Performance Research Centre, Mrs Dr J van Tongeren of Nederlands Omroepproduktie Bedrijf nv, Hilversum, Jeff Walden of the BBC Written Archives Centre, Caversham, Malcolm Walker, the Librarian and Pam Wheeler of the Britten-Pears Library, Aldeburgh, Suffolk, William Wilcox, Kenneth Wilkinson and Reg Williamson.

Special thanks are due to Bryn Terfel, himself a winner of the Kathleen Ferrier award in 1988, who has generously contributed a Foreword for this new edition. Dame Janet Baker kindly wrote a Foreword for the first edition, retained here without alteration. The help of both these top performers, and the warmth of their appreciation of Kathleen Ferrier's work, has been very much appreciated.

During 2004 a number of the same people have further assisted my research, several of them by now having become good friends; in addition, I have been in close touch with other Ferrier enthusiasts, who have helped me in many ways. Among them must particularly be mentioned John Pickstone of Tasmania, whom I have never met but who, with the wonders of the internet, has helped assemble the increasingly complex discography in Part Two, and has unstintingly advised, assisted and encouraged me over a long period, Roger Beardsley who has prepared the commercial release of the BBC broadcast of *The Rape of Lucretia* on Pearl, Peter Land for his encyclopaedic knowledge of Ferrier facts and recordings, and Derek Pain, who discovered some unique 'new' Ferrier discs and readily made them available for commercial release. I offer my warm thanks to my new publisher, Richard Elkin, of Thames Publishing and to John Saunders, the designer, for invaluable guidance during the preparation of this book.

Others who have advised, and been immensely supportive during this busy year of writing, are:

Sylvia Alexander of the Kathleen Ferrier Society, Julia Aries, Archivist of Glyndebourne Festival Opera, Katie Avey, administrator of the Kathleen Ferrier Memorial Scholarship, BBC Written Archives Centre in Caversham, Lady Barbirolli, Chris Bennett of the Elgar Birthplace Trust, Lady Berkeley, Michael Berkeley, Alan Blyth, Paul Brooks of the Barbirolli Society, Sarah Broughton, Valerie Croft and Suzanne Phillips of Forget About It TV and Films Ltd, Richard Caniell of Guild Historical (Immortal Performances Recorded Music Society), Bryan Crimp of APR, Andrew Dalton, Raymond McGill and Ben Pateman of the Decca Music Group Limited, Timothy Day and Jonathan Summers of the National Sound Archive and their patient colleagues in the Listening Service, the Earl of Harewood, David Heather, Rebecca Hill of Blackburn Museum and Art Gallery for helpful advice and the use of several photographs, James Jolly and Rob Cowan of *The Gramophone*, Ted Kendall, Michael Letchford for reading a late manuscript and advising on textual improvements, Larry Lustig editor of *The Record Collector*, Richard Mangan of the Raymond Mander and Joe Mitchenson Theatre Collection, Don McCormick, Curator of Rodgers & Hammerstein Archives at NYCL for the Performing Arts, Mark Obert-Thorn, James Rattray, Myriam Scherchen of Tahra Records, Anthony Shuttleworth, Barabara Simpson, Professor Robert Souhami, Professor Jeffrey Tobias and Dr Daniel Hochhauser, for their contributions on the Kathleen Ferrier Cancer Fund, and Adrian Yardley. Others not mentioned here have provided help and permission for photographs and illustrative material; these are listed on page xxvi.

Very many other people, I regret too numerous to mention individually, have taken time and trouble to reply to my letters, phone calls and emails; although they were not necessarily able to provide me with new information, their interest and enthusiasm for this project have been very supportive. I thank them all.

Finally, my deepest gratitude is to Winifred Ferrier, who was a close and wonderful friend for twelve years until her death in 1995. She made available to me Kathleen's diaries, correspondence, photograph albums and cuttings books, welcomed me into her home on many occasions, and recalled anecdotes and memories of events which had taken place over forty years earlier. Without such generosity and support the first edition of this book could not have been written – and certainly no second version would have been forthcoming either!

Paul Campion
April 2005

The Kathleen Ferrier Memorial Scholarship
by Winifred Ferrier and Katie Avey

THE PRESTIGIOUS KATHLEEN FERRIER MEMORIAL SCHOLARSHIP competition takes place every year in the spring. It is now open to singers of any nationality who have completed at least one year of study at a UK conservatoire or with a recognised vocal coach in the UK. They must be under 29 years of age at the time of the final auditions.

The auditions usually take place over five days. During the first three days the adjudicators hear all the singers who are eligible and decide on 10 to go forward to the semi-finals, which are held in public at the Wigmore Hall. From these, five are then selected for the final auditions two days later, also held before an audience at the Wigmore. Besides the prestigious First Prize, a second prize and a recital prize are awarded and there is also an accompanist's prize.

Candidates can choose their own programme subject to certain repertoire requirements, which include an aria/song by Bach or Handel, at least one operatic aria and two songs in different languages from the 19th, 20th or 21st century. In the final audition at least one song must be in English and all songs must be sung in their original language. The programmes last a maximum of 20 minutes. The Competition was originally organised by the Secretary of the Royal Philharmonic Society, firstly D Ritson Smith, then Sylvia East and from 1975 to 2002 Shirley Barr. The Administrator is now Katie Avey who meets several times a year with the Trustees to discuss matters concerning the Trust Fund and developments and alterations to the Competition itself. The current Trustees are Paul Strang (Chairman), Sir Thomas Allen CBE, Sheila Armstrong, Valerie Beale, Vernon Ellis, Catherine Goode, Sir Nicholas Goodison, Graham Johnson OBE, Yvonne Kenny AM, Joan Rodgers CBE, John Shirley-Quirk CBE and Martin B Williams.

The Competition attracts a remarkably high standard of singing. It also attracts a dedicated audience of cognoscenti who gather together after the finals in the Bechstein Room at the Wigmore to congratulate singers and to dissect and discuss performances; it has been suggested that a book should be run on the result as everyone has such strong opinions!

All this stemmed from a letter to *The Times* in 1953, suggesting that there should be a musical memorial for Kathleen. An appeal for funds was launched by Sir John Barbirolli, Roy Henderson, Gerald Moore, Sir Malcolm Sargent and Hamish Hamilton, who became Chairman of the Trustees. In September 1954 he published *Kathleen Ferrier – A Memoir*, edited by Neville Cardus, for which five of her closest musical friends each wrote a chapter. The book went into five impressions and all the proceeds from its sale were devoted to the Kathleen Ferrier Memorial Scholarship. Hamish Hamilton was also instrumental in arranging for HRH The Duchess of Kent to become Patron, and she attended both the twenty-fifth anniversary final in 1980 and Kathleen's 'eightieth birthday' commemorative final in 1992. Myers Foggin, too, was involved from the earliest days and took over from Hamish Hamilton as Chairman of the Trustees. Paul Strang became a Trustee in 1978 and later succeeded Myers Foggin as Chairman.

From the beginning the Scholarship Fund was supported by Kathleen's friends and admirers. There have been donations, covenants and legacies which have helped to maintain the prizes at their current level; in particular there were regular donations from the RVW Trust and from Decca by way of a special Prize which ran for twenty-one years from 1978 to 1998. Since 1986 Mrs Lise Rueff Seligman, an enthusiastic follower of Kathleen's, has contributed most generously towards the fund; sadly she died in 2003 but the Competition is indebted to her for her support during this period which, with the addition of an anonymous donation, enabled the Trustees to raise the sum of the First Prize in 1992 to £10,000. Most recently, the fund has been boosted by generous donations from two of the current Trustees; however, still further donations and legacies are vital if the current level of prize-giving is to be maintained.

A great deal of careful preparation goes into making the Competition the foremost event of its kind in the UK, not only behind the scenes by the administration but also by the artists taking part, both singers and their accompanists. A glance at the list of past winners will show that the adjudicators have had a remarkable degree of success in 'getting it right'. It features such names as Margaret Price, Della Jones, Felicity Palmer, Yvonne Kenny, Joan Rodgers, Bryn Terfel, Sarah Fox, Sally Matthews, Jonathan Lemalu and the 2004 winner Kate Royal, to mention just a few.

A notable aspect of the KFMS has been the warmth and dedication that Kathleen's memory has inspired in all those who are involved. This very much came to the fore in 2003, the 50th anniversary of her death, when there were celebrations in Blackburn and a special exhibition was mounted in the Art Gallery there, which attracted visitors from around the world. A documentary film *An Ordinary Diva* was made with contributions from many people who had known Kathleen and had heard her sing, and this was shown to great critical acclaim on BBC 2 and BBC 4; it was subsequently issued as a special double DVD/CD by Decca, including some of Kathleen's most famous recordings, and is currently enjoying great commercial success. 2005 hosts the 50th Competition and there are plans to make it a noteworthy occasion, including this reissue of Paul Campion's book. The Kathleen Ferrier Memorial Scholarship Fund indeed has a great future to look forward to.

Kathleen Ferrier Memorial Scholarship Awards – Winners

Joyce Barker, Elizabeth Simon (1956)

John Mitchinson, Neil Howlett (1957)

Maureen Jones, John Wakefield (1958)

Victor Godfrey, Elizabeth Vaughan (1959)

Elizabeth Harwood, Lorna Elias (1960)

Lorna Haywood, Audrey Deakin (1961)

Robert Bateman, Maureen Keetch (1962)

Janice Chapman, Ann Cooper (1963)

Alfreda Hodgson, Richard Angas (1964)

Sheila Armstrong, Margaret Price (1965)

Malvina Major, Hugh Sheena (1966)

William Elvin (1967)

Gwynneth Griffiths (1968)

Della Jones, Brian Rayner Cook (1969)

Felicity Palmer (1970)

Sandra Browne (1971)

Glyn Davenport (1972)

Linda Esther Gray (1973)

Linda Finnie, Anthony Smith (1974)

Yvonne Kenny (1975)

Keith Lewis (1976)

Lynda Russell (1977)

Jacek Strauch (1978)

Alexander Garden (1979)

Penelope Walker (1980)

Joan Rodgers (1981)

Anne Dawson (1982)

Louise Jackson (1983)

Peter Rose (1985)

Janice Close (1986)

Janice Watson (1987)

Bryn Terfel Jones (1988)

Paul Clarke (1989)

Stephen Gadd (1990)

Mary Plazas (1991)

Gwyn Hughes Jones
Second: Nathan Berg (1992)

Ruby Philogene
Second: Sara Fulgoni (1993)

Susan Gritton
Second: Roderick Williams (1994)

Garry Magee
Second: Lorna Rushton (1995)

Geraldine McGreevy
Second: Alison Buchanan (1996)

Sarah Fox
Joint Second: Felicity Hammond, James Rutherford (1997)

Emma Bell
Second: Andrew Foster (1998)

Sally Matthews
Second: Arlene Rolph (1999)

Gillian Keith
Second: Roland Wood (2000)

Stephanie Marshall
Second: Rachel Nicholls and Lianne-Marie Skriniar (2001)
Song Prize: Lianne-Marie Skriniar
Accompanist's Prize: Christopher Glynn

Karen Cargill and Jonathan Lemalu
> *Joint First and Second Prizes* (2002)
> *Song Prize*: Julianne de Villiers
> *Accompanist's Prize*: Simon Lepper

Wendy Dawn Thompson
> *Second*: Elizabeth Franklin-Kitchen and Robert Murray (2003)
> *Song Prize*: Gudrun Ólafsdóttir
> *Accompanist's Prize*: John Reid

Kate Royal
> *Second*: Andrew Kennedy (2004)
> *Song Prize*: Susanna Andersson
> *Accompanist's Prize*: Annabel Thwaite

Anna Stéphany
> *Second*: Lucy Crowe (2005)
> *Song Prize*: Andrew Staples
> *Accompanist's Prize*: Jonathan Beatty

Decca – Kathleen Ferrier Prize Winners

Decca Prize awarded as second prize from 1978-1991 and third prize from 1992 to 1999.

Jacek Strauch (1978)	William Dazeley (1989)
Lesley Garrett (1979)	Alison Hudson (1990)
Stewart Buchanan (1980)	Jane Irwin (1991)
Brian Scott (1981)	Alice Coote (1992)
Matthew Best (1982)	Ruth Peel (1993)
Carol Smith (1983)	Catrin Wyn Davies (1994)
Susan Bullock (1984)	Kerrie Sheppard (1995)
Judith Howarth (1985)	Konrad Jarnot (1996)
Alastair Miles (1986)	Matthew Hargreaves (1997)
Elizabeth McCormack (1987)	Mark Stone (1998)
Amanda Roocroft (1988)	Richard Burkhard (1999)

Other Award Winners

The Baroness Ravensdale Prize

Helen Kucharek (1982)	Ian Platt (1984)	Jane Webster (1986)

Jury's Prize

Timothy Wilson (1985)

Third Prize

Bethan Dudley (1989)	David Mattinson (1990)	Gail Pearson (1991)

The Kathleen Ferrier Cancer Research Fund

by Winifred Ferrier, with contributions from Professor Robert Souhami, Professor Jeffrey Tobias and Dr Daniel Hochhauser

DURING THE LAST TWO YEARS OF HER LIFE Kathleen had radiotherapy whenever it became necessary, under the care of Dr Gwen Hilton and her assistants at University College Hospital. Great pains were taken to ensure that Kathleen was able to continue singing and to do an amazing amount, despite the treatment. She travelled in this country and overseas, giving recitals, taking part in oratorio and opera and making a series of incomparable recordings.

Kathleen was so grateful for all the skill and care lavished on her at University College Hospital that she intended to give a concert for the funds of the Radiotherapy Department. Unfortunately this was never possible. So, after her death, it was decided to establish a cancer fund in her name. An appeal was launched by Hamish Hamilton, Sir John Barbirolli, Sir Laurence Olivier, Dame Myra Hess, Sir Benjamin Ormerod and Dr Bruno Walter. The response was astounding. Amounts of money came in, large and small. The Hallé Orchestra gave a concert conducted jointly by Dr Bruno Walter and Sir John Barbirolli, and from this and many other sources the money to establish firmly a Kathleen Ferrier Cancer Fund at University College Hospital was raised. Many subsequent donations have been made to the Fund and the royalties from some of Kathleen's recordings have been dedicated specifically to this purpose.

Dr Nicholas Godlee succeeded Dr Gwen Hilton as Director of the Department, and in 1993, shortly before it merged with its much larger counterpart at the Middlesex Hospital, Professor Jeffrey Tobias was invited to become the first Clinical Director of the joint Department – a post he held until 1997. Since the merger there has been a major expansion, with over twice the number of consultants offering a comprehensive service to patients. The radiotherapy equipment and support facilities now available are particularly valuable for children and adolescent patients with rare cancers, including those from Great Ormond Street Children's Hospital. Exciting research continues in many aspects of cancer treatment and the department has been successful in bidding for additional input from Cancer Research UK, now Britain's largest public charity. A fully staffed clinical trials centre has been inaugurated to develop and implement new studies in a whole range of cancers, in order to produce better ideas and treatment outcomes with novel drugs or other new approaches.

In 1987 the Trustees of the Kathleen Ferrier Cancer Research Fund and the Administrators of London University founded a Kathleen Ferrier Chair of Clinical Research. Dr R L Souhami, who was appointed as the first Professor, writes:

'Following the endowment of the Kathleen Ferrier Chair in 1987, new research laboratories were established in the Courtauld Institute in 1988. These laboratories have housed teams of investigators, who have had particular interest in the way in which anti-cancer drugs react with DNA. The department expanded considerably during the 1990s since when the Department of Cancer Medicine has joined with that at the Royal Free Hospital in Hampstead, close to Kathleen's home in Frognal Mansions; this was part of the amalgamation of the Medical School at University College with that of the Royal Free, a beneficial move that has led to greatly expanded research capability.

'At the clinical level, the endowment of the Chair was followed quickly by the establishment of a ten-bedded ward which was especially designed for the care of adolescents with cancer – the first of its kind in the UK. The next, and largest, development will be the opening of the new University College Hospital on the Gower Street site, which will expand clinical facilities for the treatment of patients and provide a first-class environment.

'Throughout this period, the Kathleen Ferrier Chair has been a focal point of the clinical and laboratory cancer research at University College, London. It is a particular pleasure for me, as the first holder of the Chair, to go every year to the concert given by the winner of the Kathleen Ferrier prize. Win Ferrier came to my inaugural lecture, and I came to know her quite well. I know she would be delighted with the way in which the department that treated Kathleen over fifty years ago has expanded and developed both in the care of patients, and in research into causes and treatments of cancer.'

In 2002 Dr Daniel Hochhauser was appointed to the position of Kathleen Ferrier Reader in Medical Oncology at the Royal Free and University College London Medical School. Funding for his research programme has been obtained from several sources and a key collaboration has been with Professor John Hartley who started his work at the Middlesex Hospital in close co-operation with Professor Souhami. Dr Hochhauser also recalls a valued family connection:

'The Kathleen Ferrier endowment forms a critical node in the integration of academic cancer research and we will be continuing in the traditions of Professor Souhami in strengthening the research output of our group. I am also particularly glad to be holding the Kathleen Ferrier Readership in view of the fact that my father – Victor Hochhauser – was the impresario who presented Kathleen Ferrier on many occasions at the Royal Albert Hall over fifty years ago.'

The Kathleen Ferrier Archive

by Rebecca Hill, Keeper of Art at Blackburn Museum and Art Gallery

THROUGHOUT HER ADULT LIFE Kathleen Ferrier's sister Winifred collected press cuttings, photographs and records relating to the life and career of her beloved sister. Together with Kathleen's letters and diaries, the collection formed a fascinating archive. Following Winifred's death in 1995 the archive was given to the joint custody of the Kathleen Ferrier Society and Blackburn Museum and Art Gallery.

Winifred Ferrier also bequeathed money to maintain and promote the archive. This has made possible the purchase of high quality archival boxes in which the archive is now stored. It has enabled us to acquire a number of items which have recently appeared, such as a copy of the programme from the final performance of *Orpheus* at the Royal Opera House in 1953.

In addition to this we are very grateful to the Kathleen Ferrier Society members who have donated items over past years, in particular John Hart. Mr Hart has donated to the archive an entire set of all available recordings in CD format, having tirelessly sourced a comprehensive collection including a number of rarities.

Blackburn Museum and Art Gallery are pleased and proud to house the archive. We have on permanent display a small selection of memorabilia relating to Blackburn's most famous daughter. The rest of the archive is kept in storage, and is available to view by appointment.

For further details please contact:

> Blackburn Museum and Art Gallery
> Museum Street
> Blackburn
> BB1 7AJ
>
> Tel: +44 (0)1254 667130
> Fax: +44 (0)1254 685541
> Email: museum@blackburn.gov.uk

The Kathleen Ferrier Society
by Sylvia Alexander, Joint Chairman

1993 WAS THE 40TH ANNIVERSARY of the death of Kathleen Ferrier. Out of the renewed interest in one of England's greatest singers sprang the Kathleen Ferrier Society. Kathleen's sister, Winifred, was still alive and was delighted to become the first President of the Society. In 1996, after Winifred's death, international soprano Sheila Armstrong (a former Memorial Scholarship winner) was invited to become the second President; she has proved to be devoted and supportive in the role and takes a great interest in the progress and careers of the singers who take part in the Bursary Competitions.

The Kathleen Ferrier Society exists to provide an information service, to award bursaries to young singers, to collect memorabilia for the Blackburn Museum Archives, to send newsletters to members and to raise money for the Kathleen Ferrier Cancer Research Fund. The Society has more than 200 members, drawn from the United Kingdom and fifteen other countries as far away as Australia and New Zealand. In the first ten years, three residential weekends were held, major ones being the Launch Weekend in 1993 and the 50th Anniversary Celebration Weekend held in October 2003. Plans have been made to hold an annual mini-weekend to coincide with the Bursary for Young Singers, which takes place on the last Sunday in October in Blackburn, where Kathleen Ferrier lived for twenty years from the age of two. The first such mini-weekend was held in 2004.

The Bursary for Young Singers is open to vocal students just beginning their second year of study at each of the eight major Music Colleges in England, Scotland and Wales. Each college sends two singers who present a varied programme of no more than 20 minutes. The winner receives a bursary of £3,000 spread over three years. Owing to the generosity of Winifred and two major donors, the Society, which is a charity, has maintained the level of the bursary and, indeed, through the continued generosity of members, has been able to present second and third awards in 2003 and a second prize in 2004.

The Society was overwhelmed by the amazing response to the 50th anniversary of Kathleen's death; a flood of letters, telephone calls and emails came from many people who still cherish memories of her. The Society can step out into the next 50 years supported by the knowledge that Kathleen Ferrier's unique voice and warm personality are still greatly loved.

Kathleen Ferrier Society contacts:

Sylvia Alexander   Joint Chairman Telephone: +44 (0) 1254 262293
    Email: esa@freenet.co.uk

Robert Langstaff   Joint Chairman Telephone: +44 (0) 1625 573761
    Email: evenwood@tiscali.co.uk

Shirley Parker   Treasurer   Telephone: +44 (0) 1254 202069
    Email: parker92055@aol.com

PAST WINNERS OF THE KATHLEEN FERRIER SOCIETY BURSARY

Year	Name	School	Voice
1996	Elliott Goldie	(Guildhall School of Music and Drama)	Tenor
1997	Rory O'Connor	(Royal Academy of Music)	Tenor
1998	Clint van der Linde	(Royal College of Music)	Countertenor
1999	William Berger	(Royal Academy of Music)	Baritone
2000	Simona Mihai	(Royal College of Music)	Soprano
2001	Fflur Wyn	(Royal Academy of Music)	Soprano
2002	Nicky Spence	(Guildhall School of Music and Drama)	Tenor
2003	Sophie Bevan	(Royal College of Music)	Soprano
	Second and Third prizes shared by Ben Johnson (RCM)		Tenor
	and Njabulo Madlala (GSMD)		Baritone
2004	Rhydian Roberts	(Birmingham Conservatoire)	Tenor
	Second prize winner David Thaxton (Royal Welsh College)		Baritone

Illustration Sources and Credits

We acknowledge the following with thanks:
Page

2. Decca
5. EMI
9. Tassell/Winifred Ferrier
12. EMI
13. Author's collection
15. Radio Times
16. Author's collection
17. John Vickers/Roy Henderson
18. EMI
21. William Parsons/Joan Taylor
24. Royal College of Music (Boyd Neel)
24. Peter Land (Test pressing)
25. Winifred Ferrier
27. Author's collection
28. Hulton-Deutsch Collection
30. Roger Beardsley/The Earl of Harewood
32. Radio Times
37. Anefo, Amsterdam/Winifred Ferrier
38. Winifred Ferrier
39. Covent Garden Books
41. Reeves, Lewes/Author's collection
47. Bath Evening Chronicle
49. Decca
52. Norward Inglis/Barbara Simpson
53. Roger Beardsley/Derek Pain
56. BBC Written Archive Centre, Caversham
59. König/Hulton-Deutsch Collection
61. Fayer, Vienna/Decca
64. Norward Inglis/Blackburn Museum and Art Gallery
67. BBC/Royal College of Music (Lennox Berkeley)
67. BBC Written Archive Centre, Caversham (BBC confirmation)
71. Roger Beardsley/Derek Pain
73. Decca
75. Author's collection
78. Author's collection (Programme)
78. Woburn Studios Ltd/Author's collection (Royal Albert Hall)
82. Decca
87. Particam Pictures, Amsterdam
88. Norward Inglis/Barbara Simpson
97. Little Beat Records/Archives, Denmark
99. Blackburn Museum and Art Gallery
103. Kemsley House, Glasgow/Winifred Ferrier
107. Radio Times
109. Roger Beardsley/Derek Pain
117. Erich Auerbach/EMI
120. Angus McBean/EMI
125. Winifred Ferrier
128. Reg Wilson/EMI
137. Anefo, Amsterdam
139. Author's collection (Concertgebouw)
139. Author's collection (Jo Vincent)
142. Michael Letchford
146. Winifred Ferrier
150. Winifred Ferrier
152. Nottingham Evening Post/Blackburn Museum and Art Gallery
155. Author's collection
156. Author's collection
170. Decca
171. Author's collection
180. Dr Howard Ferguson (Howard Ferguson)
180. Vaughan-Spencer/Boosey & Hawkes (Edmund Rubbra)
180. Colin G Futcher/Jill Wordsworth (William Wordsworth)
190/1. David Heather
192. Nederlandse Omroep Stichting
198. Houston Rogers/Decca

The following companies' record and CD booklet covers have also been used as illustrations, with thanks:

APR, BBC Artium, BBC Legends, Danacord, Decca, Dutton, EMI, Foyer, London, Music & Arts, Naxos and Tahra.

We thank all those photographers whose work we have been unable to identify individually.

Foreword to the First Edition by
Dame Janet Baker

I WAS TALKING WITH A GROUP OF YOUNG SINGERS the other day and asked them during our conversation what Kathleen Ferrier meant to them. One, a true contralto (rare bird!), immediately began to speak in the most passionate and vivid terms about her memories of being brought up with the sound of her mother's Ferrier records, and told us how totally overwhelmed she had been by Kathleen's glorious voice; she had decided to develop her own gift and to study the same repertoire as a direct result of Ferrier's artistry. It was fascinating to see the depth of feeling and the adoration this young student held for a performer who could only be known to her through the medium of recording but who, nevertheless, had been inspired by her to a marked degree.

There has been another indication during the past few months of the effect Kathleen Ferrier's work had on someone who did know her performances from personal experience, and who loved them so much that as a result of this devotion a truly enormous gift has been made to the memorial prize fund, a gift so magnificent that the prize has now become one of the most valuable in the world. Two reactions from people separated by a large gap in age, but which reflect unmistakably the power this beloved performer has had, and still has, over the hearts of those who hear her.

Paul Campion's book sets out in the clearest terms to show us not only the extent and variation of Kathleen's recording career, but also makes it blindingly obvious to us the miracle she achieved in the very brief time she was allowed to develop it. We must just feel grateful to destiny, as in the case of Mozart, that she was spared to the world long enough for this legacy to be created. Although I never met her, I feel I knew her; I expect many of us share that. As a fellow Northerner, I like to imagine that if, as a young singer, I had ever shared the same platform with her, we would have had much in common. I'm quite sure we would have laughed a lot.

January 1992

On Recording

'Miss Ferrier first recorded for Columbia and is now with Decca. Like many highly-strung artists she finds recording "the most difficult thing under the sun. If you sing a song at a concert there are always snags, but they are surmounted. But when the same song has to be sung over and over again, the snags increase. A breath held too long, the anxiety of singing quietly, then sometimes the roughness which creeps momentarily into the voice through dryness and which, when recorded, sounds like a foot scraped over a floor. But to hear a record made by yourself is the best and most salutary lesson one can have, even if it is also the most depressing. One listens technically, not as one would listen to an ordinary singer. And the second listening is worse than the first. With the first comes a feeling of relief at having got through the song, and that perhaps it is not so bad as one thought it was going to be. But recording is now easier, with the introduction of the tape, than it was, and at least one can now decide at a session whether or not the record can be passed. But whatever the record, when I hear it in my own home, I always wish that I could have done it once more! Perhaps the best record I have made is the Brahms *Alto Rhapsody* [with Krauss]. It was recorded in a large hall and my voice floated out naturally. One or two passages in the *St Matthew Passion* [with Jacques] aren't too bad! I think the folk songs I have recorded, particularly the unaccompanied *Blow the wind southerly* and *The keel row* are good." '

Kathleen Ferrier in conversation with W S Meadmore in *The Gramophone*, March 1951

Part I
THE CAREER

Chapter One
January–June 1944

10.30am on 30.6.44
EMI Studio 3, Abbey Road

KF 1 **GLUCK**/Calzabigi (translated)
What is life? (Orpheus and Euridice)/English
Piano: Gerald Moore
Matrix 2EA 10249-<u>1</u>

KF 2 **BRAHMS**/Reinick (translated)
Constancy (Liebestreu), Op. 3, No 1/English
Piano: Gerald Moore
Matrix 0EA 10250-<u>1</u>

KF 3 **BRAHMS**/Traditional (translated)
Sweetheart (Feinsliebchen)/English
(No 12 of *49 Deutsche Volkslieder*)
Piano: Gerald Moore
Matrix 0EA 10251-<u>1</u>

KF 4 **ELGAR**/Cardinal Newman
My work is done ... to ... *earth to Heaven*, and
It is because ... to ... *the agony*
(*The Dream of Gerontius Op. 38*)/English
Piano: Gerald Moore
Matrix 2EA 10252-<u>1</u>

Kathleen Ferrier's recording career was due to have begun earlier than it did. The archives show that, at 1pm on 19 May 1944, she was booked to record a test session, with Gerald Moore as her accompanist, at EMI's Abbey Road Studios in St John's Wood, London. It is not noted why the booking was postponed, but Kathleen's diary reveals that the previous day she was broadcasting in Manchester and the following day she was singing in Swansea – typical of the pressure of the work that she was already undertaking. Neither is it known what was to have been recorded on that occasion; but at 10.30am on Friday 30 June the two musicians *did* meet at Abbey Road, Studio 3, and made four titles. Those

3

four recordings were allocated HMV matrix numbers, not Columbia numbers, as Bryan Crimp explains below; it was for Columbia that Kathleen's first *issued* 78s were made. The prefixes '2EA' and '0EA' refer to the diameter of the matrices – 12" and 10" respectively.

These test records, then, were never published as 78s, and were first released in 1978, when they formed a substantial part of an EMI LP, *Great British Mezzo-Sopranos and Contraltos*. They first appeared on CD in 1997, included in a delightful joint recital with Isobel Baillie, based on Columbia 78s made between 1941 and 1945, issued by APR – duets and solos sung by two great ladies of the concert platform.

Bryan Crimp, Product Manager, EMI Records (UK) in 1978, re-discovered these tests in the company's archives, and here recalls the background to his find:

'There are, of course, many reasons why 78rpm matrices remain unpublished; perhaps an interpretative shortcoming, a minor technical fluff (which invariably assumes an irritating significance on repeated hearings) or even a recording fault. In most instances these matrices are destroyed and the title scheduled for re-recording at a later date. Fifty or more years on, these matrices are occasionally discovered, serendipitous survivors of managerial oversight. Surviving matrices of test recordings are an even rarer breed. As the name implies, these were experimental recordings, usually made to determine an artist's presence and capability in front of a microphone or to secure a correct balance between soloist and accompaniment.

'Walter Legge, EMI's recording producer, obviously impressed by the potent mix of radiant innocence and melting naivety, allied to a natural, God-given voice he discovered in the young singer fresh to London, decreed these tests should, to use EMI's terminology of the time, be 'held' rather than "destroyed". His decision is nevertheless surprising given that there was not the remotest chance of a commercial release for the two 12" matrices: with the Elgar matrix comprising two unconnected, "suspended" fragments, the Gluck aria was left without a coupling and so consigned to limbo. The two Brahms songs could have been released as a 'domestic' Columbia 10" disc though there appears to have been no intention on EMI's part to do so.

'The supposition that Legge recorded the Elgar extracts because he was then preparing for the British Council-sponsored première complete recording of *The Dream of Gerontius* conducted by Malcolm Sargent (recorded in April 1945) is a strong one. Indeed, if Legge had not offended Ferrier by his notorious womanising during one taxi ride with her, it is more than conceivable that this recording of *Gerontius*, released just two months after recording, would have boasted Ferrier's Angel alongside Heddle Nash's searing Gerontius, rather than the underwhelming Gladys

Recording sheet from KF's first test session, 30 June 1944

THE GRAMOPHONE CO. LTD., HAYES, MIDDX.
TECHNICAL RECORDING DEPARTMENT.

The following Selection was made on __30th **June** 1944__ at _____ Abbey Rd.

Matrix No. (and Recording Mark.)	Red Form No. _____
	Listed Record No. _____
Size	12"
	Date Issued _____
Category	Vocal — COMMERCIAL TEST Wear Test Report _____
Title	MissKathleen Ferrier
	with Gerald Moore at the Piano
Artist ... ... (In the case of Dance Band or similar recording state if with vocal refrain.)	
Subject to Artist's Royalty (If more than one artist, state names and proportion payable to each.)	2EA 10249 –1 Have I lost thee"Orfeo" (Gluck)
Language of Text	2EA 10252 –1 Angel's Address "Gerontius" (Newman/Elgar)
† Accompaniment (see footnote) (State name of Orchestra or Accompanist.)	OEA 10250 –1 Constancy (Brahms)
	OEA 10251 –1 Feinsliebchen (Brahms)
† Conductor (see footnote)	

Ripley. Indeed, Ferrier only honoured her Columbia contract by persuading Isobel Baillie to join her in duet recordings. Baillie was never to forget Ferrier's earthy invective against Legge: "I'm certainly not going to give that bugger any solo material."

'That these "tests" were given HMV matrix numbers, although Ferrier became a contracted Columbia artist, is of little significance. EMI usually designated HMV matrix numbers for their tests. It was only after an artist had been accepted that they would be assigned to HMV, Columbia or another affiliated label.'

These four titles give an indication of the repertoire that Kathleen was developing: Brahms songs (sung here in English, as much German music was at that time) were to play a very important part in her career. Among her surviving recordings, there are more individual works by Brahms than any other composer. *Feinsliebchen* or *Sweetheart* is usually referred to in Kathleen's diary by its opening words – *Nay, why go barefoot?* ; she seems to have dropped it from her repertoire after 1946. Gluck's *What is life?* (also sung in English) was effectively to become Kathleen's theme song. Six versions of her singing this have survived, more than any other individual song or aria (though recent CD issues and further rumours indicate that Mahler's complete *Das Lied von der Erde* may now equal that number; see Chapter Seventeen). This *What is life?* is in no way comparable with her later interpretations of the aria; it lacks tension and dramatic interest and Kathleen avoids the two climactic top Fs.

The two brief excerpts from Elgar's *The Dream of Gerontius*, both recorded on a single 12" wax are, as Crimp acknowledges, particularly interesting. Although the Angel was to become one of Kathleen's finest roles, and one in which she was greatly acclaimed, she never recorded any further music from the oratorio. The second excerpt, beginning *It is because ...* stops suddenly, ending with the words *... the agony*, almost as if a silent signal had been given – 'Thank you, we'll let you know ... ' Her first public performance of the work was apparently in Newcastle upon Tyne just three months earlier, on 26 March, and although in later years Kathleen sang works by Elgar such as *The Apostles*, *The Kingdom*, *Sea Pictures* and *The Music Makers*, these *Gerontius* fragments, together with the incomplete *Land of Hope and Glory* from Manchester in 1951, remain her only Elgar recordings.

Making records during those June days of 1944 was a hazardous occupation. Earlier in the month, the first of the pilotless V1 flying bombs had been launched against Britain from occupied Europe, and to spend time in a soundproofed recording studio must have been an unnerving experience for any musician, so near to the centre of the capital. Indeed, just three hours after these sides were recorded, two such V1 incidents caused considerable loss of life in the West End of London, only a short distance from the studio; terrible times indeed.

Kathleen's four EMI sessions, held between June 1944 and September 1945, were her only fruitful visits to those famous premises at 3 Abbey Road. Still used extensively today, their history goes back to November 1931 when a stuccoed Victorian villa was extended to create a group of studios of various sizes, and they have since been the venue for some of the world's most famous recordings. The photograph of Elgar and the young Yehudi Menuhin at the main entrance, taken after their celebrated 1932 sessions for the composer's *Violin Concerto*, is almost as evocative as that of the Beatles crossing the street on the 1969 *Abbey Road* album – their final collaboration. Abbey Road has now developed as probably the most technically advanced recording complex in the world and remains a byword for sound recording of the highest quality.

Entirely appropriately, then, the sound quality of these four test sides of Kathleen's is excellently clear, and almost entirely free from surface noise – thanks, surely, to Bryan Crimp's use of vinyl in pressing the transfer copies.

The recording producer for this session was Walter Legge.

Chapter Two
July–December 1944

KF 6 **GREENE** (arranged by Roper)/The Bible
I will lay me down in peace
(from the anthem *O God of righteousness*)/English
Piano: Gerald Moore
Matrix CA 19599-1-2

KF 7 **GREENE** (arranged by Roper)/The Bible
O praise the Lord
(from the anthem *Praise the Lord, O my soul*)/English
Piano: Gerald Moore
Matrix CA 19600-1-2

Another commercial test session was booked at Abbey Road, again with Moore, for 3.15pm on 25 September. As Kathleen had already recorded four test sides in June, it might seem puzzling as to why it was thought necessary to make more. Indeed, the session may never have taken place; no recordings from it have survived, and apart from an official memo in the archives, no other reference has been traced at EMI.

But two interesting entries in Kathleen's diary are relevant here. That for 25 September itself notes a lunchtime meeting with her teacher and colleague Roy Henderson, with the word *Gerontius* written next to the time of 3.15pm. Perhaps Legge still had hopes of finding his Angel in Kathleen and planned (in vain) to record further excerpts with her on this occasion. Even more enigmatic is the entry for the following day – 26 September – marked simply 'Decca 2pm'. Was Kathleen, even at this stage of her recording career, considering moving to Decca? Had an early meeting already been booked? Perhaps Henderson had been discussing the matter with her at the previous day's lunch. Whatever, it was fifteen months before her first Decca recording was made, but perhaps the first idea of a forthcoming change of company was already in her mind.

Exactly three months to the day after Kathleen first visited Studio 3, she returned to record what proved to be her first published 78rpm record.

This time she was recorded on Columbia matrices, and all her commercial recordings were on that label until she transferred to Decca in February 1946. The Columbia matrix prefix CA indicates a 10″ disc; the prefix CAX, used for her recording session the following April, refers to a 12″ disc.

Two excerpts from anthems by the London-born composer and organist Maurice Greene had been selected for this session, which took place at 2.30pm on 30 September, with Gerald Moore again at the piano. Kathleen had first met Moore in 1943; he was by then a most celebrated accompanist, who had for nearly twenty years worked with many of the world's finest singers and instrumentalists, and Kathleen was in some awe of him. As their musical partnership developed, they became great friends and performed frequently together, giving recitals in London and around the British Isles, at the Edinburgh Festival, in the Netherlands, France and Germany. Their shared sense of humour was a great support on many tiring tours and Moore, with his wife Enid, became very close to Kathleen and her family circle. All of their joint recordings, with one exception, are from Kathleen's short time as an EMI artist. After Kathleen's death Moore took a keen interest in the Memorial Scholarship founded in her name and he died at the grand age of eighty-eight in 1987, remembered still as the doyen of accompanists.

These extracts by Greene appear to achieve no mention either in Kathleen's diary or her correspondence. Were they in her regular repertoire or did she, perhaps, learn them specifically for the recording? At least *The Gramophone* magazine, reviewing this record in November 1944, approved of the results: 'This young singer has already won golden opinions and should gain another for having the courage to make her first appearance on records in little known music. Kathleen Ferrier possesses a sense of the value of words: being perhaps rather too near the microphone, her tone in the vigorous *O praise the Lord* has a little edge on it which does not really belong to the voice.' Subsequent EMI reissues of the record have removed the artificial edge, and restored the true timbre of Kathleen's voice.

Two hours after the session was completed, Kathleen was travelling again, this time by a late train to Crewe, where she was singing the next day in a joint recital with the bass Norman Lumsden.

The recording producer for this session was Walter Legge.

Chapter Three
January–June 1945

2.30pm on 20.4.45
EMI Studio 3, Abbey Road

KF 11 **HANDEL**/N. Haym (translated by Arthur Somervell)
Spring is coming (*Ottone*)/English
Piano: Gerald Moore
Matrix CAX 9276-1-2

KF 12 **HANDEL**/N. Haym (translated by Arthur Somervell)
Come to me, soothing sleep (*Ottone*)/English
Piano: Gerald Moore
Matrix CAX 9277-1-2-3

After the critical approval of her first published record, Kathleen was invited to make more sides for Columbia in the spring of 1945. The studio

*A recital in Carlisle
with Gerald Moore*

was booked for 6 March, when she and Gerald Moore were scheduled to record two Brahms songs, *Sapphic Ode* and *May Night*, both apparently in English; but the session was postponed, presumably at short notice, as EMI archives report that it was too late to prevent Moore attending the studios. It is tempting to wonder if he still required his fee. The same Brahms items were rescheduled for 20 April 1945, but even then they were not recorded, as two Handel arias were substituted. *Sapphic Ode* was eventually recorded, but not until December 1949, for Decca, when it was sung in German. *May Night* never was.

The two arias that *were* performed are from Handel's opera *Ottone*, sung in a spurious English translation by Arthur Somervell; both featured regularly in recitals at that stage of Kathleen's career and continued to be programmed (on some occasions together, on others separately) until 1952.

Winifred Ferrier remembered hearing the original copy of the 12" 78 with Kathleen: 'She laughed at the way she had over-emphasised the words "Spring is coming" and said, "With some arm movements, it would make a nice little jazz number," and proceeded to show us how it would go!'

The recording producer for this session was Walter Legge.

Chapter Four
July–December 1945

2.30pm on 21.9.45
EMI Studio 3, Abbey Road

KF 16 **PURCELL**/? Tate
Sound the trumpet
(*Come ye sons of art away* – extract from *The Ode for Queen Mary*)/English
Piano: Gerald Moore, Soprano: Isobel Baillie
Matrix CA 19861-1-2

KF 17 **PURCELL**/Dryden and Howard
Let us wander (*The Indian Queen*)/English
Piano: Gerald Moore, Soprano: Isobel Baillie
Matrix CA 19862-1-2

KF 18 **PURCELL**/Dryden
Shepherd, leave decoying (*King Arthur*)/English
Piano: Gerald Moore, Soprano: Isobel Baillie
Matrix CA 19862-1-2

KF 19 **MENDELSSOHN** /Heine (translated)
I would that my love, Op. 63, No. I/English
Piano: Gerald Moore, Soprano: Isobel Baillie
Matrix CA 19863-1

KF 20 **MENDELSSOHN**/Eichendorff (translated)
Greeting, Op. 63, No. 3/English
Piano: Gerald Moore, Soprano: Isobel Baillie
Matrix CA 19864-1-2

KF 21 **MENDELSSOHN**/Burns
O wert thou in the cauld blast? Op. 63, No. 5/Scottish
Piano: Gerald Moore, Soprano: Isobel Baillie
? Sung as a solo by Isobel Baillie
Never issued/Destroyed
Matrix CA 19865-1

KF 22 TRADITIONAL

Turn ye to me/English
? Piano: Gerald Moore, Soprano: Isobel Baillie
Never issued/Destroyed
Matrix CA 19866-1

Kathleen was becoming increasingly disillusioned at Columbia, and did not enjoy a good relationship with Walter Legge, finding his attentions rather more personal than she cared for; his two wives, however, were both valued colleagues. The first was Nancy Evans, whom Kathleen had already known for about a year, and to whom she was to become even closer when they both sang at Glyndebourne in 1946; (it was at this time, too, that Nancy got to know her second husband, Eric Crozier, the producer of *The Rape of Lucretia*); the second Mrs Legge – soprano Elisabeth Schwarzkopf – knew Kathleen but briefly, appearing together, according to Dame Elisabeth, in just a handful of performances in Vienna, Milan and Manchester.

Isobel Baillie (left) and Kathleen Ferrier, whose delightful Mendelssohn duets form an important issue for November.

ISOBEL BAILLIE (Soprano) and
KATHLEEN FERRIER (Contralto)
With Gerald Moore at the Piano

I WOULD THAT MY LOVE (Music, Mendelssohn ; Words, Heine) ....
GREETING (Mendelssohn)..............**DB2194●**

MENDELSSOHN WAS successful with practically every form of musical composition except opera. He was one of the few composers of the classical school whose music became universally popular during his lifetime, although he lived for only 38 years, and his early death created a profound sensation throughout Europe, so wide had been the appeal of his music.
Now, nearly a hundred years afterwards, much of the vast output is forgotten, and this delightful record by Isobel Baillie and Kathleen Ferrier may well lead to a revival in interest in

Mendelssohn part songs. They are charming and have a lovely melodic flow. No wonder they were popular in the Victorian drawing rooms! To anyone with an ear for melody they are quite irresistible.

*Columbia catalogue
publicity, November 1945*

Isobel Baillie

After deciding to make no more solo records for Columbia, but needing to fulfil her contract, Kathleen asked Isobel Baillie to sing some duets with her, which Baillie agreed to do. Kathleen did not want to risk recording important solo material in her last session for Legge, knowing that Decca, the recording company she had decided to join, would give her the opportunity to sing some of her best concert and oratorio pieces. Kathleen and Isobel Baillie (1895-1983) first sang together in December 1941, in a performance of *Messiah*, but many years earlier than that, when Kathleen's principal musical interest had been the piano, she had acted as Baillie's accompanist at one of the soprano's recitals in the north of England. The two singers gave many performances together, and were much in demand as soloists in concerts and oratorios, but they were not close friends; mutual admiration, rather than affection, might fairly describe their working relationship.

Three duets by Purcell, three by Mendelssohn, and one traditional song were recorded in Studio 3 on 21 September 1945; in the event, two of the sides were never issued, and no copies of them appear to have survived. Although it is a duet, the recording sheet for *0 wert thou in the cauld blast?* names Baillie only, with Moore as the accompanist; and, again according to the sheet, the duet *Turn ye to me* may have been sung unaccompanied, as Moore is not mentioned. Copies of the music of both songs were in Kathleen's collection (now in Blackburn Museum), written in her own hand, perhaps prepared specifically for this session. Unless test pressings are found, it cannot be confirmed exactly how the works were performed.

The Purcell duets are short: indeed, there is space for two of them on one side of a 10" record. *Let us wander* was originally a duet for two sopranos with chorus entitled *We the spirits of the air*, and is performed here in an arrangement by Moffat. *Shepherd, leave decoying*, which follows *Let us wander* on the 78 side, was included in, but not listed on, the 1988 EMI Références CD which contains of most of Kathleen's EMI recordings. It is to be found at Index number 11 on CDH 761003 2, and follows *Let us wander*.

Of the issued Mendelssohn duets *I would that my love* is the better known, but *Greeting* is no less charming. That made all the more regrettable its omission from the above-mentioned CD of Kathleen's Columbia recordings. There was sufficient space for it, as the total time for the CD as issued was only 72'04. Happily, on EMI's 1999 release CDM 566911 2, *Greeting* is restored; this duet was also included on an EMI LP in February 1967, as part of a tribute to Gerald Moore, around the time of his retirement from the concert platform.

These two issued 10" records with Baillie mark the end of Kathleen's contract with EMI, but they were not the last records she was to make for the company. As we shall see, in 1949 she was temporarily released by Decca to record Mahler's *Kindertotenlieder* with the Vienna Philharmonic under Bruno Walter, and that performance, in due course, also appeared on the Columbia label.

The recording producer for this session was Walter Legge, and the balance engineer Arthur Clarke.

7.45pm-9.00pm on 7.11.45
BBC Maida Vale Studio 1, West London

KF 23 **SHAPORIN**/From mystic poems by Block
(English translation by D. Miller Craig)
On the Field of Kulikovo, a Symphony Cantata/English
Conductor: Albert Coates, Soprano: Laelia Finneberg,
Tenor: Frank Titterton, Baritone: Roderick Jones
BBC Symphony Orchestra, Leader: Paul Beard
BBC Choral Society, Chorus Master: Leslie Woodgate
Never commercially issued/BBC Sound Archives Reference:
Tape T 28115
NSA Reference: NSA Tape T9184W+R

The BBC Sound Archives contain a wealth of historical material, including some recordings of broadcasts dating back to the 1920s. The earliest of Kathleen's radio performances to have survived there is of a huge, impressive work that she sang in November 1945 – *On the Field of Kulikovo* – by the Soviet composer Yury Shaporin.

This Symphony Cantata, composed in 1938, has nine movements. There are solos for soprano, contralto, tenor and baritone, and a considerable amount of music for the large chorus. As recorded, the work lasts for a little under an hour; Kathleen sings in two of the movements. To quote the spoken introduction: 'In simple, expressive music, mother and children weep for husband and father fallen in battle.' A beautiful woodwind

14

introduction precedes the contralto's solo, with the men's chorus singing between verses. Kathleen also makes a contribution to the epilogue, together with the other soloists and the chorus.

Apparently performed and broadcast as a token of Anglo/Soviet friendship after the horrors of the Second World War, this major British première not surprisingly required four rehearsal sessions of three hours each; generous time given to a work that was unlikely to receive a second local performance – at least in the immediate future.

The choice of Albert Coates as conductor seems appropriate for this piece. He was born in St Petersburg in 1882, and worked extensively in Germany before the First World War. He continued to conduct in Russia up to 1917, and returned occasionally after the Revolution; he died in 1953, two months after Kathleen.

The performance was broadcast simultaneously on the BBC Home Service and in the Soviet Union. Winifred Ferrier, who was present, commented: 'There was no need to broadcast it to Russia: it was so loud that I'm sure it could have been heard from England!' The Maida Vale suite of studios, situated in Delaware Road, an elegant and principally residential district of west London, was created by the BBC in 1934 on the site of a former ice-rink and is used mainly for large orchestral and choral performances;

*Radio Times
advance publicity,
7 November 1945*

15

Mahler's *Third Symphony* (**KF 52**), in which Kathleen sang with Sir Adrian Boult conducting in November 1947, was also broadcast from there, as were several of her smaller scale Lieder recitals – that with Benjamin Britten recorded in February 1952 (**KF 196-198**) being an example. The studios, still used for public broadcast concerts and recordings, are the home of the BBC Symphony Orchestra, which regularly performs there, nearly sixty years after Winifred Ferrier was almost deafened by their playing in Shaporin's Symphony Cantata. Part of Kathleen's solo from that long distant post-war transmission was broadcast again during Radio 3's fiftieth anniversary tribute programme on 8 October 2003 – surely its first radio repeat in almost 58 years.

Yury Shaporin

Chapter Five
January–June 1946

5.30pm on 6.2.46
Kingsway Hall, London

KF 26 **J.S. BACH**/The Bible (translated)
Have mercy, Lord, on me (Part 1)(*St Matthew Passion BWV 244*)/English
Matrix AR 10042-1-2
Have mercy, Lord, on me (Part 2)
Matrix AR 10043-1-2
Conductor: Dr Malcolm Sargent; Solo violin: David McCallum
National Symphony Orchestra

In 1945 (or maybe even earlier – see Chapter Two) Kathleen had spoken to her teacher in London, the baritone Roy Henderson, about her unhappiness at Columbia; he suggested that she join Decca, to which company he was contracted. She did, and made her first record for them in February 1946 although, according to an article by Henderson in the Summer 1998 edition of *International Classical Record Collector*, she did not sign her first Decca contract until after the recording of Pergolesi's *Stabat Mater*, three months later. It is a sad irony that Kathleen and Henderson never recorded together as soloists; Henderson conducted the Pergolesi work, which was made in May 1946, but that was their only joint recording, despite the many public performances that they gave of oratorio during the 1940s.

Roy Henderson

Another incentive for Kathleen to sign with Decca was their assurance that they would include her in a complete recording of Handel's *Messiah*, a work she greatly loved. In the event, this *Messiah* project never came to fruition, and the only parts that she recorded were the two arias which she sang during her final commercial session, in October 1952.

Kathleen's first session for Decca was rich indeed. She recorded the aria *Have mercy, Lord, on me* from Bach's *St Matthew*

Dr Malcolm Sargent

Passion, with the National Symphony Orchestra conducted by Malcolm Sargent (1895-1967). It was her first commercial recording with an orchestra; and the choice of conductor was appropriate, as it was Sargent who had, in May 1942, auditioned Kathleen in Manchester and recommended that she move to London, to pursue her career in the capital, rather than in the north of England. Through him she had an introduction to Ibbs and Tillett, the concert agency who continued to represent her throughout her life. She first sang under Sargent's baton in 1944, and as well as frequently appearing on concert platforms together, they recorded five published sides for Decca. (The 1949 Brahms *Four Serious Songs* was not originally a Decca performance, but was taken from the BBC Sound Archives.)

The Bach aria recorded on 6 February 1946 was probably regarded as a test for the complete *St Matthew Passion* that Decca were intending to record. Although it was given a 78 issue number, and was released at some stage, Decca archives do not reveal an issue date, and no contemporary review of the 78 has been traced in *The Gramophone*.

In 1954 the performance was issued as a 45rpm record, and has since been transferred on to LP, cassette and CD. Clearly Kathleen and Decca were pleased enough by the results to make plans for the (almost) complete version of the *Passion*, the recording of which started in June 1947.

Kathleen's diary shows that *Laudamus Te* (from the *Mass in B Minor*) was also planned for the same session, but that idea was shelved before the recording took place; it was an aria that she never recorded commercially, although just one version has survived, in the 1951 complete *Mass*, now available on BBC Legends.

6.00pm on 27.2.46
Kingsway Hall, London

KF 27 **HANDEL**/Salvi, altered by Haym (translated)
Art thou troubled? (*Rodelinda*)/English
Conductor: Dr Malcolm Sargent, London Symphony Orchestra
Matrix AR 10092-1-2

KF 28 **GLUCK**/Calzabigi (translated)
What is life? (*Orpheus and Euridice*)/English
Conductor: Dr Malcolm Sargent, London Symphony Orchestra
Matrix AR 10093-1-2

Sargent was again the conductor when Kathleen revisited Kingsway Hall three weeks later to record favourite arias by Handel and Gluck. These have remained extremely popular performances, and *What is life?* is certainly one of her best known recordings. Generations of British radio listeners have come to know and love Kathleen's voice from the almost continual broadcasts of this aria during the 1950s, and the same surely applies to admirers the world over. Its poignant sentiments caught the public's imagination in a way that none of her other records (excepting only *Blow the wind southerly*) has done. *What is life?* was already one of her favourite recital pieces at the time of the recording and it remained in her concert repertoire until almost the end of her career. Whilst five other versions of the aria by her survive, the Sargent version is by far the most celebrated, if not the most artistically distinguished.

Despite her evident enjoyment of Handel's baroque arias, Kathleen never sang in a complete performance of any of his operas.

Decca's re-issues continue to use their 1950 tape transfers, which do the performances no service at all; Dutton's versions, re-mastered from original 78s, bring these two celebrated arias freshly to life on the CD *Stars of English Opera Volume 2*.

Afternoon on 8.5.46 and 10.00am on 28.5.46
Decca studios, Broadhurst Gardens

KF 29 PERGOLESI

Stabat Mater, complete (orch. Scott)/Latin
Conductor: Roy Henderson, Soprano: Joan Taylor
The Boyd Neel String Orchestra, Nottingham Oriana Choir

Matrix/Take	Date	Auto	Straight	Title	Singers
AR 10287-1-2	8.5.46	AK 1517	K 1517	*Stabat mater*	Chorus
AR 10288-1-2	8.5.46	AK 1518	K 1517	*Cujus animam*	JT
				O quam tristis	Chorus
AR 10289-1-2	28.5.46	AK 1519	K 1518	*Quae moerebat*	KF
				Quis est homo	JT
				Quis non posset	KF/JT
AR 10290-1-2	8.5.46	AK 1520	K 1518	*Pro peccatis*	Chorus
				Vidit suum	JT
AR 10291-1-2	8.5.46	AK 1521	K 1519	*Eia mater*	KF
				Fac ut	Chorus
AR 10292-1-2	28.5.46	AK 1521	K 1519	*Sancta mater*	KF/JT
AR 10293-1-2	28.5.46	AK 1520	K 1520	*Sancta* (contd)	KF/JT
AR 10294-1-2	28.5.46	AK 1519	K 1520	*Fac ut portem*	KF
AR 10295-1-2	28.5.46	AK 1518	K 1521	*Inflammatus*	KF/JT
AR 10296-1-2	8.5.46	AK 1517	K 1521	*Quando corpus*	Chorus

KF 29a   *Quae Moerebat*
KF 29b   *Eia, Mater*
KF 29c   *Sancta Mater* with Joan Taylor, soprano
KF 29d   *Fac ut Portem*

By May 1946 Kathleen had already started preparing the title role in Britten's *The Rape of Lucretia*, which was to receive its world première at Glyndebourne in July. Time was found, however, to spend two days recording Pergolesi's *Stabat Mater*, in a version re-orchestrated in 1927 by Charles Kennedy Scott (1876-1965), the noted conductor and choirmaster. The performance was conducted by Roy Henderson.

Joan Taylor and KF – taken by William Parsons

The first LP release of
Stabat Mater, *1978*

Of the ten sides that were needed for *Stabat Mater*, Kathleen sang on six. Stylistically this version is highly 'unauthentic' (the original is believed to have been performed by soprano and alto soloists, without extra chorus), but that it was recorded complete at all showed some courage on Decca's part. It was a favourite work of Henderson's during the war, as the chorus in this version is for women's voices; at that time it may well have been difficult to find men who were free to sing. He had conducted the work at two National Gallery concerts with the Nottingham Oriana Choir and Joan Taylor, although it was Astra Desmond, and not Kathleen, who sang the alto part on those occasions.

The sides that involved the chorus were recorded on 8 May, and those involving only the two soloists on 28 May. Roy Henderson, who died aged 100 in the year 2000, remembered: 'The Oriana Choir travelled from Nottingham for a 10.15am rehearsal (on 8 May) at Southwark Cathedral, followed by a lunchtime concert there, had a picnic lunch in the Cathedral grounds, and made their way to Broadhurst Gardens, West Hampstead, where the recording was made. I don't know what time they got back to Nottingham! They sang everything from memory. Joan Taylor was a pupil of mine at the Royal Academy of Music, so I had two pupils and my own small choir which I founded just to make music, and we had a lot of fun together.' Joan Taylor also recalled: 'The actual recording went well; it was always a joy to sing with Kathleen, as she was such a fine musician, and I felt we phrased and blended almost instinctively.'

Henderson's links with Decca went back to 1929 when he had been the baritone soloist on their first classical release – Delius's *Sea Drift* – and for many years he visited the studios at 165 Broadhurst Gardens, close to West Hampstead Underground Station in north London, to make records of song, opera and oratorio. (These studios were situated about a mile north of EMI's Abbey Road headquarters in St John's Wood, where Kathleen made her first records.) The building comprised a suite of large halls and smaller spaces where all types of classical music, West End shows and big bands were recorded and where, shortly after the end of the second world war, Full Frequency Range Recording – Decca's proud technical achievement – was inaugurated. The Broadhurst Gardens premises are now perhaps best remembered by followers of some of the great pop bands of the 1960s, notably the Rolling Stones, one of Decca's most successful signings, who also recorded there. The studios closed in 1980 and have since become a rehearsal space for English National Opera – still certainly within the spirit, if not the letter, of Kathleen's principal repertory.

Like many 78 sets of the time, *Stabat Mater* was issued in two formats: 'automatic coupling' and 'straight coupling'. The layout above illustrates how the two different couplings were presented.

In 1999 Dutton remastered this *Stabat Mater* in excellent sound, and issued it as part of a three CD set, also featuring the 'complete' 1947/48 *St Matthew Passion*. It presents the recording with a new clarity and presence, entirely appropriate for the era of the compact disc.

Chapter Six

July–December 1946

3.30pm on 2.9.46
? Decca studios, Broadhurst Gardens

KF 31 **MENDELSSOHN**/Paraphrase of Psalm 37, verses 1, 4 & 7
O rest in the Lord (*Elijah, Op. 70*)/English
Conductor: Boyd Neel, The Boyd Neel Orchestra
Matrix AR 10544-<u>1</u>-<u>2</u>

KF 32 **MENDELSSOHN**/The Bible – Hosea vii, verse 13
Woe unto them (*Elijah, Op. 70*)/English
Conductor: Boyd Neel, The Boyd Neel Orchestra
Matrix AR 10545-<u>1</u>

By September 1946, when Kathleen made her next recordings, she had already appeared in her operatic stage début as Lucretia. The first performances at Glyndebourne in July were followed by a tour of the English regions, Edinburgh, Glasgow, and almost three weeks at Sadler's Wells Theatre in London.

It must have proved something of a respite to record two arias from Mendelssohn's *Elijah* during this short London season, after so many performances of Britten's testing music. The oratorio was one in which Kathleen often sang; indeed, it was the work that had introduced her to Roy Henderson when they performed it together in Runcorn in Cheshire in 1942. It always remained a favourite with Kathleen, as well as with audiences, but seems since to have gone out of fashion and is now seldom heard in Britain. Dutton's CD issue of these two arias, on *Stars of English Oratorio*, re-mastered from good quality 78s, brings new clarity to Kathleen's performances.

The English-born conductor Boyd Neel (1905-1981) founded his orchestra in 1932 and toured with it extensively both before and after the Second World War. Visits to the 1937 Salzburg Festival and to Australia and New Zealand in 1947 were particularly notable. Neel performed at the wartime National Gallery Concerts and it may well have been at one of these that he first met Kathleen; he was appointed dean of the Royal

Decca's hitherto unpublished test pressing of O rest in the Lord – *take 2*

Boyd Neel

Conservatory of Music in Toronto in 1953 and became a naturalized Canadian in 1961.

Ferrier enthusiast Peter Land is fortunate to own a test pressing of take 2 of *O rest in the Lord* (or, as Kathleen impishly referred to it, *O rust in the Lard*) and this probably-unique disc will be released on a Pearl CD in autumn 2005.

Decca's archives give the date for this recording as 3 September, but Kathleen's diary is marked very clearly on the 2nd – 'Recording *Elijah* 3.30' – The recording venue cannot be confirmed; it was probably Decca's studios.

7.45pm – 11.00pm on ?4.10.46
Stadsschouwburg, Amsterdam

KF 33 BRITTEN/Ronald Duncan (after Obey's play *Le viol de Lucrèce*)
The Rape of Lucretia, *Op. 37*/English
Soprano: Joan Cross, Female Chorus
Soprano: Margaret Ritchie, Lucia
Mezzo: Anna Pollak, Bianca
Tenor: Peter Pears, Male Chorus
Baritone: Edmund Donlevy, Junius
Bass: Owen Brannigan, Collatinus
Bass: Otakar Kraus, Tarquinius
Conductor: ?Hans Oppenheim, The Glyndebourne Opera Orchestra
Dutch Radio Sound Archives NOB: Reference EM-HM-0030
Representative excerpts have been issued from the complete recording, which is in NOS (Dutch Radio) Archives.

KF 33a Act 1 From ***Rome is now ruled*** *... to ...* ***Christ's own tears***
KF 33b Act 1 From ***My horse! My horse!*** *... to ...* ***Good night, Lucretia***
KF 33c Act 2 From ***She sleeps as a rose*** *... to ...* ***Tarquinius is drowned***

KF 33d Act 2 From *Hush, here she comes* ... to ... *Do you remember?*
KF 33e Act 2 From *Lucretia, Lucretia* ... to ... *It is all. It is all.*

Of the five extracts, all except *KF 33a* include Kathleen.

Benjamin Britten first heard Kathleen sing in 1943, when she and Peter Pears were two of the soloists in a performance of *Messiah* in Westminster Abbey. He was impressed by the quality of her voice and musicianship, and when he began composing *The Rape of Lucretia* he felt sure that she was the right singer to undertake the title role. At first Kathleen was apprehensive about the difficulties of the music, and equally concerned about making her stage début in such a modern work. At this point in her career, acting in opera did not come naturally to her but, nonetheless, the opening night at Glyndebourne on 12 July was a critical (if not a great public) success. Gleaning information from her diary and correspondence, it seems that she sang forty performances of the opera in 1946 and eight in 1947, including her Covent Garden début. She appears never to have sung Lucretia subsequently, but occasionally included the *Flower Song* from Act 2 in recitals. Gluck's *Orfeo ed Euridice* was the only other opera that Kathleen sang in staged productions.

Glyndebourne, July 1946: l to r: Owen Brannigan, KF, Reginald Goodall,
Nancy Evans and Hans Oppenheim

Two separate casts were assembled to perform the opera at Glyndebourne and on the subsequent British tour. This was to avoid undue strain on singers who would otherwise be on stage virtually every evening, with some matinées, for a period of nine weeks. Kathleen was the Lucretia of what was called the 'first' cast, although both casts had superb singers, selected by Britten. Her opposite number in the 'second' cast was Nancy Evans, a good friend (and the first wife of EMI's Walter Legge), who later married Eric Crozier, the opera's producer. Whilst singers of each cast tended to stay together for performances, there were occasions when a member of the other cast would appear instead, to replace his opposite number.

At the end of September 1946 Kathleen paid her first visit overseas, when she and the other participants in the *The Rape of Lucretia* travelled to Holland to give performances in Amsterdam and The Hague. The first broadcast performance of the opera was given from Stadsschouwburg (the Municipal Theatre) in Amsterdam and featured the entire 'first' cast. Since the issue by Educ Media of the first LP of excerpts in 1981, there has been considerable dissension among record companies and their customers in trying to establish its true recording date and conductor.

Dutch broadcasting company archives (NOS) state that the recording was made on 5 October with Britten conducting; but in a letter dated 18 September 1946, Peter Diamand (organiser of the visit in Amsterdam) wrote to Rudolf Bing, General Manager at Glyndebourne, confirming arrangements: '... As I informed you, the performance of October 4th is going to be broadcast; I should appreciate it if you would be helpful in the matter of additional fees ...' A cutting from *De Radiobode* (which published Dutch radio programme listings for that week) in Kathleen's scrapbook also indicates that the broadcast was to be on 4 October, via the radio station Hilversum II. The only performance that Britten conducted of the opera in the Netherlands was the first, on 2 October, the remainder being shared between Reginald Goodall and Hans Oppenheim; Oppenheim on 4 and 5 (matinee) October, and Goodall on 3, 5 (evening) and 6 October, as confirmed both by Glyndebourne's archives and by theatre programmes for those performances. (A memo at Glyndebourne shows that Britten was originally intended to conduct on the 4th, but his name was deleted and replaced by Oppenheim's).

It is conceivable (though inconsistent with Diamand's letter quoted above) that the performance which Britten conducted was recorded, and not broadcast until 4 October, but that still does not account for the 5th being quoted as the recording date in the Dutch Radio archives. With a work such as *The Rape of Lucretia* there would have been considerable difficulty in recording on discs at a live performance, and then playing them back on the air at a later date, coping with the awkward side changes that the format dictated. It would have been easier to broadcast

STADSSCHOUWBURG

VRIJDAG 4 OCTOBER
DES AVONDS 8 UUR

CONTINENTALE PREMIÈRE

BENJAMIN BRITTEN

THE RAPE

OF

LUCRETIA

UIT TE VOEREN DOOR

THE GLYNDEBOURNE OPERA

Amsterdam, the
recorded performance of
The Rape of Lucretia
– or was it?

RAPE OF LUCRETIA

An opera in two acts

ic by BENJAMIN BRITTEN

Libretto by RONALD DUNCAN

after the play 'Le Viol de Lucrèce' by André Obey

Conductor: HANS OPPENHEIM

Producer: ERIC CROZIER   Designer: JOHN PIPER

Male Chorus	Peter Pears
Female Chorus	Joan Cross
Collatinus, a Roman General	Owen Brannigan
Junius, a Roman General	Edmund Donlevy
Tarquinius, an Etruscan Prince	Otakar Kraus
Lucretia, wife to Collatinus	Kathleen Ferrier
Bianca, nurse to Lucretia	Anna Pollak
Lucia, maid to Lucretia	Margaret Ritchie

the first performance live, on 2 October, and have done with it. A contrary view might assert that if the performance was not intended for delayed, rather than live, broadcast, there would have been no need to record it at all; (compare with the 1951 Dutch recordings of Mahler's *Second Symphony* and *Orfeo ed Euridice*, both of which were recorded specifically for later transmission); or that the performance of 4 October was indeed broadcast live, but that the opera was recorded by Dutch Radio the following night for archival purposes – surely impractical as well as unlikely – and Britten was not conducting on that occasion in any case.

27

*Rehearsing Lucretia
at Glyndebourne*

Information offered in different CD booklets confuses the issue further. In
their regrettably inaccurate notes, Educ Media (LP) and Music & Arts
(CD), which offer five extracts from the performance, give the date as
5 October, with Britten; however, they also claim that the opera's first
performance was on 7 June 1946 (it was on 12 July); that the libretto
issued with their recording is complete (it is of the later revised version
of the opera and thus is missing significant passages); and that the
orchestra is that of the English Opera Group (which was not founded
until well after this Dutch tour was concluded). Gala now offer the
complete performance on two CDs (with extracts from an early Covent
Garden performance of *Billy Budd* as filler) and they too claim the English
Opera Group orchestra, but give Goodall as conductor and 2 October as
the date. Willem Smith Productions have also issued the complete

performance on two Wisp CDs (claiming 5 October/Britten), with *Der Abschied* from the 1948 New York *Das Lied von der Erde* as filler.

But, after all, the most important aspect of this recording is that here at last is *The Rape of Lucretia* complete in its original version, before Britten amended the score ready for the 1947 series of performances, whoever the conductor may have been on that particular evening. In his sleeve notes to the Educ Media LP issue of excerpts in 1981, the Earl of Harewood explained the composer's revisions, which

'... were extensive but, one scene apart, more cosmetic than structural or dramatic. Wholly beneficial was the removal from the libretto of certain elements of attempted persiflage ... Other [changes] represent the kind of second thoughts a composer may be expected to have once he has heard a work relatively often: an example is the intervention (later cut) of the Male and Female Chorus in the confession of Lucretia, when with cries of 'No, no, Collatinus' they attempt to restrain her husband's magnanimity as something which will increase rather than assuage her grief ... More important was the dropping of the original aria for Collatinus in the first scene and its replacement with new music. The composer did not want Collatinus seen as a natural cuckold in his too ready acceptance of Junius's protestations and so an aria with a beautiful flowing tune in triple time disappeared, to be replaced, it is true, by another, but representing a different side of the composer's invention ...'

It must be emphasised that none of these revisions affected Lucretia's music, so in this recorded performance Kathleen is heard in her role as she sang it both in 1946 and 1947 and as a member of the cast that had taken part in the opera's première three months earlier.

7.15pm-10.25pm on 11.10.46
The Hippodrome, Camden Town, London

KF 34 **BRITTEN**/Ronald Duncan (after Obey's Play *Le viol de Lucrèce*)
The Rape of Lucretia, Op. 37/English
Soprano: Joan Cross, Female Chorus
Soprano: Margaret Ritchie, Lucia
Mezzo: Anna Pollak, Bianca
Tenor: Peter Pears, Male Chorus
Baritone: Frederick Sharp, Junius
Bass: Owen Brannigan, Collatinus
Bass: Otakar Kraus, Tarquinius
Conductor: Reginald Goodall,
The Glyndebourne Opera Orchestra.

The surviving parts of this version are:

Act 1 From *Rome is now ruled* ... to ... *is love! Is love! Is love!*

Act 1 From *To the chaste Lucretia* ... to ... *Good night Lucretia*

Act 2 From *The prosperity of the Etruscans* ... to ... *know our knife*

Act 2 From *She sleeps as a rose* ... to ... *and wakes to kiss again*

Act 2 From *Oh! What a lovely day* ... to ...

to harness song to human tragedy (The End)

In addition to the omissions indicated, other occasional words and phrases are missing, due possibly to the difficulty of changing acetate discs during the recording of the broadcast.

BBC Sound Archives Reference: Tape T 39584

NSA Reference: NSA Tape T9202W+R

KF 34a From Act 2 *Flowers bring to every year*

KF 34b From Act 2 *Lucretia, Lucretia, O never again must we two dare to part*

Bass: Owen Brannigan, Collatinus

After the performances in Amsterdam, the second cast travelled to The Hague, to continue the Dutch tour, while the first cast returned to London. In *Reggie*, his biography of Sir Reginald Goodall (published by Julia MacRae Books in 1993), John Lucas sets down the circumstances of the opera's first UK broadcast:

'On 11 October, Goodall conducted a studio performance of *Lucretia* for the BBC's Third Programme, which had been inaugurated only twelve days earlier. The BBC wanted to broadcast the opera direct from Glyndebourne, but had been stymied by the fact that the second act clashed with the nine o'clock news in the Home Service. As far as the BBC

The Rape of Lucretia – a disc from the Earl of Harewood's collection, 11 October 1946

30

was concerned, there was no question of changing the time of the news for *Lucretia*; there would be a national outcry. Nor was Glyndebourne prepared to delay the start of the second act; members of the audience would miss the last train back to London … [and so] … the opera had to await the arrival of the more flexible Third Programme.'

The broadcast was given live from Camden Hippodrome, then used as a BBC studio; a letter in Glyndebourne's archives addressed to Rudolf Bing confirms the arrangements that had been made for the rehearsal (10.30am–1.30pm), and for the broadcast (Act 1: 7.15pm and Act 2: 9.15pm). The cast, with one exception, was that which had broadcast in Amsterdam a week earlier; Frederick Sharp from the second cast replaced Edmund Donlevy. In the small orchestra were some well-known names from the immediate post-war (and later) musical world, including Emanuel Hurwitz, Peter Schidlof, Kenneth Essex, John Francis and Edward Downes (now Sir Edward, and a conductor of international renown). In a conversation with the author in 2004, Sir Edward recalled that he played the French horn in every Glyndebourne performance of *Lucretia* except the first two, and continued with the company on its subsequent tour. He remembered a further link with Kathleen's career when, in 1953, he was in the prompt box at Covent Garden during her last two performances of *Orpheus*.

At the request of George Lascelles (now the Earl of Harewood), a friend of Britten's, the broadcast was recorded off the air on acetate discs. Unfortunately not all the opera survives in this version, but the extant parts (see above) have long been available for listening at the National Sound Archive of the British Library. In August 2005 they will be released commercially for the first time on two Pearl CDs, with Britten's lost (but now re-discovered) incidental music to the play *Stratton*, by Ronald Duncan, as principal filler. The sound quality on this version of *The Rape of Lucretia* is markedly better than that of the Amsterdam performance of the previous week; the difference is clearly audible at the points where sound restoration engineer Roger Beardsley has skilfully inserted extracts from the Dutch recording to complete the missing sections. Thus both Juniuses – Donlevy and Sharp – are on parade here at different points in the opera.

One excerpt from Act 2 was issued on the BBC LP *The Singer and the Person*, but the sleeve notes inadvertently gave the date of the broadcast as 4 October 1946; the same duet has since appeared on a variety of CDs from different companies. Additionally, Lucretia's *Flower Song* is included on a Memoir CD of Kathleen's 1944-6 recordings.

In the early summer of 1946 David Bicknell of EMI wrote to Rudolf Bing expressing an interest in recording Britten's opera commercially. Negotiations proceeded falteringly, largely because three of Britten's preferred artists were contracted to Decca – Kathleen, Peter Pears and

FIRST BROADCAST PERFORMANCE OF
Benjamin Britten's new opera

'The Rape of Lucretia'

By the company and orchestra from the Glyndebourne Opera

Libretto by Ronald Duncan, after the play 'Le Viol de Lucrèce' by André Obey

CAST (*in order of singing*)

Male Chorus	Peter Pears
Female Chorus	Joan Cross
Collatinus, a Roman General	Owen Brannigan
Junius, a Roman General	Frederick Sharp
Tarquinius, an Etruscan Prince	Otakar Kraus
Lucretia, Wife to Collatinus	Kathleen Ferrier
Bianca, Nurse to Lucretia	Anna Pollak
Lucia, Maid to Lucretia	Margaret Ritchie

Conductor, Reginald Goodall

The Glyndebourne production by Eric Crozier

7.15—8.15 ACT I

Prologue
Scene 1: The generals' tent in the camp outside Rome
Interlude: The ride to Rome
Scene 2: Lucretia's house in Rome, the same evening

9.15—10.10 ACT II

Scene 1: Lucretia's bedroom the same night
Interlude: A Chorale
Scene 2: Lucretia's house, next morning
Epilogue

Radio Times *announces the first* **British** *broadcast performance,*
11 October 1946

Ernest Ansermet (who conducted the first performance at Glyndebourne). Decca themselves then contacted Bing, indicating that *they* would like to record *Lucretia*, but by that time negotiations with EMI were already too far advanced to change plans. Eventually, in 1947, EMI indeed made the first commercial recording, of excerpts only, conducted by Reginald Goodall and, of course, Kathleen was unable to participate. It has however preserved, among other interpretations, that of Nancy Evans in the title role, Norman Lumsden as Collatinus, Dennis Dowling as Junius and Frederick Sharp, who by that time had graduated to the role of Tarquinius.

Chapter Seven
January–June 1947

2.30pm on 14.3.47
Decca studios, Broadhurst Gardens

KF 36 **SCHUBERT**/Goethe
Gretchen am Spinnrade, Op. 2, D118/German
Piano: Phyllis Spurr
Matrix AR 11096-1-<u>2</u>

KF 37 **SCHUBERT**/von Craigher
Die junge Nonne, Op. 43, No. 1, D828/German
Piano: Phyllis Spurr
Matrix AR 11097-<u>1</u>

Kathleen's reputation as a singer of German Lieder is far greater than her reputation as an opera diva; few of her recitals were without at least one item by Schubert, Schumann or Brahms.

On 14 March 1947 she made her first recording of Schubert songs, with Phyllis Spurr as accompanist. They first worked together in 1945, and over the next few years theirs became a very happy and successful musical association. Phyllis accompanied Kathleen on tours in Britain and Europe, and to Scandinavia in October 1949, which included the broadcast recitals from Copenhagen and Oslo; they recorded together at several sessions in the Decca studios at Broadhurst Gardens. Socially, too, Kathleen and Phyllis spent time together and the pianist would frequently visit Kathleen's home in Frognal Mansions, Hampstead, to help her learn new repertoire and rehearse for forthcoming recitals. During the 1940s and 1950s Phyllis was one of Decca's 'house' pianists – the equivalent of her erstwhile teacher Gerald Moore at EMI – and she recorded with several of their top artists. Two years older than Kathleen, Phyllis had studied piano at the Royal Academy of Music and, after too short a career, died in 1965.

Kathleen's diary reveals that she started taking German lessons on 27 April 1942, whilst still living in Carlisle. She seems to have enjoyed her studies, making rapid progress, and this record was the first of the many that she sang in that language.

10.00am-1.00pm and 2.30pm-5.30pm on 22.6.47
10.00am-1.00pm on 23.6.47
10.00am-1.00pm and 2.30pm-5.30pm on 29.6.47
Decca studios, Broadhurst Gardens

KF 38 GLUCK/Calzabigi
Orfeo ed Euridice, Concise version/Italian
Soprano: Ann Ayars, Euridice
Soprano: Zoë Vlachopoulos, Amor
*Flute solo: John Francis
Conductor: Fritz Stiedry,
Southern Philharmonic Orchestra, Leader: David Martin
Glyndebourne Festival Chorus

Side	Matrix/take	Date	No (auto)	No (straight)	Title	Singers
					ACT 1	
1.	AR 11392-1-2	22.6.47	AK 1656	K 1656	Ah se intorno	Chorus
					Euridice!	KF
					Amici, quel lamento	KF
2.	AR 11393-1-2	22.6.47	AK 1657	K 1656	Ritornello	Orchestra
					Euridice!	KF
					Piango il mio ben	KF
					Io sapro	KF
3.	AR 11394-1-2-3	22.6.47	AK 1658	K 1657	Amore assisterà	ZV
					Della cetra	KF/ZV
					Ascolta	ZV
					Che disse!	KF
					ACT 2	
4.	AR 11395-1-2	22.6.47	AK 1659	K 1657	Chaconne	Orchestra
					Ballet	Orchestra
5.	AR 11396-1-2	22.6.47	AK 1660	K 1658	Chi mai dell'Erebo	Chorus
					Deh Placatevi!	KF/Chorus
6.	AR 11397-1-2	22.6.47	AK 1661	K 1658	Misero giovane	Chorus
					Mille pene	KF/Chorus
					Men tiranne	KF/Chorus
7.	AR 11398-1-2	23.6.47	AK 1662	K 1659	Dance of the Blessed Spirits	*Orchestra
					E quest'asile	AA/Chorus
8.	AR 11399-1-2	23.6.47	AK 1662	K 1659	Che puro ciel!	KF/Chorus

Side	Matrix/take	Date	No (auto)	No (straight)	Title	Singers
9.	AR 11400-1-2	23.6.47	AK 1661	K 1660	Vieni a'regni	Chorus
					ACT 3	
					Ah vieni, o diletta	KF/AA
					Si, or il passo	KF/AA
10.	AR 11401-1-2	23.6.47	AK 1660	K 1660	Sol uno sguardo	KF/AA
					Vieni con me	KF/AA
11.	AR 11402-1-2	29.6.47	AK 1659	K 1661	Ah, potess'io	AA
					Che fiero	AA/KF
					Avezzo al contento/	
					Qual dolor	AA/KF
12.	AR 11403-1-2	29.6.47	AK 1658	K 1661	Ah! per me il duol	KF/AA
					Qual pena	KF/AA
					Che feci mai	KF
					Che farò	KF
13.	AR 11404-1-2	29.6.47	AK 1657	K 1662	Ah! Finisca	KF
					Non più!	KF/ZV
					Frena, frena	KF/AA/ZV
					Usciam di qua	ZV
					Trionfi Amore	KF/AA/ZV/ Chorus
14.	AR 11405-1-2	29.6.47	AK 1656	K 1662	Gaudio, gaudio	KF/AA/ZV
					Trionfi Amore	Chorus

KF 38a	From Act 1	Euridice ... Piango il mio ben
KF 38b	From Act 2	Deh placatevi!
KF 38c	From Act 2	Mille pene
KF 38d	From Act 2	Che puro ciel
KK 38e	From Act 3	Che farò?

Kathleen's success in *The Rape of Lucretia* at Glyndebourne led to an invitation for her to sing there again during the summer of 1947, in nine performances of a new production of Gluck's *Orfeo ed Euridice*. Originally the plan was that Ernest Ansermet, conductor of many performances of *Lucretia* the previous year, would be in charge of the musical direction but, after he cancelled in early March, the Viennese-born Fritz Stiedry (1883-1968) was booked to take over.

In a letter to Audrey Mildmay – co-founder, with her husband John Christie, of Glyndebourne Festival Opera – Kathleen wrote on 4 May: '...I am staggering through *Orfeo* – the memorising of the Italian was a struggle at first with all the other work I had to do – but I have been going to an Italian, Mr Gibilaro, who has helped me terrifically, and now I feel

35

I'm getting the upper hand. (Fingers crossed!) The music, I think, is wonderful – and oh dear, I <u>do</u> hope I can do justice to it, and to the standards that Glyndebourne is famed for. I'm ready to work like a Trojan for you all!' It seems that this may have been her first venture singing in the Italian language.

The difficulties that Kathleen encountered with this production were not with the music, which she is quoted as saying 'lies in the fat of my voice', but with Maestro Stiedry. He was very highly regarded but, it seems, not easy to work with. During rehearsals for *Orfeo*, he continually criticised Kathleen's acting, and changed words that she had spent hours learning – an approach that upset her badly – but she and the other members of the cast were more fortunate in having as their Italian language coach Renato Cellini who, in the 1950s, became a celebrated conductor himself. Carl Ebert was the opera's producer.

The edition of the opera that Stiedry intended to use was, in his own word, the 'usual' one, printed by Peters, edited by Dorffel, which is a blend of both the Italian version for alto and the later one for a high tenor Orfeo. 'In only one place I propose to use the old Italian version' he wrote, 'in the big C Major aria of Orfeo. It is longer than the version in French.'

The Amor of this production was the Greek soprano Zoë Vlachopoulos, who spoke virtually no English except for the then popular phrase 'Don't be vague, ask for Haig', a slogan advertising whisky which she learnt from stage hands at Glyndebourne. Ann Ayars (1918-1995), the American soprano who sang Euridice, also partnered Kathleen in concert performances of the opera in New York in 1949 and 1950. As a young actress she had appeared in a number of Hollywood movies during the Second World War and in 1950 sang the role of Antonia in Powell and Pressburger's film *The Tales of Hoffmann*, conducted by Sir Thomas Beecham, in which Kathleen was also invited to take part, but declined.

In letters to Winifred and to an old friend in Silloth, Kathleen related some of her Glyndebourne experiences:

'I am doing *Orfeo* here with an American Euridice, a Greek God of Love, a German producer and conductor (*sic*) and an Italian coach. Talk about the Tower of Babel! ... I was so pleased with myself because I'd memorised two acts while travelling, but when I arrived here, much of it was changed. I've cried for three days! ...' – 'The stage manager has brought me a lovely lyre of heavy plywood to get used to carrying, and it's going to make a lovely weapon when Stiedry tries me too far. One of these days he won't know what's hit him! He still shrugs his shoulders in despair, calls me an oratorio singer, and shouts himself hoarse ... I've been to bed each night after dinner to alter my score – stick bits in and take bits out and have been doing about 14 hours a day, but last night I

Orfeo, Glyndebourne, 1947

Summer 1947 at Glyndebourne: KF, Renato Cellini, Ann Ayars and
Zoë Vlachopoulos

went to the local with the stage manager and had a dirty big pint. Did me
a lot of good! Ayars, the American, is a love I think – she hasn't had
Stiedry yet, but I should say she's pretty tough.'

During May, before rehearsals began, there were discussions between
Rudolf Bing (Glyndebourne's General Manager), Stiedry and Decca
about how the opera might be abridged for the proposed recording. The
original plan was for it to be issued on six 12" 78s (although this was
eventually increased to seven). A little over one hour's music was to be
recorded in this way – approximately two thirds of the score. The first
night of the new production of *Orfeo* brought Kathleen great personal
success and three days later the cast began to make their 'concise'
recording at Decca's studios (not, it seems, as stated in the first edition of
this book, at Kingsway Hall). A memo dated 13 June from Rudolf Bing to
the performers finalised the dates, times and venue of the sessions, whilst
Kathleen's diary merely notes the times and dates of recording but is not

specific about the studio. Bing's note surely confirms the matter. Two further sessions in June were used to complete the fourteen sides of 78s which made up the set. Decca archives indicate that two takes were made of each side; on the published discs, however, one matrix (AR 11394) is clearly marked as a third take.

The score is, of course, drastically cut, so the recording does not truly represent Glyndebourne's full-length production; the main arias are, however, complete and the sense of dramatic continuity is preserved. The original 78 rpm labels do not specify which musical numbers are found on which sides, but show simply, for example, *Act 2 continued*, or *Act 3 conclusion*. With the cuts as they are, it would have been virtually impossible to list each side's music and make sense of it. Stiedry's tempi in this set have often been criticised, particularly that of *Che farò*, which is taken at a much faster speed than was usual in the 1940s, although by the standards of some of today's performances, it seems he judged it about right. Whether this was part of his interpretation, or was dictated by the constraints imposed by the playing time of a 78 side, is unclear.

Until the re-discovery of the Dutch set of *Orfeo* in the 1970s, this 'concise' version was thought to be the most complete recording of Kathleen singing the title role; yet another, less concise version, recorded in New York in 1950, has also been traced – (see **KF 135**, Chapter Thirteen).

Orfeo was recorded on days when it was not being performed at Glyndebourne – two Sundays and a Monday – and Bing alerted the musicians that '...the [Decca] Company warns me that they will not be able to supply refreshments in the Studio during Sunday recordings owing to the fact that the Staff, with the exception of the recording engineers, will not be available. Anybody who may want refreshment therefore must, I am afraid, bring this with them'. For Glyndebourne's and Decca's purposes the orchestra was known as the Southern Philharmonic but it was, in fact, the Brighton Philharmonic (whose chief

Fritz Stiedry

conductor and founder was Herbert Menges), working under a temporarily assumed name. The conductor and composer Berthold Goldschmidt was in charge of the chorus during this, his only Glyndebourne season.

Orfeo was issued in both straight and automatic 78 rpm coupling systems but when it came to re-issuing it at 33rpm in February 1954, it was cut further, presumably to suit the playing time of two early 12" LP sides. So, on all subsequent Decca LP, cassette and CD re-issues of this set an orchestral section of side 4

Dutton's restored Orfeo

has been excised, as has the whole of side 7, with *The Dance of the Blessed Spirits*, and Euridice's solo with chorus; the chorus *Trionfi Amore* on side 13 has also been omitted, but the same chorus at the close of the opera, recorded on side 14, has been retained. Surely it is time for Decca to reassemble the whole set in a new dubbing from original 78s. Happily, in 1998 Dutton released a superbly re-mastered single CD of Decca's original performance – without their later excisions – in excellent sound, with a total playing time of almost 63 minutes, thus demonstrating the high quality of Decca's original shellac discs. Another re-issue on two Document CDs includes several other of Kathleen's Decca recordings on the second disc.

Kathleen's own set of *Orfeo* 78s, still showing the original postage label on the box, is now a treasured item in Glyndebourne's archives; it is part of a collection of *Lucretia* and *Orfeo* material which was generously donated to the archive by Terence Hodgkinson CBE, in April 1999. The records originally belonged to Hans Schneider, who worked for Taylor & Penton, and who realised the costume designs for *The Rape of Lucretia*.

In 1995 a set of twenty-two test pressings of *Orfeo* was found at Glyndebourne among John Christie's own record collection, including eight unpublished takes. These were generously given by the Christie family to Blackburn Museum and Art Gallery for safe keeping in the ever-growing Ferrier collection in Kathleen's home town.

The above listing gives an indication of the music recorded on Decca's original seven-record set. Harry Sarton was the recording producer and Arthur Haddy the sound engineer for these sessions.

5.35pm-6.35pm and 8.10pm-9.00pm on 27.6.47
Glyndebourne Opera House, Sussex

KF 39 GLUCK/Calzabigi

Orfeo ed Euridice/Italian
Conductor: Fritz Stiedry, Southern Philharmonic Orchestra
Soprano: Ann Ayars
Glyndebourne Festival Chorus

Side 1. Act 2 *Deh placatevi con me* ... to ... *al mio cor.* with Chorus
Side 2. Act 2 Orchestra only (1' 45") *Che puro ciel* (first part)
Side 3. Act 2 *Che puro ciel* (concluded), with Chorus/Ballet music –
  Orchestra
Side 4. Act 3 *Vieni, vieni con me o cara*, with Ann Ayars/*A dovessi* ...
  to ... *oscuro fassi gia.* – Ann Ayars

Never commercially issued. In a private collection.

In 1991 a discovery was made of some privately recorded acetate discs, owned by an anonymous enthusiast. They date from 27 June 1947, when the BBC broadcast a performance of *Orfeo* direct from Glyndebourne on the Third Programme. The discs contain excerpts from Acts 2 and 3; all the vocal music also featured on Decca's commercial recording made the same month, and the interpretation is naturally very similar.

In 2004 Derek Pain purchased a set of four acetates recorded on the private label TNHG. Whether these are the identical discs referred to above is not yet clear, but their sound quality is, for the most part, quite good; a necessary side turn loses a section of *Che puro ciel* and the chorus's overloud contribution distorts at several points, but perhaps a commercial issue will nevertheless result from this interesting discovery of Kathleen's only recording from Glyndebourne's stage. It is not known whether any more of the original broadcast was recorded.

*Glyndebourne –
house and theatre*

Abridged Version
30.6.47/2.00pm-5.00pm and 6.00pm-9.00pm on 4.7.47
Kingsway Hall, London

KF 40 BACH (Revised by Elgar and Atkins)/
The Bible, translated from the German by Troutbeck and Johnson
St Matthew Passion, BWV 244/English
Soprano: Elsie Suddaby, Tenor: Eric Greene (The Evangelist),
Bass: William Parsons, Bass: Bruce Boyce,
Conductor: Dr Reginald Jacques, The Jacques Orchestra, The Bach Choir,
Organ: Dr Osborne Peasgood, Harpsichord: Dr Thornton Lofthouse

Matrix/take	Date	No (auto)	(straight)	Item	Title	Singers
AR 11424-1-2	4.7.47	AK 1673	K 1673	10	*Grief for sin*	KF
AR 11412-1-2	30.6.47	AK 1674	K 1673	12	*Break in grief*	ES
AR 11413-1-2	30.6.47	AK 1675	K 1674	19	*Jesus, Saviour*	ES
AR 11414-1-2	30.6.47	AK 1676	K 1674	25	*O grief!*	EG/Chorus
AR 11415-1-2	30.6.47	AK 1677	K 1675	26	*I would beside my Lord*	EG/Ch
AR 11417-1-2	30.6.47	AK 1678	K 1675	44	*O Lord, who dares*	Chorus
				45	*Now Peter sat*	EG/ES/KF/BB
				46	*Surely*	EG/BB/Chorus
AR 11418-1-2	30.6.47	AK 1679	K 1676	47	*Have mercy, Lord* (Part 1)	KF
AR 11419-1-2	30.6.47	AK 1679	K 1676	47	*Have mercy, Lord* (Part 2)	KF
				48	*Lamb of God*	Chorus
AR 11420-1-2	4.7.47	AK 1678	K 1677	51	*Give, o give*	WP
AR 11425-1-2	4.7.47	AK 1677	K 1677	53	*Commit thy way*	Chorus
				54	*Now at that feast*	ES/EG/BB/Ch
AR 11416-1-2	30.6.47	AK 1676	K 1678	70	*See ye! See*	KF/Chorus
AR 11421-1-2	4.7.47	AK 1675	K 1678	72	*Be near me, Lord*	Chorus
				73	*And behold, the veil*	EG/Chorus
AR 11422-1-2	4.7.47	AK 1674	K 1679	78	*In tears of grief* (Part 1)	Chorus
AR 11423-1-2	4.7.47	AK 1673	K 1679	78	*In tears of grief* (Part 2)	Chorus

Details of the 1948 sessions are included here, rather than in Chapter
Nine, as they comprise part of the project which commenced in June
1947.

(Almost) Complete Version
6.00pm-9.00pm on 3.5.48/6.00pm-9.00pm on 8.5.48
7.6.48/8.6.48/6.00pm-9.00pm on 9.6.48
2.00pm-5.00pm and 6.00pm-9.00pm on 10.6.48/11.6.48
Kingsway Hall, London

KF 41 BACH (Revised by Elgar and Atkins)/
The Bible, translated from the German by Troutbeck and Johnson
St Matthew Passion, BWV 244/English
Performers as KF 40, plus: Bass: Gordon Clinton,
Bass: Henry Cummings (Jesus)

Matrix/take	Date	No (auto)	Item	Title	Singers
				Volume One	
AR 12273-1-2	.6.48	AK 2001	1	*Come, ye daughters* (Part 1)	Chorus
AR 12274-1-2	.6.48	AK 2002	1	*Come, ye daughters* (Part 2)	Chorus
AR 12275-1-2	.6.48	AK 2003	1	*Come, ye daughters* (Part 3)	Chorus
			2	*When Jesus*	EG/HC
			3	*O blessed Jesu*	Chorus
			4	*Then assembled*	EG
			5	*Not upon the feast*	Chorus
AR 12276-1-2	.6.48	AK 2004	6	*Now when Jesus*	EG
			7	*To what purpose*	Chorus
			8	*When Jesus*	EG/HC
			9	*My Master*	KF
AR 11424-1-2	4.7.47	AK 2005	10	*Grief for sin*	KF
AR 11412-1-2	30.6.47	AK 2006	12	*Break in grief*	ES
AR 12277-1-2	.6.48	AK 2007	13	*Now the first*	EG
			14	*Where wilt Thou*	Chorus
			15	*And He said*	EG/HC
			16	*'Tis I*	Chorus
			17	*And He answered* (Part 1)	EG/HC
AR 12278-1-2	.6.48	AK 2007	17	*Then answered* (Part 2)	EG/HC/GC
			18	*Although our eyes*	ES
AR 11413-1-2	30.6.47	AK 2006	19	*Jesus, Saviour*	ES
AR 12279-1-2	.6.48	AK 2005	20	*And after*	EG/HC
			22	*Peter answered*	EG/HC/GC
			23	*Here would I stand*	Chorus
			24	*Then cometh Jesus*	EG/HC
AR 11414-1-2	30.6.47	AK 2004	25	*O grief!*	EG/Chorus
AR 11415-1-2	30.6.47	AK 2003	26	*I would beside my Lord*	EG/Chorus

Matrix/take	Date	No (auto)	Item Title	Singers
AR 12280-1-2	.6.48	AK 2002	27 *And He went*	EG/HC
			28 *The Saviour, low*	WP
			29 *Gladly would I*	WP
AR 12281-1-2	.6.48	AK 2001	30 *And He cometh*	EG/HC
			31 *O Father*	Chorus
			32 *Then cometh He*	EG/HC/GC
			Volume Two	
AR 12282-1-2	8.5.48	AK 2008	33 *Behold, my Saviour* (Part 1)	KF/ES/Ch
AR 12283-1-2	8.5.48	AK 2009	33 *Have lightnings* (Part 2)	Chorus
			34 *And behold*	EG/HC
AR 12284-1-2	.6.48	AK 2010	35 *O Man* (Part 1)	Chorus
AR 12285-1-2	.6.48	AK 2011	35 *O Man* (Part 2)	Chorus
AR 12406-1-2	10.6.48	AK 2012	36 *Ah! Now is my Saviour* (Part 1)	KF/Ch
AR 12407-1-2	10.6.48	AK 2013	36 *Ah! Now is my Saviour* (Part 2)	KF
			37 *And they that had*	EG
			38 *How falsely*	Chorus
AR 12287-1-2	.6.48	AK 2014	39 *Yea, though*	EG/ES/GC
			40 *He holds*	EG
			41 *Endure, endure* (Part 1)	EG
AR 12288-1-2	.6.48	AK 2014	41 *Endure, endure* (Part 2)	EG
			42 *And the High Priest*	EG/HC/GC/ Chorus
			43 *Then did they spit*	EG/Chorus
AR 11417-1-2	30.6.47	AK 2013	44 *O Lord, who dares*	Chorus
			45 *Now Peter sat*	EG/ES/KF/BB
			46 *Surely*	EG/BB/Chorus
AR 11418-1-2	30.6.47	AK 2012	47 *Have mercy, Lord* (Part 1)	KF
AR 11419-1-2	30.6.47	AK 2011	47 *Have mercy, Lord* (Part 2)	KF
			48 *Lamb of God*	Chorus
AR 12297-1-2	.6.48	AK 2010	49 *When the morning*	EG/GC/Chorus
			50 *And he cast down*	EG/GC
			52 *And they took*	EG/HC/GC
AR 11420-1-2	4.7.47	AK 2009	51 *Give, O give*	WP
AR 11425-1-2	4.7.47	AK 2008	53 *Commit thy way*	Chorus
			54 *Now at that feast*	ES/EG/BB/Chorus
			Volume Three	
AR 12289-1-2	3.5.48	AK 2015	55 *O wondrous love*	Chorus
			56 *The governor said*	EG/GC
			57 *To all men*	ES
			58 *For love* (Part 1)	ES
AR 12290-1-2	3.5.48	AK 2016	58 *For love* (Part 2)	ES
			59 *But they cried*	EG/GC/Chorus

Matrix/take	Date	No (auto)	Item Title	Singers
AR 12291-1-2	.6.48	AK 2017	60 *O Gracious God!*	KF
			61 *If my tears* (Part 1)	KF
AR 12292-1-2	.6.48	AK 2018	61 *If my tears* (Part 2)	KF
AR 12293-1-2	.6.48	AK 2019	62 *Then the soldiers*	EG/Chorus
			63 *0 Sacred Head*	Chorus
			64 *And after that*	EG
			67 *And when they* (Part 1)	EG
AR 12286-1-2	.6.48	AK 2020	67 *And set up over* (Part 2)	EG/Chorus
			68 *The thieves also*	EG
			69 *Ah, Golgotha!*	KF
AR 11416-1-2	30.6.47	AK 2021	70 *See ye! see*	KF/Chorus
AR 12294-1-2	.6.48	AK 2021	71 *Now from the sixth*	EG/HC/Chorus
AR 11421-1-2	4.7.47	AK 2020	72 *Be near me, Lord*	Chorus
			73 *And behold, the veil*	EG/Chorus
AR 12295-1-2	.6.48	AK 2019	74 *At evening*	WP
			75 *Make thee clean* (Part 1)	WP
AR 12296-1-2	.6.48	AK 2018	75 *Make thee clean* (Part 2)	WP
AR 12298-1-2	3.5.48	AK 2017	76 *And when Joseph*	EG/GC/Chorus
			77 *And now the Lord*	ES/KF/EG/WP/Ch
AR 11422-1-2	4.7.47	AK 2016	78 *In tears of grief* (Part 1)	Chorus
AR 11423-1-2	4.7.47	AK 2015	78 *In tears of grief* (Part 2)	Chorus

KF 41a	*Come, ye daughters*
KF 41b	*My Master and my Lord ... Grief for sin*
KF 41c	*Behold, my Saviour ... Have lightnings*
KF 41d	*Ah! Now is my Saviour gone*
KF 41e	*Have mercy, Lord, on me*
KF 41f	*Lamb of God*
KF 41g	*O Gracious God! ... If my tears be unavailing*
KF 41h	*O Sacred Head*
KF 41i	*Ah, Golgotha! ... See the Saviour's outstretched hands*
KF 41j	*Be near me, Lord*
KF 41k	*And now the Lord*
KF 41l	*In tears of grief*

In late June and early July 1947 Kathleen was busy with many professional commitments. In addition to singing at Glyndebourne in performances of *Orfeo* and *The Rape of Luctretia*, she was required to commute back to London from Sussex to record for Decca. The day following the last *Orfeo* session saw the commencement of one of Decca's major projects of the 78 era; the completion of this *St Matthew Passion*

took over eleven months and eventually occupied forty-two sides of 12"
discs.

Kingsway Hall was used to make this enterprising recording, ideal as it
was for accommodating the orchestral and choral forces required. It had
been opened in December 1912 as part of the extensive premises of the
headquarters of the Methodist Church's West London Mission. Apart
from regular use as a place of worship, it came to the attention of
recording companies after the advent of the electrical system in 1925 and
was soon in demand, particularly for large-scale orchestral and choral
sessions. Kingsway Hall was situated on the new, broad and elegant
thoroughfare between Holborn and Aldwych, opened in 1905, which had
been driven through a tangle of slum streets and alleys. A short walk to
the south Bush House, home of the BBC World Service, still stands
grandly facing up Kingsway and five hundred yards to the north, on
Southampton Row, a blue plaque on the wall of a restaurant marks the
birthplace in 1899 of Sir John Barbirolli. Kingsway Hall was well liked by
many musicians who recorded there; David Bicknell of EMI memorably
averred that it was better for 'beauty of tone than clarity of texture',
whilst this clarity was the virtue of Studio 1, Abbey Road; Sir Thomas
Beecham called it 'a barn of a place' but nevertheless Decca and EMI used
Kingsway Hall for recording almost equally (when not required for
religious services) until the early 1980s. It was then sold to the Greater
London Council and after a series of alterations and a further sale it was
left empty, and in 1999 demolished to make way for the new Kingsway
Hall Hotel. How many diners, enjoying their luxurious West End
evenings out, realise that on that very spot many of the great musicians
of the 20th century made some of their most famous recordings? Elgar
conducting Elgar, Flagstad in *Tristan*, Karajan conducting Gobbi in
Falstaff and Kathleen Ferrier in a landmark performance of Bach.
Fortunately, the noise of underground trains that afflicted a number of
recordings made in the Hall did not seem to intrude on Decca's *St
Matthew Passion*.

In the score, the *Passion* is divided into 78 numbers, comprising
recitatives, arias, duets, choruses and chorales. In this Decca version the
following numbers are omitted entirely:

11. Recitative for the Evangelist and Judas
21. Chorale
65. Recitative for Bass soloist
66. Aria for Bass soloist

– and numbers 10, 26, 29, 32, 63 and 73 are reduced in length; some arias,
for instance, are deprived of their full *da capo* repeat section, presumably
because of the constraints imposed by the playing time of a 12" 78rpm
side. Of Kathleen's arias, only her first – *Grief for sin* – is shortened in this
way, which may explain why, at her last commercial session for Decca in

1952, this aria was again recorded, but on that occasion included the repeat.

The first part of the set to be made was a very abridged version of only fourteen sides, just a third of the work as finally issued. These excerpts needed the services of soprano, contralto, tenor and bass soloists, another bass in the recitatives, and a choir.

After the abridged set had been issued, recording was begun, in May 1948, of the remainder of the work, and it was issued 'complete' in three volumes of 78s, each containing seven records, incorporating the earlier sides in correct sequential order. This form of presentation must have been irksome to those who had purchased the abridged set and then wished to buy the full version, although apparently Decca were prepared to assist owners of the original seven discs in some way; just how is not clear.

For the fuller version, the services of the four original soloists, Elsie Suddaby, Kathleen Ferrier, Eric Greene and William Parsons, were again used, to complete their quota of recitatives and arias, and further singers were needed in some of the recitatives.

Establishing dates for the recording of individual sides is difficult, as evidence in Decca archives conflicts with some of the details noted in Kathleen's diary. For the abridged set, fourteen consecutive matrices were allocated, which appear to have been used in chronological order,

St Matthew Passion *at Bath Abbey, 14 October 1950. Not the recorded performance, but showing Kathleen with some of her colleagues: l to r: Alfred Hepworth, Eric Greene, William Parsons, KF, Cuthbert Bates, Elsie Suddaby, Henry Cummings and Dr Thornton Lofthouse*

which was not, however, sequence order of the work itself. Decca's archives indicate that Kathleen recorded on both the dates which were used for the abridged version, 30 June and 4 July 1947, whilst her diary does not mention any session on 30 June – (as it was the day after the completion of the recording of *Orfeo* she might well have deserved a day off, and she was due anyway to sing the role on stage at Glyndebourne that evening) – but it mentions two sessions – from 2.00pm to 5.00pm and from 6.00pm to 9.00pm – on 4 July.

For the 1948 sessions, three sets of dates were needed, as detailed in Decca's archives: 3 May; 8 May; and 7, 8, 9, 10 and 11 June. On 3 May Kathleen returned to London from a brief visit to Holland, arriving back just in time to attend a recording session at Kingsway Hall from 6.00pm to 9.00pm, at which she apparently recorded one side. In the archives, no differentiation is made between the set of five days in June; they are blocked together as a unit, but Kathleen's diary shows her intended participation in sessions from 6.00pm to 9.00pm on 9 June, and from 2.00pm to 5.00pm and from 6.00pm to 9.00pm on the 10th.

Twenty-six consecutive matrix numbers were used for the 1948 sessions, plus two completely out of sequence; Kathleen sang on these last two. The recording producer Victor Olof may have miscalculated the number of sides required, and found himself short of matrix numbers towards the end of the project. There was clearly an attempt to use these twenty-eight matrices in correct sequence of the work itself rather than chronologically, although it was not entirely successful. One curiosity apparent on the 78 set, but corrected on later issues, concerns the bass aria No. 51 – *Give, 0 give me back my Lord*. It was recorded, using one full side, for the abridged version on 4 July 1947, but when it came to 'filling in' round it in June 1948, the two previous items, Nos. 49 and 50, and the following item, No. 52, had to be recorded together on one side, putting No. 51 out of sequence.

Three labelling anomalies are apparent on the original 78s; only Eric Greene and the Bach Choir are named on the label for matrix AR 12287, although Gordon Clinton and Elsie Suddaby are both heard to sing a few words; their names were listed on Decca's session sheets for that matrix, but were subsequently deleted; and the choir does not sing at all on that side. The label for matrix AR 11425 credits Kathleen with singing on that side, although she does not, and the label for matrix AR 12290 credits Henry Cummings and not Gordon Clinton with singing Judas's few words, although Decca's session sheets give the latter's name. These errors may have been rectified on subsequent pressings of the set.

It is also worth noting that on the abridged version take 1 is used of matrix numbers AR 11417 and AR 11418 (this latter being the first part of No. 47, Kathleen singing *Have mercy, Lord, on me*), but take 2 of both matrices is used on the complete version; these second takes were

St·Matthew Passion

(J. S. BACH)

Complete recording by

**THE BACH CHOIR and
THE JACQUES ORCHESTRA**

Dr. THORNTON LOFTHOUSE	..	Harpsichord
Dr. OSBORNE PEASGOOD	..	Organ
Dr. REGINALD JACQUES	..	Conductor

With the following artists :

ELSIE SUDDABY	..	..	Soprano
KATHLEEN FERRIER	..	..	Contralto
ERIC GREENE	..	..	Tenor
BRUCE BOYCE	..	..	Bass
GORDON CLINTON	..	..	Bass
HENRY CUMMINGS	..	..	Bass
WILLIAM PARSONS	..	..	Bass

Side Nos.

(1-2) No. 1 Come ye daughters (Pts. 1 & 2).

(3) No. 1 Come ye daughters (Concl.).
Nos. 2/5 When Jesu had finished ; O blessed Jesu ;
Then assembled together ; Not upon the feast.

(4) Nos. 6/9 Now when Jesus was in Bethany ; To what
purpose is this waste ? When Jesus understood it ;
My Master and my Lord.

(5) No. 10 Grief for sin.

(6) No. 12 Break in grief.

(7) Nos. 13/17 Now the first day ; Where, where ? And
He said, Go into the city ; 'Tis I whose sin doth bind
Thee ; And He answered and said.

(8) Nos. 17 (Concl.)/18 Then answered Judas ; Although
our eyes.

(9) No. 19 Jesus Saviour.

(10) Nos. 20, 22/24 And after they had sung a hymn ;
Peter answered and said ; Here would I stand beside
Thee ; Then cometh Jesus.

(11) No. 25 O grief.

(12) No. 26 I would beside my Lord.

(13) Nos. 27/29 And He went a little farther ; The Saviour
low before His Father bending ; Gladly would I take.

(14) Nos. 30/32 And He cometh unto the disciples ; O
Father, let Thy Will be done ; Then cometh He to
His disciples.

◆ AK.2001/7 ★

◆ *New Issue this month*

ST. MATTHEW PASSION (cont'd.)

Side Nos.

(15) No. 33 Behold thy Saviour now is taken ; Have
lightnings and thunders (Pt. 1).

(16) Nos. 33/34 Have lightnings and thunders (Concl.) ;
And behold one of them.

(17-18) No. 35 O Man, thy grevious sin (Pts. 1 & 2).

(19) No. 36 Ah, now is my Saviour gone (Pt. 1).

(20) Nos. 36/38 Oh, now is my Saviour gone (Concl.).
And they that had laid hold ; How falsely doth the
world accuse.

(21) Nos. 39/41 Yea though many false witnesses ; He
holds His peace ; Endure, endure. (Pt. 1.)

(22) Nos. 41/43 Endure, endure (Concl.) ; And the High
Priest answered ; Then did they spit in His face.

(23) Nos. 44/46 O Lord, who dares to smite Thee ?
Now Peter sat without the Palace ; Surely ; Then
began he to curse.

(24) No. 47 Have mercy, Lord, on me (Pt. 1).

(25) Nos. 47/48 Have mercy, Lord, on me (Concl.).
Lamb of God.

(26) Nos. 49/50, 52 When the morning was come ; And
he cast down the pieces of silver ; And they took
counsel.

(27) No. 51 Give me back my Lord.

(28) Nos. 53/54 Commit thy way to Jesus ; Now at
that feast Barabbas Chorus ; Let Him be crucified.

◆ AK 2008/14 ★

(29) Nos. 55/58 O wondrous love ; And the Governor
said ; To all men Jesus ; For love my Saviour (Pt. 1).

(30) Nos. 58/59 For love my Saviour (Concl.) ; But they
cried out, Let Him be crucified ; His blood be on us.

(31) Nos. 60/61 O gracious God ; If my tears be unavailing (Pt. 1).

(32) No. 61 If my tears be unavailing (Concl.).

(33) Nos. 62/64, 67 Then the soldiers ; Hail, Hail.
King ; O sacred Head ; And after they had mocked
Him ; And when they were come (Pt. 1).

(34) Nos. 67 (Cont'd.)/69 And set up over His head ;
Thou that destroyest the Temple of God ; The thieves
also ; Ah, Golgotha.

(35) No. 70 See the Saviour's outstretched hands.

(36) No. 71 Now from the sixth hour ; Eli, Eli, Lama,
Sabachthani.

(37) Nos. 72/73 Be near me Lord ; And behold the veil
of Temple ; Truly this was the Son of God.

(38) Nos. 74/75 At evening hour of calm and peace ;
Make Thee clean my heart (Pt. 1).

(39) No. 75 Make Thee clean my heart (Concl.).

(40) Nos. 76/77 And when Joseph ; And now the Lord.

(41-42) No. 78 Final Chorus—In tears of grief.

◆ AK 2015/21 ★

This recording is complete on 21 twelve-inch records arranged
in three sets of seven records in Auto-Couplings only.

★ *Auto Couplings only*

2   3

'*Full frequency range recording*': Decca's St Matthew Passion *advertising leaflet*

recorded at the 1947 sessions. It was necessary to record more than one
take, since the metalwork was sometimes damaged in the delicate
process involved in obtaining the stamper; should this happen, a back-up
was needed, and the alternative take would be used instead.

The forces assembled for this ambitious recording project were, apart from the four soloists already named: the Jacques Orchestra, the Bach Choir, Dr Osborne Peasgood at the organ, Dr Thornton Lofthouse at the harpsichord, Bruce Boyce, Henry Cummings and Gordon Clinton. The conductor was Dr Reginald Jacques. Boyce sang on two sides in 1947, but was either not available, or was not chosen to participate, the following year. As none of Jesus's words was recorded in 1947, Henry Cummings was not needed that year; his contributions to the set, and those of Gordon Clinton, are from 1948. Apart from the contralto's usual items, Kathleen also sings a phrase of recitative in No. 45, which in public performances is often allocated to another singer. The work was sung in English, and both the artists involved, and the style of performance, are representative of a good standard *St Matthew Passion* of the time.

The abridged version was issued in both straight and automatic versions. Decca's recording sheets for the 1948 sessions indicate that straight coupling was planned for the 'complete' set, although their advertising material states that it was available only as automatic.

In 1999 this performance was re-issued on three CDs by Dutton, whose skilled engineer has amply demonstrated the excellent results that can be obtained from freshly re-mastered 78s, an improvement on Decca's sonically limited CD of extracts. The unpublished take of *Oh Gracious God! ... If my tears be unavailing* is included as a bonus track on this most attractive Dutton issue, which also features the complete 1946 Pergolesi *Stabat Mater*. The informative booklet notes are by Alan Blyth.

Winifred Ferrier, present at one of these sessions, recalled the amount of time spent discussing how best to fit a particular section of music on to a 12" wax: 'It wasn't easy to make records in those days, and getting it on to a disc took priority over interpretation sometimes!'

Many years after *St Matthew Passion* was released, the engineer Kenneth Wilkinson recalled an incident that took place in a restaurant, where several of the musicians and recording crew were relaxing after one of these hard-worked sessions. Kathleen stood up and announced that she would propose a toast; perhaps her colleagues expected something to honour the memory of the composer whose work they were recording. But no; in her typically forthright way she recited a favourite rhyme – 'Here's to the girl who lives on the hill. If she won't, her sister will. Here's to her sister' – and, probably to plenty of hearty laughter, promptly sat down again.

The recording producer of this set was Victor Olof, the recording engineer Kenneth Wilkinson.

Session dates given above are from Decca's archives.

Chapter Eight
July–December 1947

8.05pm–9.15pm on 11.9.47
Usher Hall, Edinburgh

MAHLER/Translated from the Chinese by Bethge
Excerpts from *Das Lied von der Erde*/German
Tenor: Peter Pears, Conductor: Bruno Walter,
Vienna Philharmonic Orchestra

KF 46 *Der Trunkene im Frühling* (Incomplete)
KF 47 *Der Abschied* (Incomplete)

Kathleen took justifiable pride in her claim that she and her friend Gerald Moore were the only two professional musicians to take part in each of the first six Edinburgh International Festivals. The idea of the creation of a major arts Festival in the Scottish capital was first conceived by Audrey Mildmay, (co-founder, with her husband John Christie, of Glyndebourne Festival Opera in 1934), and Rudolf Bing. In the spring of 1940 the Glyndebourne Company was touring the UK with Gay's *Beggar's Opera* and, on a walk through Edinburgh during the production's run there, it struck Mildmay and Bing that the city would make a glorious setting for a celebration of music, drama, art and a wide array of other cultural activities. History has proved them right, but it was seven years before the first Festival could take place; Bing himself was its first artistic director from 1947 to 1949.

One of the principal attractions that Bing planned for 1947 was a series of performances by the Vienna Philharmonic Orchestra, conducted by Dr Bruno Walter. Before the war, orchestra and conductor had enjoyed a brilliant partnership, which had ended with Walter's move to the USA in 1939. Now it was time for a reconciliation and Walter was keen to perform *Das Lied von der Erde*, Mahler's final vocal composition, dating from 1908-1909. In his search for the right contralto to sing at Edinburgh, Walter heard a number of singers, none of whom was thought suitable. At Bing's suggestion, he then visited the home of publisher Hamish Hamilton in London where he auditioned Kathleen informally; the rest of the story is the stuff of legend. Walter later wrote about the occasion (as

51

The Usher Hall, Edinburgh

quoted in Winifred's biography of her sister): 'I asked her to sing Lieder by Brahms and, I believe, by Schubert; after these I begged her to try also some lines of the *Song of the Earth*, which she did not know. She overcame their great difficulties with the ease of a born musician, and I recognized with delight that here was potentially one of the greatest singers of our time ...' Peter Pears (1910-1986) was selected to sing the testing – if far shorter – tenor part, in one of his rare performances of Mahler's music.

It is through *Das Lied von der Erde* that the superb artistic partnership of Kathleen and Bruno Walter is principally remembered. In addition to these Edinburgh performances and three in New York the following year, they gave the work together at the Salzburg Festival in August 1949 and twice in Vienna in May 1952, in the days around the sessions for Decca's celebrated recording. Walter was born in Berlin in 1876 and worked as Mahler's assistant in Vienna from 1901 until the composer's death ten years later. To him had fallen the honour – and responsibility – of conducting the first performance of *Das Lied* and he made its first commercial recording, also in Vienna, in 1936, with Kerstin Thorborg as the contralto soloist. His third and final commercial recording of the work was made in New York in 1960 with Mildred Miller, just two years before his death.

So, on 11 and 12 September 1947, Kathleen and Pears with the VPO conducted by Walter, performed *Das Lied von der Erde* in the Usher Hall, Edinburgh.

In early 2004, record enthusiast and discographer Derek Pain, of Warton in Lancashire (a village in which Kathleen herself lived briefly after her marriage), bought several acetate discs from a dealer about to close his business. Among the treasures he found were two privately made sides, both lasting a little under four minutes, of Kathleen and Pears singing extracts from two of their songs at this first Edinburgh Festival. The discs, on the private KJ label of 41 Downleaze, Bristol 9, were manufactured by MSS Recording Company of Colnbrook, Bucks. These fragments (maybe further sides were made, but have not yet been traced) were surely recorded from the BBC Third Programme broadcast of 11 September and are one of the major Ferrier discographical finds of recent years. No recordings of the occasion were previously known to exist and their discovery is of the greatest importance. *Der Trunkene im Frühling* fades at the words 'so schlaf' ich wieder ...' and *Der Abschied* ends during the short orchestral passage following the words 'den dunklen Fichten' – so little that promises so much.

Not only was this the first performance that Kathleen and Walter gave together, but it was also the first performance of *Das Lied* that Kathleen ever sang, a major work of the late Romantic repertory that became central to her career.

Das Lied von der Erde: a unique disc from the 1947 Edinburgh Festival broadcast

In October 2005 these two excerpts will be issued on a Pearl CD, together with other previously unpublished material.

The Usher Hall concert opened with a performance of Schubert's *Eighth (Unfinished) Symphony*, which was not, however, broadcast; the Mahler transmission began at 8.05pm.

2.30pm on 7.10.47 and 2.30pm on 8.10.47
Decca Studios, Broadhurst Gardens

KF 48 **BRAHMS**/The Bible (Ecclesiastes, Ecclesiasticus and 1 Corinthians)
Vier ernste Gesänge, Op. 121/German
Piano: Phyllis Spurr

Matrix/take	Date	No (straight)	Title
AR 11613-1-2	7.10.47	K 1742	*Denn es gehet dem Menschen*
AR 11614-1-2	7.10.47	K 1742	*Ich wandte mich*
AR 11615-1-2	8.10.47	K 1743	*O Tod, wie bitter bist du*
AR 11616-1-2	8.10.47	K 1743	*Wenn ich mit Menschen*

Never issued/Destroyed

As far as Kathleen's recordings for Decca were concerned, the second half of 1947 was considerably less successful than the first; three sets of sessions resulted in only four published sides. Fortunately, some BBC broadcast material has been preserved from this period, although its sound quality is generally poor.

Brahms' group *Vier ernste Gesänge* was a favourite recital item of Kathleen's, which she learnt soon after first seeing the score in the autumn of 1942. Three versions of Kathleen singing these songs survive; as she was dissatisfied with her performance on this occasion, these sides were never issued, but the two-record set was allocated commercial issue numbers, K 1742 and K 1743. It was almost three years later that Kathleen recorded the work again in the Decca studio, on that occasion with John Newmark as accompanist.

In his article on Kathleen's recordings in *The Gramophone* in February 1954, Andrew Porter wrote, 'Although this set is assigned ... both English and American numbers, Kathleen Ferrier told me that she had no memory of having made it. It does not appear in the English Decca catalogue, and I have failed to trace any pressings of the records.' The reason for its non-appearance is understood, but it is surprising that Kathleen failed to recall the sessions.

It is assumed that on this, Kathleen's first attempt at a complete recorded performance, the songs were sung in German; the titles are listed in that language in Decca's archives.

10.35pm-11.00pm on 3.11.47
BBC Maida Vale Studio V, West London

KF 49 **JACOBSON**/The Bible
Song of songs/English
Piano: Frederick Stone
Never commercially issued/BBC Sound Archives Reference:
Tape T 41797
NSA Reference: NSA Tape T9188W

KF 50 **RUBBRA**/The Bible
Three psalms, *Nos 6, 23 and 150, Op. 61*/English
O Lord, rebuke me not/*The Lord is my Shepherd*/*Praise ye the Lord*
Piano: Frederick Stone
Never commercially issued/BBC Sound Archives Reference:
Tape T 41797
NSA Reference: NSA Tape T4506W

Whilst being kept extremely busy in all parts of the country singing in concerts, recitals and oratorios, Kathleen was broadcasting ever more frequently on BBC radio; on 3 November she sang works by four British composers, Holst, Moeran, Jacobson and Rubbra. From this recital on the Third Programme, songs by Jacobson and Rubbra have survived. They were recorded off air on acetate discs which in 1980 were lent by the publishing company Alfred Lengnick and Co. Ltd to the National Sound Archive, for dubbing on to tape which is now in the NSA collection.

Maurice Jacobson, composer of *Song of Songs* (1946), first met Kathleen when he was adjudicator at the 1937 Carlisle Festival, at which she won both the piano and vocal classes. He accompanied her at many concerts during the war when they were touring for CEMA (Council for the Encouragement of Music and the Arts), and at her first London concert at the National Gallery in December 1942, less than a week after she moved to the capital.

Edmund Rubbra dedicated his *Three psalms* to Kathleen, and she first sang them on 23 January 1947, at the Church of St Bartholomew the Great in Smithfield, London. It was a later broadcast performance of this group

BBC PROGRAMME FORM

Please fill in this form carefully supplying ALL the information required immediately to :—

Name .... Kathleen Ferrier, ...

Permanent Address ..2, Frognal Mansions, ...

London, N W 3

Telephone No. .... Ham 2108

Date of Engagement........ Monday, 3rd Nov .... 19.47.. at.. 10.35pm .o'clock.

NOTE.—No Gilbert and Sullivan vocal items, nor songs with words by Kipling, to be used without reference to the Corporation.

IMPORTANT

	TITLE	*øComposer arranger (if any) and author	øPublisher	*øEdition or book used	Time taken to perform each item
	PORTANT.—(1) Please give all foreign titles in their original language with items please state in which language they will be sung (2) In the event of your not wishing to use the piano installed in the Corporation's premises		English translation taken from printed copy. In the case of vocal Corporation will not accept any liability for hire or transport charges, or for damage to the piano whilst on the	In the case of vocal you may provide a piano, but in that the piano whilst on the	
A. 1	Ushas (Dawn)	Holst	Chester	Vedic Hymns	$3\frac{1}{2}$
2	Three Psalms	Rubbra	Lengnick	Op 61	10
3	Flower Song	Britten	Boosey		3
4	(Rape of Lucretia)				
B. 1	Rahoon	Moeran	O U P		$2\frac{1}{2}$
2					
3	The merry green wood	Moeran	O U P	Seven poems by James Joyce	1
4					

ALTERNATIVE Items :

N.B.—These must be given as the items selected may have recently been performed

A. 1

2

3

4

B. 1

2

3

4

* If an arrangement is used the name of arranger is essential. The name of the author is required only in the case of unpublished songs where the author of the words is not the composer

* This information must be given where items are from books or collections

An accompanist will be provided.

Signature.... *Kathleen Ferrier* .... Date.... 25th Oct 1947

ø (a) It is absolutely essential that care is taken to ensure that in the case of published items the Publisher's name which is quoted is the correct one. This information must be shown in the column provided in every case. The Corporation is responsible for copyright payments in respect of such items, and incorrect information may involve serious difficulties.

(b) If you desire to broadcast a MS. item you must submit, with this form, a copy of an assignment or authority to utilise the item for broadcasting obtained from the owner of the copyright.

P/345/P 29-8-47 5000

KF's signed BBC PROGRAMME FORM for the broadcast recital of 3 November 1947. At somewhat short notice, the Flower Song *from* The Rape of Lucretia *was replaced by Jacobson's* Song of Songs (part of Kathleen's last radio recital – see Chapter Nineteen) that was issued by Decca in 1975. The sound quality of these 1947 recordings is poor, the piano accompaniment being particularly heavy and badly balanced.

7.30pm-9.00pm on 13.11.47
The Royal Albert Hall, London

KF 51 BEETHOVEN/Schiller

Symphony No. 9 in D Minor, Op. 125/German
Soprano: Isobel Baillie, Tenor: Heddle Nash, Bass: William Parsons,
Conductor: Bruno Walter, London Philharmonic Orchestra,
London Philharmonic Choir, Chorus Master: Frederick Jackson
Swedish National Radio Archive Reference: LB 8194.

The autumn of 1947 saw Kathleen preparing for her first transatlantic visit. Following her success in *Das Lied van der Erde* in Edinburgh, she was booked to sing in three more performances under Bruno Walter at Carnegie Hall, New York the following January; but there was much to do in the interim, including a handful of appearances in *Lucretia*, with which she made her Royal Opera House début on 14 October – ('From Carlisle to Covent Garden in five years – Lucky Kath!').

A further major London performance at this time was in Beethoven's *Ninth Symphony*, broadcast on the BBC Home Service from the Royal Albert Hall, the setting for so many of her oratorio and orchestral concerts. The evening also included Bruckner's *Te Deum*, which seems not to have been recorded or, if it was, has not survived.

The recording of Beethoven's *Ninth* is the only one which features Kathleen singing with her partner of so many oratorio performances, the well-loved English tenor Heddle Nash (1894-1961); the other two soloists, Isobel Baillie and William Parsons, had both recorded commercially with Kathleen by this time. This is also the only surviving example of Kathleen singing Beethoven's music.

In various writings, Kathleen made reference to three other possible performances of this symphony, none of which actually came to fruition. The first, to have been conducted by Beecham at the Royal Albert Hall on 12 May 1948, was simply marked 'cancelled' in her diary. The other two both seem to relate to the early summer of 1951 – one, a performance in Milan during May, is mentioned in a letter to Emmie Tillett her agent, and the second (as she wrote to John Newmark in the USA) 'opening the Festival of Britain hall ... with Toscanini' the same month – the whole of which she actually spent convalescing after her first cancer operation,

BRUNO WALTER
CONDUCTS

◆

BEETHOVEN
Symphony No. 9

◆

Isobel Baillie
Kathleen Ferrier
Heddle Nash
William Parsons

◆

London Philharmonic Orch.

13 November 1947

Beethoven's Ninth *– a Music & Arts CD*

having cancelled all performances. So it seems likely that this recorded 1947 performance is the only one that she sang of this perennially popular work. Towards the end of her life there was speculation that Kathleen might take part in a commercial recording of the symphony, to be conducted by Toscanini, but this plan, too, came to naught.

Both the London Symphony and the London Philharmonic Orchestras have been credited by various sources with playing on this occasion. It was, in fact, the LPO, with the London Philharmonic Orchestra Choir.

According to its booklet notes, 'This CD was mastered from a set of lacquer discs recorded in Stockholm from the broadcast of the concert … There is a missing bar (325) in the first movement due to disc damage …' The recorded sound is very reasonable for such a long distance transmission, but the issue of this disc by Educ Media many years later caused some concern to Isobel Baillie, who felt little affection for either the symphony or this performance.

8.35pm-9.45pm on 29.11.47
BBC Maida Vale (Studio 1?), West London

KF 52 **MAHLER**/Nietzsche
Symphony No. 3 in D Minor/German
Conductor: Sir Adrian Boult, BBC Symphony Orchestra,
Chesham Ladies Choir, 20 boys from the London Choir School,
Chorus Master: Maurice Barnes
Never commercially issued/
In the Music Performance Centre Archive, Barbican Centre, London
Reference: BCT 0005

On 29 November 1947, the BBC Third Programme broadcast Mahler's
Third Symphony conducted by Sir Adrian Boult and a copy was recorded
on acetate discs off the air by a listener. In 1981 this set was discovered in
Manchester in a collection of about two hundred private recordings taken
from radio transmissions between October 1947 and April 1948. The
recording of the symphony, along with others from the same collection,
is now in the possession of the Music Performance Research Centre, and
is available for listening at the MPRC Studio at the Barbican Library in
the City of London. In order to avoid clumsy side breaks, the unknown
recorder used a double turntable so that the end of one disc would
overlap the beginning of the next. This ensured that the performance was
preserved complete, but did not account for the different aural
characteristics of each recording machine; changes of sound quality are

evident from one side to another.
Although Kathleen made a number
of broadcasts during the period
covered by the 'Manchester'
collection of private recordings, this
set of discs is the only one which
preserves her voice.

In his biography *Adrian Boult*
(Hamish Hamilton, 1987), Michael
Kennedy confirms that this was the
symphony's first performance in
Britain – another première for
Kathleen; it also appears to be the
only occasion on which she sang the

Sir Adrian Boult

work; her diary and correspondence make no mention of any other performance.

Neither Kathleen's diary nor *Radio Times* indicate which studio was used for this live broadcast; Sir Adrian Boult's 'Programme Book' (preserved among his papers at the BBC Written Archive Centre at Caversham) in which he noted details of all his concerts, confirms that it was from Maida Vale.

6.00pm on 9.12.47
Decca studios, Broadhurst Gardens

KF 53 **BRAHMS**/Rückert
Gestillte Sehnsucht, Op. 91, No. 1/German
Piano: Phyllis Spurr, Viola: Max Gilbert
Matrix AR 11891-1-2
Never issued/Destroyed

KF 54 **BRAHMS**/Geibel
Geistliches Wiegenlied, Op. 91, No. 2/German
Piano: Phyllis Spurr, Viola: Max Gilbert
Matrix AR 11892-1-2
Never issued/Destroyed

Kathleen and Phyllis Spurr paid another visit to Decca's own studios on 9 December. Max Gilbert, the viola player, joined them there and the three musicians made their first (unsuccessful) attempts to record satisfactory takes of two Brahms songs. It proved extremely difficult for Kathleen and her accompanists to make versions which were suitable for publication. Further sessions were set aside in June 1948 and again in February 1949, and it was only on this last occasion that acceptable takes of both songs were obtained.

6.30pm on 18.12.47 and 10.00am on 19.12.47
Kingsway Hall, London

KF 55 **BRAHMS**/Goethe (from *Harzreise im Winter*)
Rhapsody for contralto, male chorus and orchestra, Op. 53/German
Conductor: Clemens Krauss, London Philharmonic Orchestra,
London Philharmonic Choir (Men's Voices)

Side	Matrix/take	No (auto)	No (straight)	Text	Singers
1	AR 11901-1-2	AK 1847	K 1847	*Aber abseits*	KF
2	AR 11902-1-2	AK 1848	K 1847	*Ach, wer heilet*	KF
3	AR 11903-1-2	AK 1848	K 1848	*Ach, wer heilet*	KF/Ch
4	AR 11904-1-2	AK 1847	K 1848	*Öffne den umwölkten*	KF/Ch

The only published recording that Kathleen made for Decca during the second half of 1947 was Brahms' *Alto Rhapsody* (or Brahms' *Raspberry* as she affectionately referred to it), conducted by Viennese-born Clemens Krauss (1893-1954). This was one recording that Kathleen felt did her justice. In an interview in the March 1951 edition of *The Gramophone*, she said: 'Perhaps the best record I have made is the Brahms *Alto Rhapsody*. It was recorded in a large hall and my voice floated out naturally.' The reviewer in the same magazine felt, when the set was issued in June 1948, that: 'Miss Ferrier's performance is most beautiful and tender, although her voice is recorded too strongly throughout ... but with all its defects of balance I think the recording is well worth getting for the sake of this artist's lovely performance.'

At the time of the recording Kathleen had been singing the *Rhapsody* regularly for over three years, and it continued to be a favourite work until almost the end of her career. Two other recordings, both from Scandinavia, have also been discovered, and both have been issued – one on Danacord, the other on APR. Of the three, this one for Decca is the slowest version, lasting 15' 58".

Kathleen's diary shows that two sessions were booked at Kingsway Hall; the two 78 sides on which the soloist sings alone with the orchestra may

Clemens Krauss

have been recorded at one, and the work completed, with the men's chorus, at the other. Two takes were made of each side, and it is possible that with the need to rehearse the singers and the orchestra beforehand, two sessions would indeed have been required to complete the work.

As part of a typically busy day, after the morning recording session Kathleen rehearsed for three hours in preparation for an Ernest Reed Carol Concert, to be given at the Royal Albert Hall in the evening; the next day she travelled to Sheffield for a performance of *Messiah*, of which she was booked to sing a further four performances in Birmingham, Liverpool and Blackpool before the end of the year.

Almost at the end of her career, on 17 December 1952, Kathleen sang again with Krauss, on that occasion *Kindertotenlieder* at The Royal Albert Hall, when he was deputising for an indisposed Wilhelm Furtwängler – a conductor with whom she never worked.

This Decca two-record set was issued in both straight and automatic couplings as shown above; some of these sets have been found to use Take 2 of matrix AR 11903 rather than Take 1. In addition to many re-issues by Decca, a particularly fine Dutton re-mastering has used original 78s, resulting in a beautifully clear and warm performance.

Chapter Nine
January–June 1948

3.00pm on 18.1.48
Carnegie Hall, New York

KF 56 **MAHLER**/Translated from the Chinese by Bethge
Das Lied von der Erde/German
Tenor: Set Svanholm, Conductor: Bruno Walter,
New York Philharmonic Orchestra
Complete copies are in the Rodgers & Hammerstein
Archives of Recorded Sound of the New York Public Library
for the Performing Arts, Reference: *LT10 9372
NSA Reference: 1CDR0011318

KF 56a   *Von der Schönheit*
KF 56b   *Der Abschied*

On 1 January 1948 Kathleen, with her manager John Tillett, set sail for New York, where she began the first of her three visits to North America. The earliest evidence suggesting such a visit is in a letter from Moran Caplat of Glyndebourne (perhaps writing on behalf of an indisposed Rudolf Bing) early in 1947, but the idea surely originated with Bruno Walter. Kathleen replied to Caplat on 27 February '... would be delighted to go to New York for Bruno Walter in January next year. I have asked my agents not to book me for any engagements in this country for Jan 1948 until I hear further news.'

Kathleen's principal bookings in New York were three performances of *Das Lied von der Erde* with the NYPO in Carnegie Hall, to be conducted, of course, by Walter. (These were followed by a short visit to the Chicago area for recitals and, on her return to the east coast, Kathleen socialized again with Walter and the conductor Thomas Scherman.) No sooner had she disembarked from the Mauretania at the start of her visit than she developed a cold which she feared might prevent her singing at all. All was well, however, and the third concert on Sunday 18 January was broadcast over WCBS. In the programme for these performances Kathleen was described, rather surprisingly, as a mezzo-soprano; the tenor soloist was Set Svanholm (1904-1964), who had made his reputation principally as a Wagnerian, although he also sang some of the

Italian repertory and created the part of Peter Grimes in the Swedish première of Britten's opera.

Rather to her disappointment Kathleen did not receive total acclaim for her first New York *Das Lied*: '… The audience was lousy – when I and the tenor and Bruno Walter walked on – in that order – there was a handful of clapping – I was stunned – I thought I must have dropped my pants! …' but later most of the critics relented and '… Bruno Walter was thrilled – I've never known him to open out so – he said I was making musical history (honest) …' as she wrote to Winifred. Also in this letter, written after the second performance, Kathleen quoted, perversely and perhaps modestly, from two poor reviews in the New York press, adding simply, '… I've shown you the bad ones – there are two more ecstatic ones in the *New York Tribune* and something else … I have never felt in such good trim. My soft notes came as I've never known them. I was a bit nervous, but did it all from memory except for a few words which I hid behind my programme. And Bruno W told me today my German was

Bruno Walter

pure and classic and was thrilled, so I don't really mind – only I wanted to come home sort of top of the class!'

Several libraries in the United States hold incomplete copies of the broadcast performance, but the Rodgers & Hammerstein Archives of Recorded Sound of the New York Public Library for the Performing Arts has it in its entirety; so too does the NSA in London, in sound reportedly better than that on its first complete British commercial issue, by Naxos, in 1999. Nevertheless, the Naxos CD conveys much of the freshness, energy and gravity that Kathleen brought to the music, if lighter in timbre than in Decca's commercial version from 1952. Another 1999 issue of this performance, part of a twelve disc set *The Mahler Broadcasts 1948-1982* by the New York Philharmonic Orchestra, is in fuller and more agreeable sound than the Naxos. It should be noted that the recording date of 8 January 1948, which has been quoted by various sources, is incorrect.

6.20pm-6.55pm on 16.2.48
BBC Maida Vale Studio V, West London

KF 57 **STANFORD**/Keats

La belle dame sans merci/English
Piano: Frederick Stone
(Incomplete)
Never issued commercially/NSA Reference: Tape T11540WR

Within a week of her return from New York, Kathleen was back at the BBC's Maida Vale studios to take part in a joint recital with baritone Robert Irwin on the Third Programme, accompanied by Frederick Stone. This thirty-five minute live broadcast (which was repeated on the Third Programme two days later) consisted entirely of songs by Stanford, the sole surviving extract from it being *La belle dame sans merci*, a setting of the poem by John Keats. The acetate recording was made off the air and is part of the K.H. Leech collection, which the NSA transferred to reel-to-reel tape during the 1990s. The song is preserved incomplete because of a side turn necessitated by its length, but the gap is brief and the admittedly imperfect recording offers the opportunity to hear a performance that Kathleen did not otherwise set down. Among the other songs performed on that occasion was the more familiar *Fairy Lough*, but *Radio Times* programme listings do not make clear which of the remainder were sung by Irwin and which by Kathleen.

This is the earliest of Kathleen's recordings in the K.H. Leech collection, which has preserved extracts from several of her BBC broadcasts between 1948 and 1951.

6.40pm – 7.15pm on 4.4.48
BBC Maida Vale Studio, West London

KF 58 **BERKELEY**/St Teresa of Avila, translated by Arthur Symons
Four poems of St Teresa of Avila, Op 27/English
Conductor: Arnold Goldsbrough, String Orchestra

A number of eminent British musicians wrote works specifically for Kathleen, and on 4 April 1948 she broadcast one such composition on the BBC Third Programme – the first performance of *Four Poems of St Teresa of Avila* by Lennox Berkeley. Berkeley took as his text poems by the mystic sixteenth century Spanish Carmelite nun St Teresa, translated into English by Arthur Symons.

Some little mystery still remains about the origins of the set of discs which were first commercially issued in 1978. In a letter dated 18 March 1948 to her American friend Mrs Rita Berman, Kathleen wrote '...I was thrilled the other day to know that I am possibly to sing with Tom Scherman next season. I look forward to it with intense pleasure, and hope it may be a huge success. I shall do all in my power to make it so. His manager suggested I should send some records of a new work I am broadcasting by Lennox Berkeley next month with small orchestra – so I have arranged to have the broadcast recorded ...'

In the first edition of this book it was suggested that a note in Kathleen's diary – 'Bond Street recording' – might have referred to a rehearsal in, or visit to, the Aeolian Hall for the purposes of making a special recording of the *Four Poems*, but this now seems unlikely. A recently discovered BBC memo confirms the dates and times of rehearsals at Maida Vale studios; no reference is made to any visit to the Aeolian Hall, or any other Bond Street venue, and a special recording session for the sole purpose of making a recording with string orchestra would in any case have been extremely expensive. It now seems probable that all rehearsals were indeed held at Maida Vale and that 'Bond Street' refers to the company that recorded the live broadcast of the work at Kathleen's request; there were a number of such businesses thriving at the time around the West End of London. Indeed, it might be that two sets of discs were recorded – the one for Scherman and the one later owned by the Berkeley family. In a letter to the author in 2004, both Sir Lennox's widow and their composer son Michael recalled the strong impression that Kathleen created with this work and how the discs (which, however, to Lady Berkeley's recollection, were recorded for rehearsal purposes) originally came into their possession: Michael Berkeley wrote:

'Kathleen Ferrier had mythic stature for me as a child. Not only was hers the haunting voice that seemed to stand for the art of projecting the

The BBC's confirmation of rehearsal arrangements for the world première of Four poems of St Teresa of Avila.

'Miss Bass' was the maiden name of Emmie Tillett, KF's agent

Reference: 03/M/MG   24th March, 1948.

Miss Bass,

Week 15 - BBC Third Programme
Sunday, 4th April. 6.40-7.15 p.m. and
7.35-8.40 p.m.
Kathleen Ferrier.

With reference to the above programme,
will you kindly note the following arrangements have now been made:-

Saturday, 3rd April
Rehearsal: 4.30-5.30 p.m.   Studio 1,
                               Delaware Road,
                               Maida Vale.

Sunday, 4th April
Rehearsal: 3.00 p.m.   Studio 2,
                               Delaware Road,
                               Maida Vale.

Yours sincerely,

Muriel L. Goodhall.
(for M.P.O.)

Miss Bass,
Messrs. Ibbs & Tillett,
124, Wigmore Street,
W.1.

PSD.

Lennox Berkeley

human voice at that time but she was also indelibly linked to the piece of my father's that was – and is – for me his most beautiful. The *St Teresa* songs arrived in the world at much the same time as I did (1948) and the unequivocal spiritual yearning of St Teresa's mystical words clearly struck a quite extraordinary chord in Lennox. Nowhere is this more powerful than in the third song, *Let mine eyes see Thee, sweet Jesus of Nazareth*. It would be hard to imagine a more suitably plaintive, plangent instrument than Kathleen's and whenever this music is programmed the singer I look for is the one that comes closest to Ferrier in vocal quality. Except, of course, none can – the voice is so wonderfully unique and personal, just as are the beautiful timbres of Janet Baker, Lorraine Hunt-Lieberson or Alice Coote. Recently Catherine Wyn-Rogers recorded these songs and again one can, through her sensitive singing, understand the true influence of Ferrier on those that have followed. They are few and far between, because that combination of tessitura (contralto) and natural vocal elegance is increasingly rare, as singers strive for the ever-higher registers of the mezzo-soprano. My mother, Freda, recently recalled the impact of Kathleen at the time of the first performance of the *St Teresa* songs: "Kathleen was the most enchanting human being; she radiated fun and warmth. I remember when she first performed the *Four Poems of St Teresa*, Lennox had tears rolling down his cheeks. Such a premature loss – that wonderful voice and personality. After she died, her sister, Win, brought us a record which Kath had made for rehearsal purposes. It was an old 78, which we played over and over again and inevitably it got badly scratched, much to Lennox's dismay. It was subsequently restored and made into a record by the BBC. But now, miraculously, other Ferrier recordings of the *Four Poems* have come to light, including one which Kath made with Barbirolli conducting [*KF 117*] and another with Hugo Rignold [*KF 204*]. For me, as it was with Lennox, the *St. Teresa* songs will always be Kath's piece." '

The BBC record to which Lady Berkeley referred was the LP *The Singer and the Person*, issued to commemorate the twenty-fifth anniversary of Kathleen's death, and it was Michael who re-discovered the original discs which, although in poor condition, were issued as part of that tribute. The notes on the record sleeve of *The Singer and the Person* claim that the broadcast was given on 14 April, and Kathleen's diary also refers to this being a broadcast date. According to *Radio Times*, the work was broadcast on the 4th only, and no mention is made of a repeat on the 14th. Coincidentally, a piano work of Berkeley's IS listed for a repeat performance on the 14th, having been first broadcast on 5 April. Perhaps some confusion arose at the BBC over which of Berkeley's works was being repeated, and Kathleen was wrongly informed that it was hers. This version of these songs has also been released on the Gala and WISP labels, apparently direct copies of the original BBC LP.

Rehearsals were held on 3 April at Maida Vale Studio 1 and on 4 April in Studio 2, where the broadcast itself probably took place.

The conductor of this performance, Arnold Goldsbrough (1892-1964), was a notable organist and an early supporter of authentic-style baroque performance. The small orchestra that he conducted on this occasion was described as 'Jacques String Orchestra' in a letter in BBC Archives, but for broadcast purposes it was reduced to simply 'String orchestra' in *Radio Times*. The remainder of the programme consisted of music by Bernard Stevens and Handel, with sung contributions from two of Kathleen's regular concert colleagues, Margaret Ritchie and Elsie Suddaby.

After the live Third Programme transmission, Kathleen had supper with the composer, cementing a valuable musical and personal friendship. Her diary reveals that her fee for the broadcast was 30 guineas (£31.50) and the cost of commissioning those world première discs was £3/15/– (£3.75).

9.00pm-9.45pm on 26.4.48
BBC Maida Vale Studio V, West London

KF 59 SCHUBERT/Goethe
Der Musensohn, D764, Op. 92, No.1/German

KF 60 SCHUBERT/Goethe
Wandrers Nachtlied II, D768, Op. 96, No.3/German

Both items, Piano: Frederick Stone
Neither song commercially issued/NSA Reference: Tape T11540WR

26 April 1948 brought widespread celebrations in the United Kingdom, and throughout the British Empire, as King George VI and Queen Elizabeth celebrated their Silver Wedding anniversary. In the morning a Service of Thanksgiving was transmitted from Westminster Abbey and at 8.55pm the royal couple broadcast an address to the nation on all three principal BBC radio networks. On the Third Programme this was followed immediately by a recital in which Kathleen, accompanied by Frederick Stone, sang five Schubert Lieder, Brahms' *Two Songs with Viola Op. 91*, and a chamber ensemble played a piece by Schumann. Five days later, on 1 May, the programme was repeated (but omitting the Schumann work) and it was from this second broadcast that two Schubert songs have survived as part of the K.H. Leech collection at the NSA – *Der Musensohn* and *Wandrers Nachtlied II*, this latter being the only known recording of Kathleen singing the work. Visitors to the NSA Listening Service should note that the documentation accompanying these extracts implies that the song is the *Romance* from *Rosamunde*

(which was indeed part of the original radio programme, but has not survived from this source). The original acetate disc seems to have been incorrectly annotated at the time of the broadcast, Mr Leech perhaps being under the mistaken impression that he had recorded *Der Vollmond strahlt* rather than the *Op. 96, No. 3*; both it and *Der Musensohn* are complete, and in passable sound, but there is no likelihood of their commercial release.

A rehearsal took place at Studio V, Maida Vale between 7.00pm and 8.00pm; the broadcast, starting at 9.00pm, was surely from the same studio, although BBC archives are not clear on the matter.

2.30pm on 14.5.48

Kingsway Hall, London

KF 61 **HANDEL**/Adapted from a libretto by Minato
Frondi tenere … Ombra mai fu (Serse)/Italian
Conductor: Sir Malcolm Sargent, London Symphony Orchestra
Matrix AR 12344-1-2-3
Never issued/Destroyed

On 3 May, immediately after returning from a visit to the Netherlands, Kathleen recorded her first side of the 1948 *St Matthew Passion* sessions under Dr Reginald Jacques. Over the following seven weeks all of the additional twenty-eight sides were completed to add to the original fourteen from the previous year. Kathleen sang on a total of thirteen sides, five in 1947 and eight in 1948. (Details of dates and matrix numbers are given in Chapter Seven.)

For her next commercial session, Kathleen went to Kingsway Hall on 14 May (some references in Decca's archives give it as the 13th, but Kathleen's diary indicates the later date), to record the popular *Ombra mai fu* – better, but inaccurately, known as 'Handel's *Largo*'. Sir Malcolm Sargent and the LSO accompanied three takes of the aria, none of which was judged sufficiently good for issue.

A curious anecdote about the recording was related to the author in 1992 by Dr Gareth Lewis, who had recently read the first edition of this book:

'I used to know the bass Trevor Anthony and, in reminiscing about his early recording career, he told me about sessions at Kingsway Hall in 1948, which led to his fine version of *Revenge Timotheus cries* from *Alexander's Feast*. It would appear that Decca had planned a series of Handel recordings, chiefly for the American market; Sargent took this as an opportunity to "showcase" a group of young British singers. Richard Lewis and Kathleen were joined by Anthony, soprano Ada Alsop and the

Royal Choral Society. Anthony told me that when the singers turned up for the session, Kathleen had a terrible cold, and they were asked if she could sing first. This must have been the May session, and be the explanation for the rejection of those takes of AR 12344 ... but Anthony told me that the sessions were in an evening (which was, apparently, bitterly cold), and that he only just got to Paddington in time for the last train to Wales.'

Might this explain the doubt about the date of the recording? Had Kathleen also been to Kingsway Hall on the evening of the 13 May? According to Decca's archives, Alsop, Lewis and the Royal Choral Society recorded their contributions that day, but not Anthony, who sang on the 14th. Looking again at Kathleen's diary, it seems clear that she was appearing in Bromley at 7.00pm on 13 May and could not have been in central London; if the anecdote refers to 14 May, it is surely unlikely that a 2.30pm session would stretch well into the evening, as Anthony describes. Could the incident refer to Kathleen's later takes of the aria in Kingsway Hall on 7 October 1948? That was an evening session – but, it seems, Trevor Anthony was not there that day, having no need to repeat his aria, which was successfully recorded in May. So we shall never know exactly what happened at these sessions, but Kathleen's cold might well explain why these three takes of *Ombra mai fu* were rejected.

Among the records purchased from a dealer by Derek Pain in 2004 was an unpublished test pressing of Take 3. This performance has slightly more pace than the later published take (*KF 69*), the recitative being seven, and the total side fourteen, seconds faster. It is marginally more

*The hitherto
unpublished
third take of*
Ombra mai fu,
14 May 1948

dramatic, operatic, in approach, the recitative being a slight variant of the published version; this re–mastered performance reveals the glorious bloom on the voice absent from Decca-based issues of Take 5, and it is to be issued by Pearl in October 2005.

2.30pm on 22.6.48
Decca studios, Broadhurst Gardens

KF 62 **BRAHMS**/Rückert
Gestillte Sehnsucht, Op. 91, No. 1/German
Piano: Phyllis Spurr, Viola: Max Gilbert
Matrix AR 11891-3-4
Never issued/Destroyed

KF 63 **BRAHMS**/Geibel
Geistliches Wiegenlied, Op. 91, No. 2/German
Piano: Phyllis Spurr, Viola: Max Gilbert
Matrix AR 11892-3-4
Never issued/Destroyed

Another fruitless session was held to try to record publishable versions of the two Brahms songs with viola, which had previously been attempted in December 1947. Phyllis Spurr and Max Gilbert were again the accompanists. Such long songs, both lasting over five minutes, sorely tested the playing time of a 12" 78 record, and it may be that these unsuccessful takes simply overran too far into the centre of the wax.

Chapter Ten

July–December 1948

2.30pm on 6.8.48
? Decca studios, Broadhurst Gardens

KF 66 GRUBER (arr. Gideon Fagan)/Mohr
Silent night, holy night/English
Conductor: Boyd Neel, Boyd Neel String Orchestra
Matrix DR 12581-1-2

KF 67 TRADITIONAL (arr. Gideon Fagan)/Translated from Latin
O come all ye faithful/English
Conductor: Boyd Neel, Boyd Neel String Orchestra
Matrix DR 12582-1-2

If Christmas is said to arrive earlier every year, it arrived particularly early for Kathleen in 1948. On 6 August she recorded two popular Christmas songs with Boyd Neel and his String Orchestra, which were issued in October ready for the seasonal shoppers. On 31 August the two songs were transferred from the original 10″ pressings to 12″ waxes, with matrix numbers DAR 12611 and DAR 12612, in which larger format they were issued in the United States.

It is not clear from Decca's archives that the recordings were made at their studios, but it seems safe to conclude that they were.

Decca publicising Christmas, 1948

Christmas Records

KATHLEEN FERRIER

With THE BOYD NEEL STRING ORCHESTRA
Conductor: BOYD NEEL

SILENT NIGHT, HOLY NIGHT (*Grüber, arr. Fagan*)
O COME, ALL YE FAITHFUL (*Traditional*) .... M 622

8.00pm on 26.8.48
Freemasons' Hall, Edinburgh

KF 68 **PARRY**/Anon

Love is a bable, *Op. 152, No. 3*/*English*
Piano: Gerald Moore
BBC Sound Archives References: Tape T 29270 and T 12556

Kathleen was justly proud to have sung in the first six Edinburgh Festivals – from 1947 to 1952 – and one item has survived from her 1948 appearances there. The BBC recorded Parry's setting of *Love is a bable* at a recital in the Freemasons' Hall on 26 August. The song was included among material used for a descriptive radio programme about the Festival, prepared on 6 October 1948 by John Keir Cross for the BBC Transcription Service, and still preserved in the BBC Sound Archives. Gerald Moore was the accompanist. No other items from the recital seem to have survived.

Love is a bable was first issued in 1979 on the BBC commemorative issue *The Singer and the Person*.

For the following few days in Edinburgh Kathleen enjoyed herself, met friends – Leon Goossens and the composer Berthold Goldschmidt among them – attended performances of *Belshazzar's Feast* and *Così fan tutte* and sang in Bach's *B Minor Mass* with Sargent; she then travelled to Worcester to take part for ten days in the Three Choirs Festival, where she sang in *The Dream of Gerontius*, *St Matthew Passion*, *The Blessed Damozel* and *Messiah*, before embarking on a two-week tour of Denmark. The pressure of work and her increasing popularity mounted – she was everywhere in demand.

7.30pm on 7.10.48
Kingsway Hall, London

KF 69 **HANDEL**/Adapted from a libretto by Minato

Frondi tenere … Ombra mai fu (*Serse*)/Italian
Conductor: Sir Malcolm Sargent, London Symphony Orchestra
Matrix AR 12344-4-5

On 7 October two further takes were made of the aria from Handel's *Serse*, which had previously been unsuccessfully recorded on 13/14 May (see Chapter Nine for a possible explanation of the failure of the earlier session). Fortunately, at the fifth attempt, a satisfactory version was

Under the Patronage of Their Majesties The King and Queen

EDINBURGH
INTERNATIONAL FE
of
MUSIC and DRA

IN ASSOCIATION WITH THE ARTS COUNCIL OF GREAT
AND THE CORPORATION OF THE CITY OF EDINBU

□ □

USHER HALL

Vienna Philharmonic Orc
Conductor : BRUNO WALTE

Soloists
KATHLEEN FERRIER   PETER

Thursday, 11th September 1947, at 7.

Friday, 12th September 1947, at 2.3

*The Edinburgh Festivals for 1947
and 1948 – the first two of six
consecutive years featuring
performances by KF*

UNDER THE PATRONAGE OF
THEIR MAJESTIES THE KING AND QUEEN

EDINBURGH
INTERNATIONAL
FESTIVAL
OF
MUSIC & DRAMA

*In association with the Arts Council of Great Britain,
The British Council and the
Corporation of the City of Edinburgh*

AUG. 22 — SEPT. 12
1948

EDINBURGH FESTIVAL SOCIETY LTD,
Chairman
The Rt. Hon. ANDREW MURRAY, O.B.E., J.P.
Lord Provost of Edinburgh

Artistic Organising Centre   *Administrative Centre*
Glyndebourne Society Ltd,   Synod Hall, Edinburgh
(*Artistic Director*, Rudolf Bing) (*Secretary*, John Reid)

PRELIMINARY ANNOUNCEMENT

obtained, and it was issued as a coupling for Richard Lewis's *Where e'er you walk*, from the same composer's *Semele*.

Ombra mai fu has enjoyed success for decades – centuries even – as Handel's most popular operatic aria, performed by generations of singers and instrumentalists. Few who enjoy its grave melody may appreciate its original context; as the Earl of Harewood wrote in *The New Kobbé's Opera Book* '...Once known as 'Handel's celebrated *Largo*', this Victorian sanctification does less than justice to a glorious tune ... in which Serse whimsically apostrophises the beauties of a tree in his garden in a tune of chaste simplicity and total memorability. It has been noted that Handel marks it *larghetto* and not *largo* at all.'

Admirers of another famous recording of the aria – that made in 1920 by Enrico Caruso – may enjoy the coincidence that he, too, required five takes to make a publishable version of this, the only piece common to both singers' discographies.

The introductory recitative *Frondi tenere e belle* ... was also included in Kathleen's performance on this occasion, although virtually all record labels and CD descriptions since its initial release in May 1949 omit any mention of it, giving the erroneous impression that the aria alone was recorded.

Chapter Eleven
January–June 1949

7.30pm-10.00pm on 12.1.49
The Royal Albert Hall, London

KF 71 **BRAHMS** (arr. Sargent)/
The Bible (Ecclesiastes, Ecclesiasticus and I Corinthians),
Translation from the German by Paul England
Four Serious Songs, Op. 121/English
Conductor: Sir Malcolm Sargent, BBC Symphony Orchestra
BBC Sound Archives Reference: T 13261-3
BBC Transcription Service Reference: TS 127021 (Side Number)

After a very small recorded output in 1948 (apart from the set of *St Matthew Passion*, Decca issued only three sides of Kathleen's from the whole year), 1949 proved to be most fruitful; sessions for Decca resulted in some excellent releases, and several of her broadcasts in both the UK and Europe have been issued commercially.

A series of winter Promenade Concerts at the Royal Albert Hall included a performance of Brahms' *Four serious songs* in a special arrangement for orchestra made by Malcolm Sargent. It was during the illness of his daughter Pamela, at whose bedside he spent many hours in 1944, that Sargent prepared his orchestration from Brahms' original piano accompaniment.

Nancy Evans sang the first performance of this new version in Liverpool on 10 August 1944, but to Kathleen went the privilege of giving the first radio broadcast on 26 August, from Manchester, on the day following Pamela Sargent's death; Malcolm Sargent's place on the podium on that occasion was taken by Julius Harrison. Now, four and a half years later, Kathleen broadcast the songs again, this time with Sargent himself conducting, and the recording made at the time by the BBC was held in their Sound Archives. This is the earliest of Kathleen's surviving broadcasts to have been issued by Decca and the royalties due to both her and Sir Malcolm's estates have been donated to the charity originally known as the Malcolm Sargent Cancer Fund for Children.

A release on Guild, as part of a three-CD compilation, includes the brief radio announcement at the opening and retains the original discs' surface

A winter Prom at the Royal Albert Hall, London, 12 January 1949

WINTER SERIES OF

HENRY WOOD

PROMENADE CONCERTS

Wednesday 12 January at 7.30

OVERTURE, Oberon	*Weber*
PIANOFORTE CONCERTO No. 23, in A (K.488)	*Mozart*
A LONDON SYMPHONY	*Vaughan Williams*

INTERVAL

FOUR SERIOUS SONGS	*Brahms - Sargent*
FANTASY-OVERTURE, Romeo and Juliet	*Tchaikovsky*

KATHLEEN FERRIER

Solo Pianoforte DENIS MATTHEWS

THE BBC SYMPHONY ORCHESTRA
Leader : Paul Beard

Conductor :
SIR MALCOLM SARGENT

The Royal Albert Hall

noise throughout, thereby improving the recording's sense of presence. Unlike Guild, Decca fade to silence between songs, destroying the sense of continuity, though their surfaces are less intrusive.

Kathleen's diary indicates that a rehearsal took place at 10.30 on the morning of the performance, and that the concert itself began at 7.30pm; the *Four Serious Songs* were given in the second part of the concert, which was broadcast on the BBC Home Service.

2.30pm on 10.2.49
Decca studios, Broadhurst Gardens

KF 72 **TRAD.** Arr. W.G. Whittaker
Blow the wind southerly/English
Unaccompanied
Matrix DR 13217-1-2

KF 73 **TRAD.** Arr. W.G. Whittaker
Ma bonny lad/Scottish
Matrix DR 13218-1A-1B

KF 74 **TRAD.** Arr. W.G. Whittaker
The keel row/English
Matrix DR 13218-1A-1B

KF 75 **TRAD.** Arr. Grew/Johnson
Have you seen but a whyte lillie grow?/English
Matrix DR 13219-1
Piano for all accompanied items: Phyllis Spurr

10.00am on 11.2.49
Decca studios, Broadhurst Gardens

KF 76 **TRAD.** Arr. Warlock
Willow, willow/English
Matrix DR 13220-1

KF 77 **TRAD.** Arr. Hughes
The Lover's Curse/English
Matrix DR 13221-1-2-(3)

KF 78 **TRAD.** Arr. Hughes/W.B. Yeats
Down by the salley gardens/English
Matrix DR 13222-1-2
Piano for all items: Phyllis Spurr

The month after her Royal Albert Hall performance of *Four Serious Songs*
Kathleen recorded seven folk songs, traditional airs, very different in
their simplicity from so much that was in her repertory. In the UK only
one 78 record resulted from the two sessions, one side of which is the
celebrated *Blow the wind southerly* in its arrangement by the music scholar,
conductor and composer W G Whittaker (1876-1944). This song is unique
among Kathleen's recorded legacy; it is the only one sung
unaccompanied (although on both 78 and subsequent releases, Phyllis

Spurr is credited on labels with being the accompanist), and it is the most frequently reissued of her recordings, on 45 rpm, 33 rpm 10" and 12" discs, tape cassettes, stereo 8 cartridges and on CD. It also provides a clear example of the way in which Decca used different takes for their 78 rpm and later LP releases. Any collector with a 78 copy of *Blow the wind southerly* will recall that Kathleen sings the words '… but sweeter and dearer by far when 'tis bringing …' ; LP and later collectors hear the words in a different order – 'but sweeter and dearer by far 'tis when bringing …', showing that both takes were issued, but in different formats. A Nimbus compilation from 1995, *More Legendary Voices*, issued to complement the book of the same name by Nigel Douglas (André Deutsch 1994), uses the 78 version of this song, surely a unique opportunity (at the time of writing) to hear take 1 on CD.

The two songs on the reverse are *Ma bonny lad* and *The keel row*. Issuing two numbers on one side of a 78 was by no means unusual and Kathleen had already sung two duets with Isobel Baillie on one side of a Columbia 10" in 1945. Matrix DR 13218, which features *Ma bonny lad* and *The keel row*, appears to have been created by dubbing together two separate recordings on to a new wax – hence its '1A' designation. This 78 was the only one of Kathleen's output for Decca to be issued on the 'F' label series, generally used for their more popular ranges of music; all her other Decca 10" 78s were released on the classical 'M' series, so this celebrated record might be regarded as an early example of 'crossover' repertoire, so prevalent among classical singers in more recent years.

Folk songs, with Phyllis Spurr, issued in 1951

The other four songs recorded at the sessions on 10 and 11 February were never issued in the UK as 78s, and made their first appearance in May 1951 on a 10″ Medium Play 33 rpm disc. All seven songs from these sessions were, however, issued on a set of three 78s in the United States, on the London label. Decca archives show that two takes were made of *The Lover's Curse*, but a copy of the 78 from the American set in the BBC Gramophone Library is marked 'Take 3', perhaps having been dubbed from either take 1 or 2 for technical reasons.

John Culshaw, for many years a recording manager, and later musical director, with Decca, was in charge of these sessions; he worked on other recordings with Kathleen too, but these, and the two days in October 1952, are the only sets of sessions that he specifically mentions in his autobiography *Putting the Record Straight*, published in 1981; and Decca's own archives are not forthcoming about producers and engineers for many of their sessions in the 1940s.

Kathleen's own view that '... the folk songs I have recorded, particularly the unaccompanied *Blow the wind southerly*, and *The keel row*, are good' accords with that of hundreds of thousands of record buyers since.

2.30pm on 14.2.49
Decca studios, Broadhurst Gardens

KF 79 **SCHUBERT**/Goethe
Der Musensohn, D 764, Op. 92, No. 1/German
Piano: Phyllis Spurr
Matrix DR 13234-1-2-3
Never issued/Destroyed

KF 80 **SCHUBERT**/von Schober
An die Musik, D 547, Op. 88, No. 4/German
Piano: Phyllis Spurr
Matrix DR 13235-1-2

2.00pm on 15.2.49
Decca studios, Broadhurst Gardens

KF 81 **BRAHMS**/Rückert
Gestillte Sehnsucht, Op. 91, No. 1/German
Piano: Phyllis Spurr, Viola: Max Gilbert
Matrix AR 13236-1A-2

KF 82 BRAHMS/Geibel

Geistliches Wiegenlied, Op. 91, No. 2/German
Piano: Phyllis Spurr, Viola: Max Gilbert
Matrix AR 13237-1A-2-3

Keen to record more sides before her departure for the United States on 18 February, Kathleen visited Decca's studios on the 14th and 15th, again taking Phyllis Spurr as her accompanist. Three attempts to make an acceptable version of Schubert's *Der Musensohn* were to no avail, but a

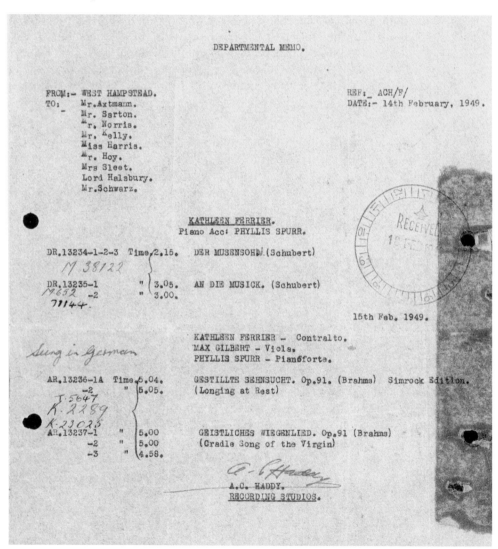

Recording sheet from the Decca sessions at Broadhurst Gardens, 14/15 February 1949

first-time success was achieved with *An die Musik*. With Max Gilbert again playing viola, two more attempts were made to obtain satisfactory performances of the Brahms songs *Op. 91, Gestillte Sehnsucht* and *Geistliches Wiegenlied*; fortunately, those, too, were successful.

By this time Decca had allocated quite new matrix numbers to those songs, rather than continuing to increase the suffix on the original number first used in December 1947. Even so, there may have been some problems with the successful takes, as they appear to have been transferred to new matrices, both with the suffix 1A. On Decca reissues, a curious addition is audible on *Geistliches Wiegenlied*, as a patch lasting thirty-eight seconds has been inserted from a different pressing, perhaps to cover a fault on the record used to make the dubbing. For his 2004 Schumann/Brahms Naxos CD, recording producer Mark Obert-Thorn has finally been able to avoid this aural scar; whilst the sources for other items on his CD were Decca LPs, he was able to trace a fair 78 rpm copy of the two Brahms songs and thus re-issue this beautiful lullaby as it was intended to be heard by the artists.

The *Opus 91* songs were originally issued by Decca on a 12" 78 in December 1949, the month in which Kathleen and Phyllis recorded the published version of *Der Musensohn*, (itself released with *An die Musik* in June 1950). It is extraordinary to think that Kathleen recorded only four of Schubert's songs commercially for Decca, although of course many others have been issued from radio broadcasts.

? 2.3.1949/New York

KF 83 ***Kathleen Ferrier at a Party***
NSA Reference: NSA Tape M7439W
In a private collection

KF 83a Moss, ***The Floral Dance***/English
Piano: Kathleen Ferrier

A tape of Kathleen exists, unique, off-stage and informal, believed to have been recorded at a party in New York at the home of her American friend the actor William Griffis. Whilst it has not proved possible to date the recording precisely, it seems to have been made during Kathleen's second visit to the United States, between late February and 26 May 1949. An entry in her diary for 2 March may give a clue; after noting an evening concert performance of *Orfeo* at New York's Town Hall, Kathleen has added '… Reception. Willie's, lovely …' But whenever it took place, there is no doubt that everyone is having a hilarious evening, being entertained by a very relaxed diva.

Although the tape lasts just six minutes forty-five seconds, Kathleen has time to sing from five songs – *Will o' the wisp, The Floral Dance, The Three Trees, Sing, joyous bird* and *Annie Laurie*. She abbreviates the first-named song by linking the first section of the first verse with the second part of the second – a fifty percent reduction at a stroke. She also omits the second verse of *The Floral Dance* for this cabaret-style performance. *The Three Trees*, referred to on the tape as *The Antelope Song*, was made popular by the American entertainer Frank Crumit; in her biography, Winifred recalled how, during the war, after practising Brahms' *Four Serious Songs*, Kathleen would 'laugh to relieve the tension. She would then sit down at the piano and perform a silly monologue' – one she obviously retained in her 'private' repertoire for a number of years. *Sing, joyous bird* receives but a brief performance and *Annie Laurie* is merely hinted at.

During this convivial evening Kathleen burlesques the overblown style employed by some singers when 'interpreting' such pieces, and accompanies herself for each item; it is the only surviving recording on which Kathleen can be heard playing the piano. Between songs, she laughs and jokes with her friends, and recalls how, when accompanying her father in years past, she would unexpectedly change key, which always amused (and probably irritated) him very much; she even manages to play a duff note in the National Anthem towards the tape's close, resulting in a typically hearty chuckle. A short ciné film was made, probably also at this party, and to see her performing (see Chapter Twenty-One) is as fascinating as to hear her.

From this tape, *The Floral Dance* was issued on the BBC tribute *The Singer and the Person* and the complete *Kathleen Ferrier at a Party* has appeared on a Gala CD and cassette compilation, and elsewhere. A release on a Wisp CD, by Willem Smith Productions in Holland, adds an extra few words to the end of this scene; a voice (probably Kathleen's, but seeming to be in a quite different acoustic), asks for some coffee to 'sober me up!' If authentic, this phrase was probably excised when the scene first became generally available on LP and CD but Mr Smith may have had access to an original copy and replaced the missing words; but most listeners will undoubtedly enjoy the party sufficiently without them.

Chapter Twelve
July–December 1949

9.10pm (UK broadcast starting time) on 14.7.49
Concertgebouw, Amsterdam

KF 86 **BRITTEN**/Various poets
Spring Symphony, Op.44/English
Soprano: Jo Vincent
Tenor: Peter Pears
Netherlands Radio Choir and Boys' Choir of St Willibrorduskerk,
Rotterdam, Concertgebouw Orchestra
Conductor: Eduard van Beinum
NSA Reference: NSA Tape T10543

In the summer of 1949 Kathleen spent five weeks in the Netherlands
singing at the Holland Festival, the culmination of which was the first
performance of Benjamin Britten's latest work, *Spring Symphony*. It was
composed for the Boston Symphony Orchestra at the request of Serge
Koussevitzky, who had hoped to conduct the world première in the
United States. However, that honour went instead to Eduard van Beinum
(1901-1959) in Amsterdam, as part of the Festival. Some sources give the
date of the performance as 9 July but others, including the Britten-Pears
Library in Aldeburgh and Kathleen's own diary, confirm that it was in
fact 14 July. Such an error is understandable, as both *The New Grove
Dictionary of Music* and Britten himself in *Kathleen Ferrier – A Memoir*
(published by Hamish Hamilton in 1954) quote the earlier date.

Spring Symphony is composed for three soloists – soprano, contralto and
tenor – mixed chorus, a separate chorus of boys' voices and orchestra.
The texts used are British poems and include works from the 13th
century (*Soomer is icoomen in* – anonymous) through to the 20th,
represented by W.H. Auden (*Out on the lawn I lie in bed*).

On 5 May Kathleen wrote to Britten from Cuba, clearly anticipating the
difficulties of the work ahead '… looking forward enormously to
Holland! Getting worried about seeing my notes and getting used to the
augmented 19ths I know await me! Hope I don't let you down mi darlin'!
Will try awful hard not to! …' Once in Amsterdam, on 5 July she confided
to her Canadian accompanist and friend John Newmark '… I still haven't

really started on the Britten, but have been so tired and hardworked, I could only tackle one job at a time … but after tomorrow I really must get down to it!' And in a letter to Winifred on 12 July she admitted '… working … at the Britten – not thrilled with my bits and I can get mi 'oo' but I'm buddered if I can get mi 'cuck'! Poor Kaff! I'm a shadow! Oh yea!' The comment on 'oo's and 'cuck's refers to the section *Spring*, in which Kathleen was joined by the other two soloists; each had to sing imitation birdsong in turn – a different bird for each of three verses.

Kathleen did not start seriously learning the symphony until the first week of July; she had been fully occupied with a new production of *Orfeo ed Euridice* and several concerts and recitals, but the first performance with Jo Vincent and Peter Pears as her fellow soloists seems to have been a considerable success. The presence of Field Marshal Montgomery, who was not apparently noted for his interest in modern music, irritated Britten, who feared that the reception given to the respected military leader might detract from the artistic acclaim that the occasion deserved. The concert opened with a performance of Mozart's *Symphony in E Flat* (K 543); Britten's new symphony comprised the entire second half of the programme.

At the request of Lord Harewood a private recording was made of the BBC Third Programme broadcast of the Amsterdam première and in 1991 he gave the acetate discs to the National Sound Archive in London. He was keen that the performance should be made publicly available, both at the NSA and commercially. In a letter written in 2004, Lord Harewood recalled the occasion: 'With my first wife Marion, I was in Amsterdam for rehearsals and the first performance of Britten's *Spring Symphony* in summer 1949. It was a splendid occasion, beautifully performed in the very good acoustics of the Concertgebouw and with exemplary soloists of Britten's choosing. Kathleen's performance was on the highest level, a wonderful example of her ability to convey serenity and intensity in the same performance. I rank her performance of Britten's setting of the Auden poem as one of the finest things she ever did.'

In his 1992 biography of Britten, published by Faber and Faber, Humphrey Carpenter quoted Ronald Duncan, librettist of *The Rape of Lucretia*, who had earlier written about this concert: 'I recall Ben's concern with the chorus of boys, and how he repeatedly interrupted the rehearsals … because he was worried about the articulation … "You want to bite your consonants as though they were an apple," he said emphatically.' Such close involvement of the composer leads one to question why he was not himself conducting the performance.

In August 1994 this *Spring Symphony* was first released by Decca. Britten's *Four Sea Interludes* from *Peter Grimes* and *Young Person's Guide to the Orchestra*, also conducted by van Beinum, completed the CD. The accompanying booklet is furnished with the full text of the symphony

With Benjamin Britten in Amsterdam. In the background is the Earl of Harewood, who attended Spring Symphony's *première*

and valuable notes by John Steane, although the incorrect date is quoted; no matter. That the performance should have been issued at all is most heartening and the imperfect technical quality is a small price to pay for the historical value of such an issue. At the time of writing this Decca CD is no longer in their catalogue but a similar issue, on the Audiophile label released in 2003, appears to be currently available.

Six weeks after this première Kathleen sang with Julius Patzak in two concerts at the Salzburg Festival, with Bruno Walter conducting the Vienna Philharmonic Orchestra. It would seem to be one of those performances of *Das Lied von der Erde* that was recorded and allegedly survives in Austrian Radio archives (see the discussion concerning **KF 210** in Chapter Seventeen), but about which ORF are unwilling to comment.

7.30pm-9.00pm on 7.9.49
Usher Hall, Edinburgh

KF 87 **SCHUBERT**/Craigher
Die junge Nonne, D 828, Op. 43, No. 1/German

KF 88 **SCHUBERT**/Von Chézy
Der Vollmond strahlt (Romance from *Rosamunde*), D 797, Op. 26/German

The Usher Hall recital, 7 September 1949: signed for the
photographer, Norward Inglis

KF 89 **SCHUBERT**/Platen
Du liebst mich nicht, D 756, Op. 59, No. 1/German

KF 90 **SCHUBERT**/Claudius
Der Tod und das Mädchen, D 531, Op. 7, No. 3/German

KF 91 **SCHUBERT**/Willemer adapted by Goethe
Suleika 1, D 720, Op. 14, No. 1/German

KF 92 **SCHUBERT**/Rückert
Du bist die Ruh', D 776, Op. 59, No. 3/German

KF 93 **SCHUMANN**/Chamisso
Frauenliebe und Leben, Op. 42 (Eight songs)/German

KF 94 **BRAHMS**/Lingg
Immer leiser wird mein Schlummer, Op. 105, No. 2/German

KF 95 **BRAHMS**/Heine
Der Tod, das ist die kühle Nacht, Op. 96, No. 1/German

KF 96 **BRAHMS**/Daumer
Botschaft, Op. 47, No. 1/ German

KF 97 **BRAHMS**/Wendish poem, German version by Wenzig
Von ewiger Liebe, Op. 43, No. 1/German

All items, Piano: Bruno Walter
BBC Sound Archives Reference: T 14015-20
BBC Transcription Service Reference: BBC TS 127021
(Side Number) *Du liebst mich nicht* only
BBC Transcription Service Reference: BBC TS 101490
(Side Number)

This recital, broadcast by the BBC and recorded by the Transcription Service on 7 September 1949 from the Edinburgh International Festival, is the best surviving demonstration of the way in which Kathleen responded to a live audience. Like most singers, she was able to interpret her material far more vividly during a public performance than in a recording studio; valuable comparisons can be made between versions of Lieder sung at this recital and those made at other times with only the microphone and an accompanist present.

With Bruno Walter at the piano, Kathleen sang as she never could in the cold solitude of a studio and she held the audience at the Usher Hall enthralled. In the form in which it has survived, the recital comprises six Schubert Lieder, Schumann's song-cycle *Frauenliebe und Leben* and four Lieder by Brahms. Both *Radio Times* and Kathleen's diary list two further Brahms pieces – *Wir wandelten* and *Am Sonntag Morgen* – which, if performed, appear not to have survived. Indeed, even with these two numbers included, the recital seems to have offered rather short measure.

Six days later Kathleen wrote to her agent Emmie Tillett, '… wish you had been here. I missed you because I felt the recital with Bruno Walter was a peak to which I had been groping for the last three years! He was pleased and so were the critics, so everybody's happy …' She certainly appreciated the privilege of appearing with Walter in this, one of the major events of the third Edinburgh Festival.

Decca first issued this recital in November 1975, taken from original recordings in the BBC archives. It required three sides of a double LP album, the fourth side being devoted to another BBC recital, Kathleen's last radio recording, from January 1953. Subsequent re-issues of the Edinburgh Liederabend omitted the 1953 broadcast, enabling it to be

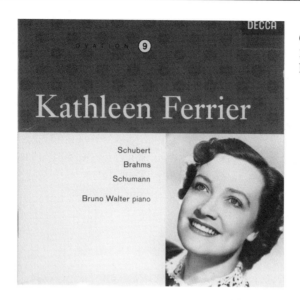

CD booklet from Decca's 1992 Kathleen Ferrier *Edition*

released complete on a single LP, cassette and CD. Before Decca's issue, an earlier LP of the performance was available from the Bruno Walter Society in the USA, though this version did not include Kathleen's short broadcast talk, which is such an attractive addition to Decca's. *Frauenliebe und Leben* was issued on yet another American issue, with a different coupling. More recent Decca CD releases have enabled this fine recital to be heard in improved sound.

Kathleen recorded one of the Schubert Lieder commercially for Decca and three others survive in BBC studio performances, but these are the only extant versions of *Der Tod und das Mädchen* and *Du bist die Ruh'*. *Frauenliebe und Leben* was recorded by Decca with John Newmark as accompanist in July 1950 – Walter had previously made a recording with the soprano Lotte Lehmann in June 1941; and the incomplete 1951 version, in which Walter again accompanied Kathleen, survives in the Leech collection at the NSA (*KF 181*). In this 1949 Edinburgh recording, Walter's playing seems unsubtle – eccentric even – but is perhaps representative of the style in which he was taught at the end of the 19th century. The evident rapport between singer and pianist gives this live 1949 performance a vitality that is missing from Ferrier's commercial recording (but see Chapter Fourteen, in which this apparent lack of energy is discussed). Kathleen recorded one of the Brahms Lieder commercially three months after the Edinburgh performance, with Phyllis Spurr; and another survives in an incomplete version from Denmark from October 1949, but neither *Immer leiser wird mein Schlummer* nor *Der Tod, das ist die kühle Nacht* was otherwise recorded.

The order above is that of the original LP issue in 1975. According to *Radio Times*, *Du bist die Ruh'* was sung second in the programme and *Der*

Vollmond strahlt was sung after *Suleika 1*. The two (?) missing Brahms items were sung after *Der Tod, das ist die kühle Nacht*; on reissue in 1986, *Frauenliebe und Leben* was placed at the end of the recital, which order has been retained for later CD versions. The master tape in the BBC Sound Archives retains the original radio announcements, although they have been omitted on the commercial releases; a pity perhaps, as they would have added an authentic period quality and contributed to the immediacy of the occasion. Some items from this recital also survive in the Leech collection at the NSA, but the sound on the BBC's Transcription Discs is far superior to the home-recorded acetates.

12.15pm-12.55pm on 11.9.49
BBC Studio, Edinburgh

KF 98 *What the Edinburgh Festival has meant to me*
Talk broadcast by the BBC
BBC Sound Archives Reference: LP 27264
NSA Reference: NSA Tape M7439W
KF 98a Extract from talk

Not all of Kathleen's surviving recordings are of her singing. There are four brief examples of her speaking voice, of which this short talk, given during the 1949 Edinburgh Festival, is the only one preserved by the BBC; it lasts just two minutes fifty-two seconds. Kathleen spoke several times on BBC radio and appeared on television on at least one occasion; but like so many broadcasts which would now be considered of historical interest, most were either not recorded at the time or, if recorded, were not long saved in the archives.

This talk was broadcast on a Scottish Home Service *Arts Review* programme, entitled simply *Edinburgh International Festival*; it was issued commercially by Decca in 1975 as an introduction to the Lieder recital with Bruno Walter and an extract was issued in 1979 on the BBC's *The Singer and the Person*.

Kathleen's speaking voice is as warm and rich as her singing voice. She reveals a slight hesitation at some points, as if diffident about broadcasting, and an audible smile is heard when she mentions Bruno Walter's comments on her recital in New York. She tells how much she values working and learning with her musical mentor and of her pleasure at singing once again in Edinburgh. Kathleen wrote the talk herself and both its content and delivery convey the amazement she felt at having achieved so much, particularly overseas, in such a short time. One reference in the BBC Sound Archives indicates that the talk was given on 8 September, and another that it was the 11th; an entry in her diary '… 12.00 broadcast' on the 11th surely settles the matter.

2.30pm-5.30pm on 4.10.49
Kingsway Hall, London

KF 99 MAHLER/Rückert

Kindertotenlieder/German
Conductor: Bruno Walter, Vienna Philharmonic Orchestra

Side	Matrix/take	No (auto)	Title
1	CAX 10624-1A-1B-2	LX 8939	*Nun will die Sonn'so hell aufgeh'n*
2	CAX 10625-1-2	LX 8940	*Nun seh'ich wohl, warum so dunkle*
3	CAX 10626-1	LX 8941	*Wenn dein Mütterlein tritt zur Tur*
4	CAX 10627-1A-1B	LX 8941	*Oft denk'ich, sie sind nur ausgegangen*
5	CAX 10628-1-2	LX 8940	*In diesem Wetter, in diesem Braus* (Pt 1)
6	CAX 10629-1A-1B	LX 8939	*In diesem Wetter, in diesem Braus* (Pt 2)

KF 99a   *Nun will die Sonn'*
KF 99b   *Oft denk' ich*

After appearing together at the Edinburgh Festival, Kathleen and Bruno Walter travelled to London to give two more concerts, and in Kingsway Hall on 4 October they realised one of their dearest artistic ambitions; to record Mahler's *Kindertotenlieder*.

*KF on HMV –
the 1972 LP issue*

Walter had introduced Kathleen to these songs in 1947 and she first performed them on BBC radio on 25 November that year. Early in 1949 Kathleen had asked Decca to release her temporarily from her contract so that she might be 'lent' to American Columbia, the company for which Walter worked, so that this recording might be made. After receiving their refusal, Kathleen wrote from New York on 19 May to Harry Sarton, manager of Decca's Artists Department.

'... I can't tell you how disappointed I am that you have decided not to release me for this recording with Bruno Walter. I rang Mr Lieberson up this morning and agreed with him when he said it was too uneven an exchange of artists – Bruno Walter for me! I told him you had lent artists before and had no-one in exchange and that it was too one-sided and he said he was willing to exchange any pianist, singer or other executant, in this case as BW has asked for me personally.

'... If you don't release me to do this, they will have an American singer – of whom there are many – to do it. Can't you see, that with all this competition, what an honour it is, for you as well as for me, to be singled out – to have to borrow an artist? When I came to Decca at first it was with the promise of a recording of the *Messiah* – which never materialised. This same recording is the biggest hit in America and one of the largest money-makers.

'... I never expect to make money with this recording of the *Kindertotenlieder* but the honour of appearing on a label with Bruno Walter would put me in the top flight of artists both here and in Europe and would compensate for my disappointment over the *Messiah* recording.'

Kathleen also used the letter to make a firm point about Decca's overseas sales policy.

'... My records – when they are purchasable – are going like wildfire here, but there are just not enough to go round this huge country. I hope you are pleased with my latest recordings of folk songs. I have been singing them from Canada to the Middle West, Florida and Cuba, so send a lot – they'll sell too!'

So Decca relented and Kathleen made her first commercial recording with Walter; in 1952 the compliment was returned when American Columbia 'lent' Walter to Decca so that these two friends and devoted Mahlerians could record *Das Lied von der Erde* and three *Rückert Lieder*, again with the Vienna Philharmonic. After all this discussion, however, there was a strangely long delay in releasing *Kindertotenlieder* in the UK. It first appeared on a set of three 78s and on a 10inch 33rpm disc in November 1952.

Kathleen wrote a letter home to Winifred, from Beverley Hills, on 3 February 1950, in which she referred to the recording. By that time she had been sent test pressings of the 78s.

'... the first record is not the one to be published as I run out of breath in one phrase ... I do hope you like the records – I was rather pleased with them myself, for once, but will probably change my mind when I hear them again.'

In his book *Walter Legge – A discography*, published by Greenwood Press, Alan Sanders points out that matrix CAX 10624 (the first of the set) was transferred on to another wax and allocated the number CAX 10624-1B. The recording sheets in EMI's archives emphasise that there was a problem with a matrix of the first side, but do not specify its nature. If this is the side to which Kathleen referred in her letter, then the fault with her breathing would still be heard on the newly-made wax (which it is not); as this session was recorded on tape as well as disc (almost certainly the first of Kathleen's recordings at which the new medium was used) it may be that the transfer was made from the tape of a different take of the first song. Another possibility is that the flawed take that she had been sent was the *second* take on wax (which is known to have been made), and that the transfer to CAX 10624-1B was made for a technical rather than a vocal reason. EMI archives confirm that two other sides (CAX 10627 and 10629) were transferred from the tape source on to wax, and were issued with the suffix 1A. Yet another factor which confuses the issue is the ambiguity of the meanings of 1A and 1B; these terms were also used when more than one wax was made of a given take, the number denoting the take number, and the suffix letter denoting which turntable had been used. It is thus not entirely clear in this case just what 1A and 1B signified.

Whatever the truth or supposition about it, EMI's engineers did full justice to the artists; this *Kindertotenlieder* is in excellent sound and contains some wonderful singing and playing. It was the only recording that Kathleen made for Columbia after leaving that company for Decca in 1946; on 78s it was issued on automatic couplings only. In November 1987 Decca issued a further version of Kathleen singing the work, taken from a live performance in Amsterdam in July 1951, with Otto Klemperer conducting.

In their Centenary Edition of 11 CDs, issued in 1998 to celebrate 100 years of record making, EMI Classics selected the fourth song of the Ferrier/Walter performance – *Oft denk'ich* – to represent Kathleen's contribution to their unique musical heritage.

The producer for this recording was Walter Legge and the balance engineer Douglas Larter.

8.00pm on 6.10.49
Denmark's Radio Studio No.1, Copenhagen

KF 100 **BRAHMS**/Goethe (from *Harzreise im Winter*)
Rhapsody for contralto, male chorus and orchestra, Op. 53/German
Conductor: Fritz Busch, Danish Radio Symphony Orchestra,
Danish Radio Male Chorus

KF 101 **BRAHMS**/Wendish poem. German version by Wenzig
Von ewiger Liebe, Op. 43, No. 1/German
Piano: Phyllis Spurr
(Incomplete)

KF 102 **BRAHMS**/Hungarian poem, German translation by Daumer
Wir wandelten, Op.96, No.2/German
Piano: Phyllis Spurr
(Incomplete)

On the day after recording *Kindertotenlieder*, Kathleen, with her accompanist Phyllis Spurr, flew to Denmark on the first leg of a Scandinavian tour. In a letter to Emmie Tillett, her agent, Kathleen wrote '… our plane was an hour late leaving! You should have seen us skid through the Customs and the traffic to the Radio for immediate rehearsal!'

The next evening Kathleen sang Brahms' *Alto Rhapsody*, with two Lieder as encores, for a broadcast which was recorded by Danish Radio. Unfortunately, none of the three works was satisfactorily preserved, but all have been issued commercially, shortcomings notwithstanding. Despite the use of a double turntable so that long performances could be recorded complete, with overlapping sides, not all of *Alto Rhapsody* survived. Some discs suffered damage and there seemed to be no chance of assembling a complete version until a tape of the broadcast, recorded by Dr Bengt Andreas in Malmö, Sweden, was discovered. This enabled the engineers to fill in the gaps but with the result that several times during the work the sound quality changes very noticeably. Apparently filters and digital processors were used to minimise the problem but with only modest success. Both Brahms songs, with Spurr's accompaniments, are shorn of their opening bars. In the case of *Von ewiger Liebe*, thirty-two bars (approximately eighty seconds) are missing, comprising most of the first stanza. From *Wir wandelten*, three bars, of piano introduction only, are lost. Perhaps the sound engineer failed to position the recording head on to the wax in time, or maybe parts of the discs were irreparably

The Danish Brahms broadcast
– a Danacord LP

damaged. The performance of *Alto Rhapsody* is of special historical significance as the only surviving recording of Kathleen singing a performance conducted by Fritz Busch (1890-1951). In 1950 he again conducted the *Rhapsody* with Kathleen as soloist at the Edinburgh Festival, a performance given shortly after his return to Glyndebourne as Music Director, following an absence of eleven years.

On the issued LP, cassette and CD these performances are coupled with a 1950 broadcast of Beethoven's *Fifth Symphony* conducted by Furtwängler, also recorded in Copenhagen. Danacord, the issuing company, have donated funds from the sales of the recordings to cancer research.

The recording engineer for Danish Radio was Frederic Heegaard.

14.10.49/Studio of Norsk Rikskringkasting, Oslo

KF 103 **BRAHMS**/Goethe (from *Harzreise im Winter*)
Rhapsody for contralto, male chorus and orchestra, Op. 53/German
Conductor: Erik Tuxen, Oslo Philharmonic Orchestra,
Men of The Oslo Philharmonic Chorus
Norsk Rikskringkasting Reference: Ark.Nr.9189

Another stop on this Scandinavian tour was in Oslo. Kathleen gave a further performance of *Alto Rhapsody* on 12 October – her diary mentions that Berkeley's *Four poems of St Teresa* were also performed – but does not

Erik Tuxen

Das Lied von der Erde *and*
Alto Rhapsody *on APR, 2003*

specify a venue; and although not shown in the diary, Norwegian Radio claim yet another *Rhapsody* from their studios on 14th, conducted by Erik Tuxen. Whether these two Brahms performances might, in fact, be one and the same should be considered, for it could simply be that the later date was mistakenly entered on the studio's documentation; no mention is made in Kathleen's diary of a performance on 14th – simply a reference that she was in Oslo.

The *Rhapsody* remained in their archives and is the finest of the three extant versions of the work. It is in excellent sound, if slightly bass-heavy, and has appreciably more pace than that recorded by Krauss for Decca in 1947. Kathleen seems in better voice than in the Danish version of the previous week and the studio audience applauds enthusiastically at the work's close.

Erik Tuxen (1902-1957) enjoyed an interestingly varied career for, after studying music in various European cities and conducting opera in Copenhagen, he formed his own jazz orchestra, which performed successfully for several years before the Second World War. He later became an advocate of the music of Nielsen, recorded several of his symphonies and composed several film scores and incidental music for a number of stage performances in Denmark.

As a 50th anniversary tribute to Kathleen, this performance of *Alto Rhapsody* was issued commercially for the first time in 2003 (together with the Barbirolli *Das Lied von der Erde*) by Appian (APR), an English record company based in Northumberland. The piece has transferred beautifully to CD and is one of the great Ferrier treasures to have been released in recent years.

16.10.49/Studio of Norsk Rikskringkasting, Oslo

KF 104 PURCELL/Settle? after Shakespeare
Hark! The echoing air (*The Fairy Queen*)/English
Matrix AR 22959

KF 105 HANDEL/Adapted from Valerian,
English version by Albert G Latham
Like as the love-lorn turtle (*Atalanta*)/English
Matrix AR 22960

KF 106 HANDEL/English version by M X Hayes
How changed the vision (*Admeto*)/English
Matrix AR 22961

KF 107 PURCELL (arr. Britten)/
from *Choice Ayres and Songs to sing to the theorblute, or bass-viol*
Mad Bess of Bedlam (*From silent shades*)/English
Matrix AR 22962

KF 108 WOLF/E Mörike
Verborgenheit, *Mörike-Lieder No.12*/German
Matrix AR 22963

KF 109 WOLF/E Mörike
Der Gärtner, *Mörike-Lieder No. 17*/German
Matrix AR 22964

KF 110 WOLF/E Mörike
Auf ein altes Bild, *Mörike-Lieder No. 23*/German
Matrix AR 22965

KF 111 WOLF/E Mörike
Auf einer Wanderung, *Mörike-Lieder No. 15*/German
Matrix AR 22966

KF 112 L I JENSEN/Moren
Altar/Norwegian
Preceded by a brief spoken introduction
Matrix AR 22967
Norsk Rikskringkasting Reference: Ark.Nr.9202
On all items – Piano: Phyllis Spurr

A postcard from Oslo:
'a bluidy marvel!'

All still well with us. sat: hope
it is with you aussi. Concerts have
gone well so far, and crits. wonderful.
K.K! Am singing a song in Norweigan
temorrow. I'm a bluidy marvel!
leave temorrow for Stockholm &
home on 29th – whispee! have
from littul Phyll – she's spoiling
me to death. Much love to
you both. Kaff.

On 16 October Kathleen was again in the Oslo studios, this time to broadcast a recital with Phyllis Spurr. On tour she often performed two contrasting programmes, and in Scandinavia in 1949 the two consisted of

(a) Schubert, Schumann and Brahms – indeed, the very group that she sang at the Usher Hall, Edinburgh the previous month, and (b) a mixed recital consisting principally of Purcell, Handel, Wolf and Britten, together with some other English and Italian songs. It is part of the latter programme that has survived from this Norwegian broadcast. It seems that it was judiciously cut, perhaps to fit a broadcasting schedule, but what remains provides an opportunity to hear Kathleen sing six songs that she did not otherwise record. After the concert, for Kathleen's benefit, the engineer played the recording that had been made; as so often, she claimed to be disappointed by her efforts, and so it was consigned to a distant shelf in the archives. Seven years later, after her death, it was re-discovered and sent to Winifred, so that she might hear and enjoy it. With the permission of Norsk Rikskringkasting, she in turn offered it to Decca who issued it (with one omission) on an LP in May 1957.

The surprising omission from this LP was *Mad Bess of Bedlam* by Purcell, in an arrangement by Benjamin Britten; it surely cannot have been for reasons of space on the record as the complete recital lasts little over 34 minutes. *Mad Bess* was, however, first released by Decca in April 1963, coupled with two folk songs accompanied by John Newmark. Even in the 7-LP boxed set AKF 1-7, issued in 1973, *Mad Bess* does not appear on the same disc as the rest of the recital and is not acknowledged as having originally been part of it. Only on the CD and cassette issues of 1992 was the whole recital reassembled. A strange situation, as Kathleen might have observed using her pet name for this song, ... a *Bad Mess*.

Kathleen sang little Wolf, but *Verborgenheit* (*Secrecy*) was the song for which she was awarded the Gold Medal at the Millom Festival in 1938, although on that occasion it was performed in English. (The adjudicator commented '... her voice ... makes me imagine I am being stroked'!) The final item, which Kathleen sang as an encore, is particularly intriguing. It is *Altar* by Jensen, learned shortly before the performance, as she explained on a postcard to Winifred on 15 October '... Concerts have gone well so far and crits wonderful ... am singing a song in Norwegian tomorrow – I'm a bluidy marvel!' Kathleen introduced the song with a few words, which for several years were believed to be the only surviving example of her speaking voice. Some Decca re-issues of *Altar* omit this introduction: 'I should like to sing a song for you, if you will bear with some very bad Norwegian; it's a song called *Altar* by Jensen.' The composer Ludvig Irgens Jensen (1894-1969) was one of a number of northern European musicians who shared that surname; the writer of the words was Halldis Moren Vesaas (1907-1995).

Decca made 78rpm matrices from the Norwegian source, but the recital was never released in 78 format. The order of items above is that shown in the archives of Norsk Rikskringkasting, which is also the sequence in which the 78 matrices were prepared by Decca, whose compilations since 1992 place *Mad Bess* at the start of the recital.

A 2003 compilation of three CDs on Guild causes considerable confusion. The Norwegian recital is placed on the same disc as the BBC recital of 5 June 1952 and the booklet notes claim that both *Altar* and *Mad Bess* are taken from the latter. Several other typographical and factual errors mar this issue and the recorded sound, from tapes supplied by one Dr Elkins, is inferior to Decca's, which remains very acceptable despite light surface noise on several tracks.

6.10.49 and 6.30pm on 1.11.49
Kingsway Hall, London

KF 113 **BACH**/The Bible, translated from the German
***Praise our God**, Cantata No. 11, BWV 11*/English
(Lobet Gott in seinem Reichen)
Soprano: Ena Mitchell, Tenor: William Herbert,
Bass: William Parsons, Conductor: Dr Reginald Jacques,
Harpsichord Continuo: Dr Thornton Lofthouse,
The Jacques Orchestra, The Cantata Singers

Matrix/take	Date	No (auto)	Title	Singers
AR 14119-1	6.10.49	AX 399	Praise our God	Chorus
AR 14120-1	6.10.49	AX 400	Praise our God (contd)	Chorus
			Then Jesus	WH
			My Saviour	WP
AR 14121-1	1.11.49	AX 401	Ah, tarry yet	KF
AR 14122-1	1.11.49	AX 401	Ah, tarry yet (contd)	KF
			And behold	WH
			Now at thy feet	Chorus
AR 14123-1	1.11.49	AX 400	And while	WH
			Ye men	WH/WP
			Ah, Lord	KF
			Jesu all	EM
AR 14124-1-2	6.10.49	AX 399	When will	Chorus

KF 114 **BACH**/The Bible, translated from the German
***Praise our God**, Cantata No. 11, BWV 11*/English
Artists as above
33rpm matrices DRL 258 and DRL 259
KF 114a   Ah, tarry yet, my dearest Saviour

101

6.30pm on 3.11.49
Kingsway Hall, London

KF 115 **BACH**/The Bible, translated from the German
Hold in affection Jesus Christ, *Cantata No. 67, BWV 67*/English
(Halt in Gedaechtnis Jesum Christ)
Tenor: William Herbert, Bass: William Parsons
Harpsichord Continuo: Dr Thornton Lofthouse
Organ: Dr Osborne Peasgood, Conductor: Dr Reginald Jacques
The Jacques Orchestra, The Cantata Singers

Matrix/take	No (auto)	Title	Singers
AR 14125-<u>1</u>	AX 347	*Hold in affection*	Chorus
AR 14126-<u>1</u>	AX 348	*Lord Jesus now*	WH
		Lord Jesus Thou	KF
		Come all	Chorus
AR 14127-<u>1</u>	AX 348	*And still*	KF
		Peace be unto you	WP/Chorus
AR 14128-<u>1</u>	AX 347	*Peace be unto you* (cont)	WP/Chorus
		Lord Christ	Chorus

KF 116 **BACH**/The Bible, translated from the German.
Hold in affection Jesus Christ, *Cantata No. 67, BWV 67*/English
Artists as above
33rpm matrices DRL 260 and DRL 261

The first US issue of Cantata 67

With Dr Reginald Jacques

While Kathleen was travelling in Scandinavia, Decca began a project to record some (then) little-known music by J S Bach, in commemoration of the 200th anniversary of his death in 1750. Two cantatas, numbers 11 and 67, were arranged for Kingsway Hall sessions under Dr Reginald Jacques. On 6 October two of the soloists, William Herbert and William Parsons, with the Jacques Orchestra and the Cantata Singers, recorded three 78 sides. On 1 November Kathleen recorded on three sides, Ena Mitchell sang her aria, and the two male soloists added further contributions, making a set of three 12" 78s for *Cantata No. 11*. Two days later, again with Herbert and Parsons, but without Mitchell, Kathleen recorded *Cantata No. 67* on four 12" 78 sides; the cantatas were also issued on two separate 10" 33rpm discs.

Thanks to the perceptive listening of the reviewer in *The Gramophone* it soon transpired that the 78 and 33 versions of these cantatas are quite different performances. On 78s some of the numbers are shortened – Kathleen's solo *Ah, tarry yet* is deprived of its middle section – and the tempi of the two versions vary considerably. The decorations of the harpsichord continuos differ and, as final proof if it were needed, in *Cantata No. 67* William Herbert sings the words 'Lord Jesus' in one version, but 'Christ Jesus' at the same point in the other.

Kenneth Wilkinson, for many years Decca's Chief Recording Engineer, and Assistant Engineer Arthur Bannister both recalled the sessions for these cantatas, and confirmed that, whilst Columbia used reel-to-reel tape at Kingsway Hall for the recording of *Kindertotenlieder* on 4 October,

Decca did not use tape there until 1951. It follows that the differently issued versions of the cantatas are from different takes made at the same sessions, both using 78 waxes as their origin. The job of making LPs in the days before tape masters was an arduous one, created as they were by dubbing direct from specially pressed 78s on to 33rpm waxes. As one 78 on one turntable came to an end, the engineer had to ensure that the stylus on the next turntable was placed at the beginning of the next 78 at exactly the right moment, while the 33rpm wax continued to rotate and record. Wilkinson and Bannister recalled that the first Decca LP of Rimsky-Korsakov's *Scheherazade* took nearly two weeks to make in this way because, just as a successful 33rpm wax was being completed, a small error, perhaps on the last dubbing, would render the whole LP side useless. This must have been the method used to make the 33 versions of the cantatas; Kathleen would have had to record the central part of her aria in *Cantata No. 11* on to a 78 wax so that it could be slotted in to the LP version, even though it is not included on the 78 set. But, bearing in mind the two engineers' comments regarding the use of wax rather than tape at these sessions, it is nevertheless curious that apart from matrix 14124 only one take of each side appears to have been made; this would surely have been dangerously risky economy, particularly if one of these unique waxes had subsequently been damaged.

The original intention was to publish both these cantatas in June 1950 (the month in which Decca issued the very first 33rpm records available in the UK). *Cantata 11* was indeed released that month but there appears to have been an eight-week delay in the publication of *Cantata 67*. The 78 versions were not released until September 1950 (No. 67) and March 1951 (No. 11). When the aria *Ah, tarry yet* was issued on LP and cassette in September 1979 the full-length version was used; indeed, the full 33rpm versions of both works have been used for re-issues since 1951. The 78 sets were only in auto coupling format. *Cantata No. 67* had a choral version in English of *Jesu, joy of man's desiring* as filler on the original 33rpm disc.

Dr Reginald Jacques (1894-1969) became conductor of the Bach Choir in 1931, a position he held for thirty years, and founded the Jacques Orchestra five years later. In the 1940s and early 1950s Kathleen often sang under his baton and always tried to arrange performances with the Bach Choir, for which she had a special affection, in her heavy schedule. Jacques conducted her first important London *Messiah* in Westminster Abbey in May 1943, with Baillie, Pears and Parsons, and it was very likely that he first met Kathleen in his capacity as director of CEMA in November 1942. His work as a choral conductor, particularly in music of the 18th century, was highly innovative for its time, though later overtaken by further scholarship and the search for greater authenticity in performance.

The soprano Ena Mitchell (1903-1979) was a personal and professional friend of long standing from Carlisle days; Kathleen sang with her often before moving to London in 1942 and kept closely in touch for the remainder of her life. Mitchell took part in several concert performances of *Orfeo* that Kathleen and Sir John Barbirolli gave with the Hallé in the north of England and Kathleen's diary reveals a number of meetings with 'Ena' (surely Mitchell) up until the end of 1952. Ena it was, accompanied by Phyllis Spurr, who in 1955 paid tribute to her late friend and gave the first recital in the newly named 'Kathleen Ferrier Memorial Hall' in Etruria, Staffordshire, where Kathleen had sung on several occasions under its earlier identity of the Philharmonic Recital Hall; and Ena was also the mother of the celebrated French horn player Ifor James, who died in December 2004.

Lionel Salter, reviewer in the September 1950 edition of *The Gramophone*, commented on the release of *BWV 11*: 'Except for some of the solo works without chorus, this is, I believe, the first complete recording of a Bach cantata, and therefore all the more welcome,' and two months later he jibbed at the cost difference between the 78 and 33rpm versions of *BWV 67*; 17/3d for the former (now approximately 86 pence) and £1.9.6d for the latter (one pound, forty seven and a half pence). '... The enormous difference in price between the normal and LP versions of this work (even though the latter has a favourite tune as an additional *bonne bouche*) seems absurd to me, and will undoubtedly give pause to many intending purchasers. (I thought the idea was to *encourage* people to buy LP?) ...'

At the time of writing, neither of these cantata performances has been issued complete on compact disc. The engineers for these sessions were Kenneth Wilkinson and Arthur Bannister.

6.30pm-7.40pm on 23.11.49
Albert Hall, Manchester

KF 117 BERKELEY/St Teresa of Avila, translated by Arthur Symons
Four poems of St Teresa of Avila, Op 27/English
Conductor: Sir John Barbirolli
Strings of the Hallé Orchestra, Leader Laurance Turner

During the summer and autumn of 2004, audio restoration engineer Roger Beardsley spent several days assisting the Earl of Harewood in sorting and cataloguing his extensive collection of records at Harewood House; these included a number of acetates taken from radio performances in the 1940s and 1950s, and amongst them was a complete set of four sides of Berkeley's *Four poems of St Teresa of Avila*, made from a broadcast on the BBC North Home Service on 23 November 1949. The concert was given at the Albert Hall on Peter Street, Manchester, formerly a Methodist hall (now converted to a restaurant), which was used regularly by the Hallé for rehearsals and performances before the re-opening of the Free Trade Hall in 1951.

This most exciting find is the earliest known recording of the remarkable musical collaboration of Kathleen and Sir John Barbirolli (their three other known joint recordings date from 1951 and 1952) and it preserves the performance in excellent sound. The other pieces played during the broadcast concert were the overture to Mozart's *Così fan tutte* and Reger's *Variations and Fugue on a theme of Mozart*, but these appear not to have been recorded on this occasion.

By 1949 Barbirolli (1899-1970) and Kathleen were old friends, although their musical association did not start off entirely happily in December 1944, when they performed Elgar's *Sea Pictures* together in Sheffield. Second only to Bruno Walter, Kathleen came to recognise Barbirolli as the greatest musical influence in her life. They spent much time together; Sir John, his wife (the celebrated oboist Evelyn Rothwell) and Kathleen would play chamber music for hours, relaxing in Kathleen's Frognal flat, or at the Barbirollis' home; Kathleen never seemed happier than in the company of these two wonderful companions, with whom she also shared a number of holidays. As conductor of the Hallé Orchestra, most of Barbirolli's work was based in Manchester, with regular tours to other northern and midland towns including (as Kathleen's diary reveals) Newcastle, Sheffield, Hanley and Wolverhampton. Their performances together at the 1952 Edinburgh Festival have become legendary, but alas, no recordings of them seem to have survived; and, of course, it was Barbirolli who encouraged Kathleen throughout the arduous preparations and two fateful performances of *Orpheus* at Covent Garden in 1953.

But here, in November 1949, the forthcoming tragedy is not even dreamt of; Ferrier and Barbirolli are both at their peak, in a splendidly conducted and sung performance which will be issued on a Pearl CD in October 2005.

7.30pm-8.30pm on 8.12.49
The Concert Hall, Broadcasting House, London

KF 118 **BRAHMS**/Anon
Sonntag, Op. 47, No. 3/German

KF 119 **BRAHMS**/Daumer
Botschaft, Op. 47, No. 1/German

KF 120 BRAHMS/Reinold
Nachtigall, Op. 97, No. 1/German

KF 121 WOLF/E Mörike
Auf einer Wanderung, Mörike-Lieder No. 15/German

All items, Piano: Frederick Stone
None of these songs commercially issued/
NSA Reference: NSA Tape T11540WR

An hour's broadcast on the BBC Home Service, given in the Concert Hall on 8 December 1949, comprised nine German Lieder sung by Kathleen, and a Schubert quartet played by the Hurwitz String Quartet. In addition to the four songs which have survived as part of the K H Leech collection at the NSA, Kathleen sang three further pieces by Wolf and *Mainacht* and *Sapphische Ode* by Brahms.

This performance of *Nachtigall* is the sole example of Kathleen's interpretation of the song; neither her diary nor correspondence makes any mention of it, so she may only seldom have included it in her programmes; *Sonntag*, which she sang frequently, survives in one other version, *Botschaft*, another favourite recital piece, in two (she was to record it commercially for Decca just eleven days later) and *Auf einer Wanderung* in one. All four songs are complete and, bearing in mind their acetate disc source, are in reasonable sound.

Live at Broadcasting House, 8 December 1949, from Radio Times

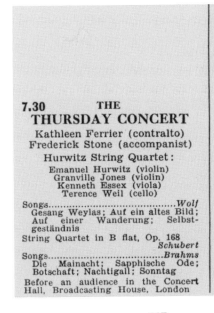

7.30   THE
THURSDAY CONCERT
Kathleen Ferrier (contralto)
Frederick Stone (accompanist)
Hurwitz String Quartet:
  Emanuel Hurwitz (violin)
  Granville Jones (violin)
  Kenneth Essex (viola)
  Terence Weil (cello)
Songs..*Wolf*
  Gesang Weylas; Auf ein altes Bild;
  Auf einer Wanderung; Selbst-
  geständnis
String Quartet in B flat, Op. 168
                              Schubert
Songs..*Brahms*
  Die Mainacht; Sapphische Ode;
  Botschaft; Nachtigall; Sonntag
Before an audience in the Concert
Hall, Broadcasting House, London

KATHLEEN FERRIER
The distinguished contralto sings two groups of songs, by Wolf and Brahms, in the Thursday Concert at 7.30

107

A rehearsal and balance test took place in the Concert Hall between 2.30pm and 3.30pm; a note from the BBC to Kathleen's agents requested that, as the recital was being broadcast in front of an audience, 'will Miss Ferrier kindly arrange to wear evening dress?'

Broadcasting House, headquarters of the BBC, was built in 1932 in Langham Place almost next door to London's beloved Queen's Hall (destroyed in the blitz of 1941) and a short walk north of Oxford Circus. The Concert Hall was incorporated into the maze of studios and offices within 'BH' and was used extensively for live broadcasts, particularly those with an invited audience; it occupied space between the first and lower ground floors, and accommodated a sizeable organ (which could not, however, be played as it was audible in studios throughout the rest of the building). Although plagued by vibration from the nearby Bakerloo Underground line, the Concert Hall was considered one of the finest broadcasting studios in London, so more's the pity that the music has mostly gone now, following its conversion into the BBC Radio Theatre.

6.00pm-7.00pm on 15.12.49
BBC Maida Vale Studio V, West London

KF 122 BACH
Vergiss mein nicht, BWV 505,
No. 71 from *Geistliche Lieder und Arien*/German
Harpsichord: Millicent Silver

KF 123 BACH
Ach, dass nicht die letzte Stunde, BWV 439,
No. 1 from *Geistliche Lieder und Arien*/German
Harpsichord: Millicent Silver

KF 124 TELEMANN
Kleine Kantate von Wald und Au, for contralto, flute and continuo/German
Flute: John Francis, Cello: George Roth, Harpsichord: Millicent Silver

A few days before her departure to North America, on what proved to be her last visit there, Kathleen pre-recorded a programme of Telemann and Bach for the BBC Third Programme. The short recital was broadcast on Boxing Day 1949 and three items were recorded privately on that occasion, the two by Bach being first issued by Decca in March 1985. Although in very poor sound, their survival and commercial release is gratifying, as Kathleen did not otherwise record these songs. Fragments of the Telemann cantata survive in a private collection, but *Bist du bei mir* from this recital seems not to have survived.

Two Bach songs, privately recorded from a BBC broadcast on 26 December 1949

In 2004 a set of four privately-recorded acetate sides, with the contents identical to the listing above, was purchased by Derek Pain; whether these are the same discs as those used by Decca for their 1985 issue of the two Bach songs is not clear, but modern transfer technology has achieved improved results, ready for commercial issue, with the cantata, on Pearl in October 2005. As Pain reports, the Telemann is spread over three sides with the two Bach songs on the fourth.

The harpsichord accompanist Millicent Silver (1905-1986) was wife of flautist John Francis (1908-1992), who often appeared in recitals and concerts with Kathleen; she (Kathleen) first refers to John in her diary in May 1942 and he played, among a host of important musical events, in the accompanying ensemble of *The Rape of Lucretia*'s tour in 1946; in Dutton's booklet notes for their CD re-issue of Glyndebourne's *Orfeo* he is also named as the solo flautist in *Dance of the Blessed Spirits*.

2.30pm on 19.12.49
Decca studios, Broadhurst Gardens

KF 125 **BRAHMS**/Schmidt
Sapphische Ode, Op. 94, No. 4/German
Matrix DR 14418-1

KF 126 **BRAHMS**/Daumer
Botschaft, Op. 47, No. 1/German
Matrix DR 14419-1

KF 127 SCHUBERT/Goethe

Der Musensohn, D 764, Op. 92, No. 1/German
Matrix DR 14420-1
On all items – Piano: Phyllis Spurr

Kathleen's first visit to the Decca studios for ten months took place on 19 December and it was to be a further seven months before she attended another session there. She and Phyllis Spurr were due to re-make *Der Musensohn*, which they had unsuccessfully recorded the previous February, and to make commercially two Brahms Lieder for the first time. Satisfactory takes were achieved of all three and the Schubert was released on 78 as a coupling for *An die Musik*; it is not clear why an entirely new matrix number was allocated to *Der Musensohn*, rather than retaining the number originally given at the earlier session.

The two Brahms items were never issued as 78s but made their first appearance on a 12" LP in November 1953, the month after Kathleen's death. It is difficult to understand why it took four years to release these two fine performances. Decca's final issue of an 'M' series 10" 78 was in June 1954, and it would have been perfectly possible for the songs to have been published together in that format shortly after they were recorded.

It is worth noting that only one take was made of each of these three sides (see also comments on *KF 113-116*). This may indicate the use of tape for the first time at one of Kathleen's Broadhurst Gardens sessions – a huge technological advance in the story of the recording industry.

Chapter Thirteen
January–June 1950

5.30pm on 8.1.50
Town Hall, New York

***KF 131* BACH** (attrib. Stölzel)
Bist du bei mir (*The Anna Magdalena Song Book, BWV 508*)/German
Piano: John Newmark
In the collection of the Library of Congress, Washington DC
Reference: Record NCP 1366

***KF 132* BRAHMS**/The Bible (Ecclesiastes, Ecclesiasticus and 1 Corinthians),
Translated from the German by Paul England
Four serious songs, Op. 121/English
Piano: John Newmark
Never commercially issued/ A tape in a private collection

Four recordings have survived from Kathleen's third (and last) North American tour, which began on 26 December 1949. The earlier two of these date from 8 January 1950 and are from a recital that she gave for the New Friends of Music in Town Hall, New York with her accompanist John Newmark.

Newmark first accompanied Kathleen in 1949, on her second transatlantic visit; he responded to her plea for help when Arpad Sandor, her pianist, fell ill and was unable to continue with the tour. Although at the time of this emergency Newmark was accompanying George London, the Canadian bass-baritone, he was released from that engagement, flew to Chicago to continue where Sandor had left off and to share much of Kathleen's taxing itinerary. They worked very happily together during the remainder of her stay in North America, and Kathleen was keen to sing with him again on her next visit. After some initial difficulty over Newmark's obtaining a work permit for the United States (he was a Canadian citizen), their second tour together was an even greater success. Early in 1950, Kathleen approached Decca with a view to his playing at recording sessions in London during the summer, and in due course arrangements were made. She was concerned about offending Phyllis Spurr, who had played on all her commercially made piano-accompanied records for Decca up to that time; but Phyllis seems not to have taken it amiss, and she recorded again with Kathleen in December 1951. Kathleen planned a fourth visit to North America and she and Newmark corresponded about her repertoire for the projected tour which, of course, never took place. She certainly had the highest regard for him as an accompanist and he earns several references in her letters home. She wrote to Winifred on 3 February; '… Johnny is fine – his playing gets better and better – I think he must be one of the finest in the world, and he enjoys it so …' and to Emmie Tillett she described him as 'absolutely superb'.

Perhaps it was because they lived so far apart that Kathleen felt able to confide in Newmark; he was distant from the local problems, strains and stresses that she encountered in her career. In the many letters to him that have survived, she shared her successes and hopes for the future, and after the onset of her illness she regularly expressed her feelings to this valued friend. On tour in North America during the early months of 1950 they socialized a great deal together, clearly enjoying each other's company, with Newmark introducing Kathleen to his social circle in Canada and the USA; he, like Kathleen, was a keen painter (though perhaps he took it rather more seriously than did she). Born in Germany in 1904, he escaped to London for political reasons in 1939 and three years later travelled to Toronto to further his studies. He finally settled in Montreal and was soon in demand throughout Canada to accompany instrumentalists and singers of the top rank. In later life he became a highly respected adjudicator in music competitions and espoused a special interest in Canadian music, of which he gave many premières. Newmark died in Montreal in 1991.

Kathleen was clearly concerned about her Town Hall recital. On 7 January she wrote to Winifred from her hotel in New York: '… My troublesome concert is tomorrow – the Bach and Brahms – and I shall be exceedingly glad when it's over …' The following week in a letter to Emmie Tillett, she declared '… Our concerts have gone well, and I've got the New Friends of Music off my chest, which was worrying me frightfully because of the fuss I had had over the programme. I thought I dithered like an un-set jelly, but the critics were good …' She even confided to her diary '… Very nervous, but staggered through …' The exact nature of the contretemps is not known, but seems to relate to some disagreement about her choice of repertoire. In the event she shared the evening with a string quintet playing Mozart, which opened the concert, after which she sang the same three Bach songs that she had recorded for the BBC on 15 December 1949, followed by Brahms' *Four Serious Songs*. Writing about this recital to Emmie Tillett on 15 January, Kathleen related the following: '… a German came up to someone and said – of course I was German, because my German pronunciation was perfect and I sang English with a marked accent. (it's true, honest!) I didn't know my

Lancashire came through quite so strongly!' Despite her trepidation she impressed the critics; the reviewer in *Musical America* wrote that: '… The quality of her vocalism was of a sort one seldom encounters these days. Her voice was equally free and richly coloured in the upper and lower ranges, her breath was endless and every tone was firmly supported …'

More's the pity, then, that only one item has been issued commercially. *Bist du bei mir*, from the *Anna Magdalena Song Book*, survived in the Library of Congress in Washington DC, on a disc displaying the label:

The Voice of America

Bach Anniversary Concerts

Programme No. 12

On the same disc is *Motet No. 6* performed by the Collegiate Chorale, conducted by Robert Shaw. It seems likely that these performances, along with all the others in the Anniversary Concert series, were taken from Voice of America radio broadcasts, to create a Bach bicentennial collection. The recording re-surfaced after enquiries to the Library in 1989 and was first issued by Decca in 1992; it reveals Kathleen in pure, velvety voice, with a wonderfully poised delivery, betraying no trace of her admitted nervousness.

The other survivor from this occasion is *Four Serious Songs*, sung in English; preserved in poor sound, this performance has never been commercially released.

? Recording venue unknown
? 24.2.50

KF 133 **MAHLER**/Collected by Brentano and Arnim

Urlicht (from *Des Knaben Wunderhorn*)
Pianist unknown
(Incomplete)
Never commercially issued/NSA Reference: Tape T11540R
NSA Reference: NSA Tape T11540WR

The date given in the Leech collection documentation at the NSA for the incomplete recording of this song is incorrect, for in February 1950 Kathleen was in La Crosse, Wisconsin, with her friends Bill and Benita Cress; no performance of *Urlicht* has yet been traced as being broadcast by BBC radio around that date. The date probably refers instead to the occasion on which Mr Leech transferred his original acetate to a new disc so, for the sake of convenience, the recording is included here, under the date that he ascribed to it.

In a letter to Bruno Walter of 27 November 1950, Kathleen wrote '… I am thrilled that we shall be making music together at the next Edinburgh Festival – I can't tell you how proud I am – and happy – that you have agreed to play for me again. It's just wonderful. Now I am being asked about a programme, and I wanted to contact you first … The only Mahler songs I have done so far are: *Wo die schönen Trompete blasen, Ich ging mit Lust, Starke Einbildungskraft,* and I know you love *Ich bin der Welt abhanden gekommen* though I haven't actually performed it.' There is no mention of *Urlicht.*

Walter replied: '… Of Mahler, I think the following songs would be just what you could wish for: *Wo die schönen Trompeten, Ich ging mit Lust, Ich atmet einen Linden Duft, Ich bin der Welt abhanden gekommen, Urlicht, Um Mitternacht* … We don't have to be afraid to include *Urlicht* in the group of Mahler songs. Although it is part of the [Second] symphony, it is at the same time a Lied which could stand on its own, and Mahler had composed it before he wrote the symphony …' This correspondence gives the impression (though perhaps a false one) that Kathleen was not at the time familiar with *Urlicht* as a song in its own right, apart from its place as a movement in the symphony. As her final choice of songs for the 1951 Edinburgh Festival recital, sent to Walter at the end of December 1950, did not include *Urlicht*, it might be inferred that she had not yet sung it as a solo Lied; but, if that were the case, Mr Leech could not have had the recording of an earlier broadcast to transfer to a fresh acetate on 24 February 1950. Until a positive identification of the (probably BBC Third Programme) broadcast is found, this brief performance, which lasts approximately one and a half minutes, will remain something of a mystery.

6.00pm on 10.3.50
CBC Studio, Montreal

KF 134 *Interview with Eric McLean*
A tape in a private collection
KF134a Interview excerpts

Kathleen's tour took her to many parts of the United States and Canada. On 10 March Eric McLean interviewed her on CBC radio in Montreal and they discussed several aspects of her career. Kathleen replied thoughtfully and with good humour to his sometimes inept questioning about the works of Benjamin Britten – *The Rape of Lucretia* at Glyndebourne and *Spring Symphony* in Amsterdam – and Chausson's *Poème de l'amour et de la mer* which she was still studying (she first performed it in public almost a year later, on 28 February 1951). Kathleen also told her interviewer about forthcoming engagements in Europe and

The Singer and the Person,
the BBC's 1979 LP tribute

the USA, of her plans for a return visit to North America in 1951 and offered her ideas about singing teachers and natural vocal gifts.

Eric McLean was a pianist, author and critic who wrote extensively in the Canadian press and broadcast frequently on CBC as a commentator and interviewer. He died in Montreal in 2002 at the age of 82.

Lasting eight minutes twenty seconds, this is both the most extended and the last surviving example of Kathleen's speaking voice; it conveys a vivid impression of her personality although, as she herself admitted, she struggled sometimes to prevent her Lancashire accent from breaking through. An edited version of the interview was first issued by the BBC on *The Singer and the Person* LP in 1979 and in this shortened form it has since appeared on several CD issues. The first complete version appeared on a hard-to-find Willem Smith Wisp CD in 1996, as one of the fillers to the 1951 Italian recital.

17.3.50, Town Hall, New York

KF 135 **GLUCK**/Calzabigi
Orfeo ed Euridice, 'Complete version' (Cut)/Italian
Soprano: Ann Ayars, Euridice
Soprano: Louise Kinloch, Amor
Conductor: Thomas Scherman
The Little Orchestra Society, Westminster Choir
Never commercially issued/In The Rodgers and Hammerstein Archives of Recorded Sound, New York Public Library
Ref: *LT10 4148-4149

Five days after the interview in Montreal, Kathleen was back on the USA's east coast ready to rehearse *Orfeo ed Euridice* for two concert performances – one in New Jersey and the other in Town Hall, New York, conducted by Thomas Scherman (1917-1979) – and to appear with Bruno Walter in a recital at Hunter College. These *Orfeo* performances must have revived memories of Glyndebourne in 1947, as Ann Ayars, Glyndebourne's Euridice, was taking the part again. They were sponsored by The Little Orchestra Society, which arranged to make a recording privately on acetates in Town Hall. Those discs are now in the Rodgers and Hammerstein Archives of Recorded Sound in New York Public Library, together with others made by the Society at live performances. Theirs seems to have been a reduced version of the opera – though surely not cut as severely as Decca's 1947 recording – but it has not been possible to establish exactly what music was included and what was omitted on this occasion.

Kathleen much enjoyed the company of Ann Ayars and her friends in New York. Her diary has many references to parties and dinners which they attended, and, while Kathleen was in Los Angeles during February and March 1950, Ann's parents and family welcomed her as one of their own. It is hardly surprising that Kathleen was keen to return to North America in 1951 for, despite the tiring travel and some badly organized bookings, she loved the New World and made many friends there.

6.00pm on 9.6.50
Musikvereinssaal, Vienna

KF 136 **BACH**/The Bible

Matthäus-Passion, BWV 244/German
Soprano: Irmgard Seefried
Tenor: Walther Ludwig, the Evangelist
Baritone: Paul Schoeffler, Jesus
Bass: Otto Edelmann
Bass: Erich Kaufmann, Petrus
Bass: Hardal Pröglhöf, Judas
Bass: Otto Wiener, Pilate
Bass-Baritone: Walter Berry, Pontifex
Soprano: Anny Felbermayer, Pilate's Wife
Soprano: Gisela Rathauscher, First Maiden
Soprano: Rosl Sterba, Second Maiden
Contralto: Magdalena Stowasser, First Witness
Tenor: Friedrich Uhl, Second Witness
Conductor: Herbert von Karajan, Vienna Symphony Orchestra,
Singverein der Gesellschaft der Musikfreunde, Wiener Sängerknaben,
Organ: Alois Forer and Anton Heiler

KF 136a   *Du lieber Heiland du ... Buss' und Reu'*

KF 136b   *So ist mein Jesus nun gefangen*/with Seefried and Chorus

KF 136c   *Ach, nun ist mein Jesus hin*

KF 136d   *Erbarme dich mein Gott*

KF 136e   *Erbarm'es Gott ... Können Tränen meiner Wangen*

KF 136f   *Ach, Golgatha ... Sehet, Jesus hat die Hand*/with Chorus

KF 136g   *Nun ist der Herr*

In June 1950 Vienna was a city occupied by Allied forces, with much of the destruction caused by advancing armies in 1945 still evident. It was here, as she later revealed, that Kathleen participated in one of the greatest musical experiences of her life.

The International Bach Festival brought to the city many fine musicians to commemorate the bicentenary of the composer's death; Kathleen was to sing in performances of three of his greatest works, *Matthäus-Passion*, *Mass in B Minor* and *Magnificat*. The conductor of the *Passion* and the *Mass* was Herbert von Karajan (1908-1989), already a celebrated musical figure, who had performed with many German, Austrian and other European orchestras since well before the Second World War. Several of the singers who appeared on the platform with Kathleen had also established successful international careers; they included Elisabeth Schwarzkopf, Irmgard Seefried, Paul Schoeffler and Otto Edelmann. The

Herbert von Karajan (foreground) with Walter Legge

Bach's Matthäus-Passion
– Foyer's 1986 LP set

twenty-one-year-old bass-baritone Walter Berry was making one of his earliest oratorio appearances in the same year as his début at the Vienna State Opera.

The Musikvereinssaal was the setting for the performances; broadcasts on Austrian Radio seem to have been the source for the complete recordings of *Matthäus-Passion* and the *B Minor Mass* which have survived, and were only in the late 1980s first made generally available. On a postcard sent to Winifred, Kathleen wrote: 'Everything fine here. Karajan very pleased with me – first performance tomorrow – <u>wish</u> you could hear it. 'Twill be broadcast – perhaps you will!' It seems that her collaboration with this charismatic conductor was limited to just three performances, all in the summer of 1950; these two in Vienna and a further *B Minor Mass* in Milan in early July.

The first work to be given was *Matthäus-Passion*. It was performed in German, the first time that Kathleen had sung it in the original language, and as the only non-native German speaker among the soloists she acquitted herself superbly. This was a more complete version than she had recorded in London for Decca in 1947 and 1948, all her arias being sung with repeats, where appropriate. There have been numerous issues on LP and CD, the finest of which is that released in 2003 on Andante. Their excellently re-mastered set of 3CDs, taken from second-generation tapes, is in wonderful sound and is presented with comprehensive essays and biographies – a work of real scholarship. Several other companies have also released the complete performance and extracts on CD. On the early Foyer four-LP set of the *Passion*, there are errors in the accompanying booklet about the position of some side turns; despite that, all the music is there. Verona, on their 1989 release of the same performance on three CDs, go one better; the aria *Gerne will ich mich bequemen* for bass soloist is given one and a half times. The aria starts towards the end of the first CD, stops abruptly at the conclusion of its first section, and begins again at the start of the second CD. In addition, seven of the eighteen cueing points on the first two CDs in the set are incorrectly shown in the booklet, making it a real achievement to find some parts of the score at all.

Whilst some reviewers have commented on Karajan's slow tempi, it should be remembered that this was a remarkable and innovative complete performance, which conformed to the style then generally favoured. Of Kathleen's comparable solos, only one is taken more slowly here than by Jacques in 1947/8 and in the heavily partial view of the present writer, the recitative and aria *Erbarm'es Gott … Können Tränen meiner Wangen* is the most inspiring of Kathleen's recordings of any Bach aria – perhaps her finest of any music.

? 9.30am on 13 or 14.6.50
Musikvereinssaal, Vienna

BACH

Excerpts from the *Mass in B Minor, BWV 232*/Latin
KF 137 *Christe eleison* (Incomplete)/Duet with Schwarzkopf
KF 138 *Laudamus Te*/Solo for Schwarzkopf
KF 139 *Qui sedes*
KF 140 *Agnus Dei* (Incomplete)
KF 141 *Et in unum Dominum* (Incomplete)/Duet with Schwarzkopf
Conductor: Herbert von Karajan, Vienna Symphony Orchestra

No recording of *Magnificat* appears to have survived, but both a rehearsal tape and the subsequent complete performance of the *Mass in B Minor* exist and have been issued commercially. During rehearsals for the *Mass* in the Musikvereinssaal, EMI were testing microphones, perhaps in readiness for taping their classic early LP recording of *Le nozze di Figaro*, featuring Schwarzkopf, Seefried and conducted by Karajan, for which sessions began on 17 June in the same hall. Walter Legge, as producer of the Mozart recording, surely had a hand in this test run. It might even be guessed that he was also holding an unofficial audition for his planned commercial recording of the *Mass*, which was eventually made by EMI in Vienna and London in 1952-3. Surviving correspondence reveals that Legge was keen to 'borrow' Kathleen from Decca for this project but, recalling the problems she encountered being 'lent' to EMI in 1949 for the recording of *Kindertotenlieder*, it seems unlikely that Decca would have even considered the idea.

Elisabeth Schwarzkopf

As part of the 1999 CD re-issue of that classic commercial recording of the *Mass*, EMI included the five surviving rehearsal extracts as a 'bonus filler'; Anthony Griffith, the recording engineer, wrote in the accompanying booklet and recalled his experiments in Vienna at that time:

'... I had been given two new ribbon microphones to try out and these I placed together, but splayed to give good coverage, some 30 to 40 feet behind the conductor ... We recorded the whole work at the rehearsal pausing only to change tapes every 30 minutes or so. Afterwards Elisabeth Schwarzkopf and Kathleen Ferrier came into the recording room and asked eagerly if they could hear their solos and duets to see if they could improve their performances for the evening concert. They were like a couple of schoolgirls, laughing and giggling; "Oh, you did that better than me!" and "That was pretty good, and together!" Ferrier said that the recording was some of the most natural sound she had ever heard. Back at Abbey Road, my senior colleague Edward Fowler congratulated me on such useful work, but no further interest was shown and, as far as I am aware, the experiments were not repeated. All that survives are these extracts – with Schwarzkopf and Ferrier in their solos and duets – taken from the experimental recording of the *B Minor Mass* rehearsal.'

Griffith's recollections imply that the rehearsal took place on the day of the concert; that may be so, but no such reference is to be found in Kathleen's diary which, however, mentions rehearsals at 9.30 (am?) on both 13 and 14 June. Richard Caniell, in the booklet accompanying Guild's issue of the complete 15 June performance, follows the same line; '... EMI recorded the entire rehearsal of the *Mass* with Schwarzkopf and Ferrier on the afternoon of the of 15 June 1950 before the evening broadcast performance ... The rehearsal tapes were then erased by EMI.' Whether this note is simply a re-writing of Griffith's essay, or is based on separate information, is not clear.

Of the five extracts in question, two are Kathleen's solos, one is a solo by Schwarzkopf, and two are duets. As published on CD, *Christe Eleison* is shorn of approximately one minute forty seconds at its opening, *Et in unum Dominum* lacks twenty-five seconds of its orchestral introduction and part of its closing orchestral section, and *Agnus Dei* starts as Kathleen sings her first 'qui tollis', at bar 10. Despite these shortcomings, they preserve in excellent sound – far better than on any published CDs of the complete performance – the radiance of the two women's voices.

As in the complete performance, Schwarzkopf sings *Laudamus Te*, frequently allocated to the alto; Kathleen sang it in many of her performances (including the 1951 BBC recording with Enesco), but clearly on this occasion either Schwarzkopf or Karajan felt it would be more appropriately sung by the soprano. As there is no other solo aria for that voice in the *Mass*, it was perhaps not unreasonable to give it to her, although some sopranos find its tessitura low.

EMI issued *Laudamus Te* and the two duets for the first time to mark Schwarzkopf's 75th birthday in December 1990. Kathleen's two solos were first published in December 1991 as part of the CD release of EMI's *The Record of Singing*, Volume 4, although they had not been part of the earlier LP version of that set.

EMI archives refer to the orchestra at this rehearsal as the Vienna Philharmonic. Foyer, Verona, Guild and other issues of the complete Mass correctly note that it was the Vienna Symphony, the name quoted in reviews of the performance in *Wiener Zeitung* on 17 June. Both styles may refer to the same body of musicians; if so, on this occasion they were called the Vienna Symphony.

6.00pm on 15.6.50
Musikvereinssaal, Vienna

KF 142 **BACH**

Mass in B Minor, BWV 232/Latin
Soprano: Elisabeth Schwarzkopf, Tenor: Walther Ludwig,
Baritone: Alfred Poell, Bass: Paul Schoeffler
Conductor: Herbert von Karajan, Vienna Symphony Orchestra
Wiener Singverein, Organ: Alois Forer and Anton Heiler
Harpsichord: Karl Pilss

KF 142a   *Christe eleison*/Duet with Schwarzkopf
KF 142b   *Qui sedes*
KF 142c   *Et in unum Dominum*/Duet with Schwarzkopf
KF 142d   *Agnus Dei*

It was her last performance in Vienna that so moved Kathleen; as Winifred wrote in her biography *The Life of Kathleen Ferrier* (Hamish Hamilton, 1955): '... Later Kathleen said that this performance of the Bach *Mass in B Minor* was one of the greatest experiences of her life. The choir and orchestra were superb, she said, they inspired the soloists.'

Elisabeth Schwarzkopf (born 1915) recalled in 1990 how, at one of the performances, either in Vienna or Milan, Karajan was seen to weep as Kathleen began to sing *Agnus Dei*, towards the close of the work. He was not, it would seem, a man easily moved to tears; it was surely as a result

121

of these performances that Kathleen was invited to record the *Mass* for EMI in 1952, a prospect she would have undoubtedly relished; but for both contractual and health reasons her presence was not a viable proposition.

Since its original release on a set of Foyer CDs, this performance has also been issued on Archipel, Verona and Guild, among other labels, but their sound quality does not bear comparison with either Andante's *Matthäus-Passion* or EMI's rehearsal recording. In his booklet notes for the Guild set, Richard Caniell wrote: 'The recording of the *B Minor Mass* was privately made by a German collector and archivist. It has sporadic short-lived defects including a loss of 2 minutes 21 seconds of choral and orchestral music at the beginning. The missing passage has been interpolated from the von Karajan recording made with the same orchestra [sic] and in the same hall in 1952.' The same passage heard on Foyer's issue (and possibly also other labels) seems to be an authentic 'live performance' passage; so was Guild's *Mass* taken from different original tapes from the others? The same imperfections elsewhere seem to afflict all makes similarly, indicating that they share the identical original source; there is occasional fade and tape stretch, but no potential purchaser should be deterred. This is one of the great Bach performances of its time, and until a similar restoration to Andante's *Matthäus-Passion* can be effected, it should certainly be gratefully accepted, as it is – warts and all.

Following this short series of performances at the Bach Festival, Kathleen, Schwarzkopf, Walther Ludwig and Karajan performed the *Mass* at La Scala, Milan on 2 July, this time with the Bulgarian Boris Christoff as bass soloist. In Kathleen's diary, the entry for 13 November 1950 reads 'Listened to broadcast of Scala *Mass* – v.g.' and *Radio Times* confirms the Third Programme transmission that evening 'By courtesy of Italian Radio'. Somewhere there may still be a tape, or sets of discs, of that broadcast – might Italian Radio be holding more treasure than they realise?

Chapter Fourteen
July–December 1950

2.30pm on 12.7.50
Decca studios, Broadhurst Gardens

KF 146 **SCHUMANN**/Chamisso

Frauenliebe und Leben, Op. 42 (eight songs)/German

Matrix	Title
AR 15209-<u>1</u>	*Seit ich ihn gesehen*
AR 15210-<u>1</u>	*Er, der Herrlichste von allen/Ich kann's nicht fassen, nichtglaube*
AR 15211-<u>1</u>	*Du Ring an meinem Finger/Helft mir, ihr Schwestern*

Piano: John Newmark

6.30pm on 14.7.50
Decca studios, Broadhurst Gardens

Matrix	Title
AR 15212-<u>1</u>	*Süsser Freund, du blickest/An meinem Hertzen, an meiner Brust*
AR 15213-<u>1</u>	*Nun hast du mir den ersten Schmerz getan*

KF 146a	**Er, der Herrlichste von allen**
KF 146b	**Ich kann's nicht fassen**

KF 147 **SCHUMANN**/Rückert

Widmung, Op. 25, No. 1/German
Matrix AR 15214-<u>1</u>

KF 148 **SCHUMANN**/Rückert

Volksliedchen, Op. 51, No. 2/German
Matrix AR 15214-<u>1</u>
All items, piano: John Newmark

2.30pm on 17.7.50
Decca studios, Broadhurst Gardens

KF 149 BRAHMS/The Bible (Ecclesiastes, Ecclesiasticus and 1 Corinthians)
Vier ernste Gesänge, Op. 121/German

Side	Matrix/take	No (auto)	Title
1	AR 15219-1	AX 563	*Denn es gehet dem Menschen*
2	AR 15220-1	AX 564	*Ich wandte mich*
3	AR 15221-1	AX 564	*O Tod, wie bitter bist du*
4	AR 15222-1	AX 563	*Wenn ich mit Menschen*

KF 150 TRAD. (arr. Roberton)
The fidgety bairn/Scottish
Matrix DR 15223-1

KF 151 TRAD. Scots tune (arr. Jacobson)/Burns
Ca' the yowes/Scottish
Matrix DR 15224-1
All items, piano: John Newmark

Kathleen's plans for Newmark's visit to London in July began to develop as hoped. She wrote to 'Dearest Johnny' on 28 April, having consulted Victor Olof, 'the musical adviser of Decca':

'… He is all for you coming to make the *Frauenliebe* with me here and doesn't think there will be difficulty about labour permit … he suggests paying your fare from Paris and your hotel room from the night before you record to the night we finish, and so much a record – I don't know yet how much but I said it must be their top fee for accompanists … OH BOY! He wants to do much more than *Frauenliebe* – lots of Lieder, so keep your fingers crossed darlint! My only slight cloud is breaking the news to Phyllis Spurr, because she's such a nice poppet … Victor told me ages ago I should have someone else – if that someone can be you, I am indeed blessed! …'

Three days later, after further discussions, she wrote to Newmark again:

'… Decca will pay your fare from Paris … three pounds a day living expenses whilst recording and pay you ten pounds for each double-sided record – and we can make as many as we can get in – until my chords start steaming in fact. That is the highest they pay for any accompanist – they don't pay by royalties – and I am terribly pleased – I do hope you are. I have asked to record in the evening, as my voice has warmed up then and

John Newmark: 'To Kaff,
with love from her Johnny'

they will do just anything to get some records on wax. Ain't that nice? I'm pickled tink! ...'

And so together they taped six works – two major groups of Lieder and four short songs – which proved to be Kathleen's only commercial sides for Decca in 1950, and were the last occasions on which she worked with Newmark. Of the recorded performances, only *Vier ernste Gesänge* and the two Scottish folk-songs were issued as 78s, although 78 matrices were made for every side; in 1947 Decca had released a version of Schumann's cycle on 78s with the contralto Astra Desmond, accompanied by Phyllis Spurr, which may have been their reason for not issuing Kathleen's performance in the same format. It was, however, released on a 12" LP in January 1951. It seems likely that the two short Schumann songs were intended to become the sixth side of the possible (but never issued) set of three 12" 78s of *Frauenliebe und Leben*; instead they were first released on a 10" 33 in March 1954.

From time to time reviewers have commented that this version of the Schumann cycle lacks the vitality and spontaneity that are such telling qualities of the 1949 Edinburgh Festival performance; record producer Mark Obert-Thorn has discovered at least part of the reason. In his notes for a Naxos Schumann/Brahms CD in 2004, he explained:

'One difference that may be noted in the present restorations concerns the pitching of the original recordings. While preparing these transfers, I was surprised to discover that previous Decca LP and CD releases of this material had been pitched shockingly flat. *Frauenliebe* and the *Serious songs*, when played on LP at 33.33 rpm, are pitched at A = 428 Hz. Their various Decca CD reissues are comparably low. This gives listeners a false impression of Ferrier's timbre, exaggerating the darkness of her voice and the pace of her interpretations. For the present transfers, all tracks were carefully re-pitched at the standard A = 440 Hz.'

So, thanks to his diligence it is now possible to re-assess both of these performances as surely they should be heard; the same problem may well apply to the four other songs recorded during the same sessions, but not then subjected to Obert-Thorn's stringent tests. But there seem to have been problems with pressings of the Schumann from the outset. On

*Naxos' Schumann/
Brahms CD, 2004*

28 February 1951 Kathleen wrote to Newmark: 'I put on our records the other night and … [Phyllis Spurr] said you ought to be furious on hearing them as anything that is wrong is obviously technical. I'm furious! I spoke to Victor [Olof] yesterday, and said there was a "wow" on the Schumann but not on the Brahms, and he said it must be my copy, but I said no as it had been mentioned in the *New Statesman* – so he's going into it – because on my short playing [78 test pressings?] there is no wow. Two crits that my Schumann was heavy, and you were insensitive and heavy – the blinking idiots – when it's obviously in the balance or manufacture … But our Brahms had good crits …' Alec Robertson would seem to have been one of 'the blinking idiots'; he highlighted some of these problems when reviewing both this Decca issue and a set of the Schumann cycle on HMV 78s (with Elisabeth Schumann and Gerald Moore), in the February 1951 issue of *The Gramophone*. Robertson closed his critique of the HMV recording thus: '… Gerald Moore is here at his best, never sentimentalising his part, but following all the changing moods the singer is expressing. The balance and recording are, in general, very good, the piano tone being very much superior to the Decca LP issue.'

The recording of *Vier ernste Gesänge* is the only one of Kathleen's three surviving versions to be sung in German, and both the others are public performances. As in the case of *Frauenliebe*, the interpretive advantages of hearing her singing in front of a live audience must be weighed against the better quality of sound of the Decca studio version. The two 78 record set of *Gesänge* was issued in automatic coupling only, but was not released in that format until October 1951, ten months after its appearance on LP, coupled with *Frauenliebe und Leben*.

The two charming Scottish songs were recorded, Newmark admitted, as a special favour to him from Kathleen. Beautifully sung (and accompanied) they have never gained the ubiquitous circulation of some of Kathleen's other folk-song records. *Ca' the Yowes* (more literally, but less poetically, understood by Sassenachs as 'Call the sheep') was selected by EMI to represent Kathleen's art in their major LP project *The Record of Singing*, of which Volume 4 was reviewed in *Gramophone* in April 1989.

Decca's archives indicate that these recordings took place over three days: 12, 14 and 17 July. Once again, Kathleen's diary yields different information; it mentions 12, 13, 14, 17, and 18. It seems unlikely that these twelve sides would have taken five days to record, so some of the sessions may have been cancelled. In view of her comments to Newmark '... we can make as many [records] as we can get in ...' she may have been disappointed that the sessions reserved for them were not more fruitful – just the equivalent of twelve 78rpm sides – but in March 1952 Newmark wrote to Kathleen with some heartening news: '... May I congratulate you right on the spot on the Grand Prix du Disque 1951 which, according to the Paris weekly *Opera* of 5 March, was given to "our" recording of Schumann and Brahms. Maybe you have not heard about it yet and I am the first to tell you, which would please me even more! You can imagine how proud I am ...' What a rewarding outcome to this fine artistic partnership – one which lasted but fifteen months.

The dates above are from Decca, the times from the diary; the recording producer for these sessions was John Culshaw.

Sir John Barbirolli

Chapter Fifteen
January–June 1951

KF 156 **HANDEL**/Congreve
Where'er you walk (Semele)/English

KF 157 **HANDEL**/Adapted from Valerians/
English version by Albert G Latham
Like as the love-lorn turtle (Atalanta)/English

KF 158 **PURCELL**/? Settle after Shakespeare
Hark! The echoing air (The Fairy Queen)/English

KF 159 **MONTEVERDI**/Rinuccini
Lasciatemi morire (Arianna)/Italian

KF 160 **LOTTI**
Pur dicesti (Arminio)/Italian

KF 161 **GLUCK**/Calzabigi
Ah diletta, Euridice ... Che farò senza Euridice?
(Orfeo ed Euridice)/Italian

KF 162 **SCHUBERT**/Rückert
Lachen und Weinen, D 777, Op. 59, No. 4/German

KF 163 **BRAHMS**/Anon
Sonntag, Op. 47, No. 3/German

KF 164 **PARRY**/Anon
Love is a bable, Op. 152, No. 3/English

KF 165 **STANFORD**/M O'Neill
The fairy lough, Op. 77, No. 2/English

KF 166 **TRAD.** Scots tune (arr. Jacobson)/Burns
Ca' the yowes/Scottish

KF 167 **TRAD.**/Traditional
The Spanish Lady/English
All with Piano: Giorgio Favaretto

1951 was an unkind year to Kathleen. In January she braved bad weather and flew to the Netherlands for performances of *Orfeo ed Euridice* and, after recitals in Paris and Zurich, arrived in Rome, only to receive a telegram from Winifred with news that their father was seriously ill, and was not expected to live. She decided not to return to London, but to continue with her tour of Italy, and it is from one of her engagements shortly after her father's death that the enigmatic recording of a recital originates. In their LP catalogue, Rococo Records described this recording of Kathleen's as a 'live performance' recital in Italy. Kathleen visited Italy twice only; for the first time in June and July 1950 when she sang Bach's *B Minor Mass* under Karajan at La Scala, Milan, following the successful performance in Vienna, and now again at the end of January and early February 1951. That appears to limit the possible periods for the recital to two, and there is no trace of her having performed anything other than the *B Minor Mass* on the earlier occasion.

Kathleen gave a public recital in Rome on 2 February (where her long-standing friend from Liverpool, Rick Davies, appears to have joined her); her diary confirms that it included all the items on the Rococo disc, as well as four additional songs, but there is no indication that it was broadcast or recorded. However, in Milan on 6 February, Kathleen pre-recorded a programme for Italian Radio, and although it has not been possible to confirm what was sung on that occasion (the relevant page of her diary is now missing), it seems likely that it would be much the same as her Rome performance. A letter from Ibbs and Tillett, her agents in London, found among Kathleen's papers, gives the schedule for this Italian tour, and the accompanist named is Giorgio Favaretto, contracted to play for most performances. The possibility that the pre-recorded discs survived after they were broadcast, and found their way into Rococo's catalogue, seems a strong one. The lack of audience noise or applause strengthens the likelihood of a studio recording rather than a public performance, particularly as Kathleen noted in a letter to Winifred about the Rome recital that '... they are the shuffliest audience I've ever known' and to Emmie Tillett: '... I couldn't get used to the way people talked and wandered about.'

An Italian Ferrier enthusiast, Mauro Ziglioli, writing in November 2003, reported that on the occasion of a later re-broadcast of the recital (date unknown), RAI's announcer mentioned Rome as the city of origin rather than Milan, but confirmed the date of 6 February. In view of Kathleen's itinerary, this seems impossible; despite the missing diary page, details of her activities can be reassembled from her published correspondence and from information in Tahra's booklet notes, well written by Jérôme Spycket.

Thursday 1 February	Rome. 3.00pm rehearsal with Favaretto (piano)
Friday 2 February	Rome – public concert with Favaretto at the Accademia Santa Cecilia
Saturday 3 February	Travel from Rome to Florence. 5.00pm rehearsal of *Kindertotenlieder* (the day of Kathleen's father's funeral)
Sunday 4 February	Florence 5.00pm public concert (*Kindertotenlieder*), conducted by Antonio Pedrotti at the Teatro Communale
Monday 5 February	Travel from Florence to Milan
Tuesday 6 February	Milan recording of recital for later RAI broadcast
Wednesday 7 February	Milan public concert
Thursday 8 February	Travel from Milan to Turin. Rehearsal for a radio concert with Klemperer (*Kindertotenlieder*)
Friday 9 February	Turin *Kindertotenlieder* radio concert with Klemperer in the Music Academy
Saturday 10 February	Travel from Turin to Perugia
Sunday 11 February	Perugia (Perouse) recital

Some Ferrier enthusiasts have spotted a possible further anomaly. In the booklet accompanying their good CD version of the recital, Tahra acknowledge a very evident fault on *Lachen und Weinen* caused by technical problems on the original 78s. The Laserlight Classics CD (among others) suffers no such distortion at the same point; and whilst the general sound quality varies considerably from issue to issue (Laserlight's being particularly bad), some listeners claim that they detect discrepancies in different CD versions of ostensibly the same performances. A difference in note values in the aria from *Semele* is a particular case in point, the first time that the word 'into' is sung. Is it possible that more than one take was made of some or all items in this recital, in order to secure the best possible version for later broadcast? If so, have the different takes been released by different CD companies? Or maybe a transfer fault simply gives the impression of a slightly fudged note? Timings of several of the numbers also differ from make to make – is this an indicator of different performances or simply different transfer speeds? It takes an experienced and patient ear to listen for such discrepancies, and it may not be considered of much importance, even if

Hommage à Kathleen Ferrier –
Tahra's Italian recital CD

true; CD collectors may like to compare a selection of issues of this interesting recital and form their own opinions.

Gala's CD and cassette issue *Songs my Father taught me* includes only seven of the songs and asserts that their origin is 'Montreal 1950, Accompanist unknown'. Kathleen's diary confirms a concert in that city on 9 March 1950 and a letter to John Newmark dated 8 October 1949 discloses her proposed programme for that occasion; Gala and Montreal share no item in common. Perhaps this is a case of mistaken identity. On Wisp the recital is heard in good sound, with a song from the 1948 *Das Lied von der Erde*, the complete interview with Eric McLean and *Kathleen Ferrier at a Party* as enjoyable fillers; this issue has had little circulation and following the death of the proprietor Willem Smith it may regrettably disappear altogether.

Kathleen seemed to appreciate the musicality of her accompanist on this short tour of Italy. On 3 February she wrote to Winifred: '… The pianist is very good, though he <u>will</u> duet with me in a hideous falsetto all the time – but he's a trier and very sensitive, so I can bear anything,' but there is no audible evidence of duetting on any of the issued versions of the recital. Four of the twelve items performed for this broadcast were never otherwise recorded by Kathleen; the BBC included *The Spanish Lady* on their record and cassette issue *The Singer and the Person*.

8.00pm-8.50pm on 9.3.51
Milton Hall, Deansgate, Manchester

KF 168 CHAUSSON/Bouchor
Poème de l'amour et de la mer, Op. 19/French
Conductor: Sir John Barbirolli, Hallé Orchestra

Sir John Barbirolli must take the credit for persuading Kathleen to learn Chausson's *Poème de l'amour et de la mer*. He had conducted many of her performances since 1944, well understood the capabilities of her voice, and became increasingly concerned that it was not being used to its full potential. He felt there was a danger that it would gradually darken in timbre and lose the colour and freshness that had long been its radiant feature; its range deserved to be extended, its higher notes nurtured.

The first release of Poème de l'amour et de la mer, *1985*

Kathleen spent over a year preparing this intense, Romantic work; on 23 February 1950, while on tour in the USA, she confided to her diary '... Did a lot of work on Chausson ...' and by September she was able to reassure John Newmark in a letter that '... I'm working hard at the Chausson now, and am feeling particularly comfortable in my own brand of Lancashire French! ...'

Not only was its style entirely different from anything she had learnt so far, but so was the language. Up to that time Kathleen had sung nothing in French, and she sought help from Pierre Bernac, the French baritone, with both the linguistic and musical problems of the work. She wrote from Paris to Emmie Tillett on 21 January 1951: '... I'm THRILLED with my French lessons with Pierre B. He roared with mirth at first – but in the nicest way! – but now he's getting quite excited, and even I, by a series of lip contortions that might prove serious if indulged in too long, can hear an improvement. I would love a lesson a day for twelve months, then I would feel I was really getting somewhere!' To Kathleen, the discovery of the beauty of the music of Ernest Chausson was as much a milestone as had been her introduction to Mahler. It revealed not just the work of another composer, but an entirely new repertoire, one which she was not given the time to explore more fully. Her correspondence reveals that she sang only three other French songs, *Lydia, Nell* and *Après un rêve*, all by Gabriel Fauré, which apparently she first performed at a recital in Ilkley on 12 September 1951.

Kathleen gave her début performance of *Poème de l'amour et de la mer* at the Albert Hall, Manchester on 28 February 1951; as she wrote to Newmark '... Well darling, this is a great day. The first performance with Barbirolli of the Chausson. We rehearsed it last night, and oh! Boy! Is it lush!? He's pickled tink, and I'm enjoying it – there's such support for the

133

high bits – didn't worry me last night …' Nine days later she sang it again for a BBC Third Programme broadcast from the Milton Hall in the same city, with Barbirolli, of course, conducting the Hallé Orchestra. The programme, which also included works by Rossini, Fauré and Duruflé and Roussel, exuded a strongly Gallic flavour but the Chausson was Kathleen's only contribution on that occasion. Four days after this broadcast, Barbirolli was admitted to hospital for an appendectomy – he must have been suffering considerably for several days, during which time he conducted concert performances of *Orfeo* as well as the *Poème*. Kathleen wrote movingly to her good friend: '… I can't forget that you put off your appointment with [the surgeon] until *Orfeo* and the Chausson were over. Those ten days – working and being with you – were inexpressibly wonderful … It is the loveliest time I ever remember and I keep on re-living it, and purr with pleasure every time I do so.'

At Barbirolli's request a recording was made of Kathleen's broadcast on 9 March, which years later came into the possession of Mr Ian Cosens, living in Sowerby Bridge, West Yorkshire. Realising its musical and historical value, he contacted Winifred Ferrier, who in turn sent a tape dubbing to Decca, so that the technicians might assess the feasibility of issuing the performance commercially. Despite imperfect sound quality, the decision was taken to release the work on LP and cassette, and Winifred travelled to Sowerby Bridge to collect the precious discs. By this time Mr Cosens had succumbed to cancer and he never knew that his initiative would lead to the commercial release of his set of 78s. Apart from its flawed sound, somewhat improved by Decca's engineers, the performance lacks five (non-vocal) bars, nos 129-133; it was issued by Decca just thirty-four years after being recorded, in March 1985. The CD version was first released in 1992. This recording is the only extant example of Kathleen singing in French.

As the cover to their original LP issue of this performance, Decca used part of Maurice Codner's striking oil portrait of Kathleen. Her diary reveals a number of references to Codner, whom she seems to have known well socially from her earliest days in London. Entries for 10 and 12 January 1944 – 'Maurice Codner portrait' – surely indicate when the work was begun, but the finished picture has the date '1946' clearly visible. After Kathleen's death the portrait remained with Winifred, who in turn bequeathed it to the National Portrait Gallery in London, where it is now frequently on display.

Just six days after this recorded broadcast, Kathleen shared her health concerns with her companion and secretary Bernie Hammond and thus began a two-and-a-half-year battle with cancer.

Chapter Sixteen
July–December 1951

KF 171 **GLUCK**/Calzabigi
Orfeo ed Euridice/Italian
Soprano: Euridice, Greet Koeman
Soprano: Amor, Nel Duval
Conductor: Charles Bruck, Orchestra and Chorus
of the former Netherlands Opera
From a recording made available by courtesy of
Nederlandse Omroep Stichting and Katholieke Radio Omroep
Dutch Radio Sound Archives NOB Reference: EM-HM-0719

KF 171a	*Chiamo il mio ben cosi*/Act 1
KF 171b	*Chi mai dell' Erebo*/Act 2
KF 171c	*Deh! Placatevi con me*/Act 2
KF 171d	*Che puro ciel!*/Act 2
KF 171e	*Che ho fatto, ohimè – Che farò senza Euridice?*/Act 3
KF 171f	*Ah, più non m'ode – Che farò senza Euridice?*/Act 3

After an operation for cancer in April 1951, it was more than two months before Kathleen sang in public again. In the middle of the summer she began a gruelling schedule, flew to take part in the Holland Festival, and gave performances of *Orfeo ed Euridice* conducted by Charles Bruck, Mahler's *Kindertotenlieder* and *Second Symphony* with Otto Klemperer, and Bach's *B Minor Mass* under the Romanian composer and conductor Georges Enesco. By good fortune, recordings of all these works have survived from the month of July; Kathleen's arrival at Schiphol Airport was filmed for a Dutch newsreel, and is the second of the two extant examples her appearing on film (See Chapter Twenty-One).

When *Orfeo* was first issued in the UK in April 1978, it was thought to have originated from one of Kathleen's performances in Amsterdam in January 1951; however, Dutch archive material (KRO Radio Station) gives 10 July as the recording date, and seems likely to be accurate. Three performances were given of the opera that month; the first was in The Hague on the 3rd, and the two in Amsterdam on the 4th and the 10th; the opera was not transmitted live, but was broadcast by Dutch radio on 29 July – clearly the reason for making the recording in the first place. The original discs of this performance were transferred to reel-to-reel tape in 1965, and it was in this form that it was rediscovered in the archives of the NOS (Dutch Broadcasting Corporation) in the 1970s by Klaas Posthuma, the producer and technical supervisor of the release. Permission then had to be obtained from both KRO and NOS before it could be published. Decca's catalogue already included the abridged Glyndebourne recording of the opera and thus they passed the opportunity to publish this Dutch performance to EMI, who accepted with alacrity. Royalties from the EMI LPs were donated to the Kathleen Ferrier Memorial Scholarship Fund in London, which finances an annual competition and awards grants to young singers.

Kathleen was certainly not enamoured of the Dutch staging, however much she loved the music of *Orfeo*. Writing to Emmie Tillett on 9 July, Kathleen invited her to come and see the next day's performance '… but it really is a pretty awful production, so p'raps it's just as well if you don't;' and to Bruno Walter she commented in a letter '… But it's such a poor production it hurts!!'

The difference in Kathleen's interpretation between the Glyndebourne recording of 1947 and this one is astonishing. Here can be heard a fully formed characterisation, a passionate, and at times tragic hero. Kathleen's Italian had also greatly improved since the earlier version, and she really convinces that she is not just a concert singer on stage but, indeed, a fine singing actress. Against that, certain disadvantages are very evident, unavoidable in the recording of a staged performance. The sound is excellent, considering its source, but not of studio standard; the other singers competent but certainly not excellent, and the corps de ballet and chorus are decidedly heavy-footed. Greet Koeman (Euridice) and Nel Duval (Amor) were sisters, who often sang with the former Netherlands Opera, and appeared with Kathleen in both the January and the July performances of *Orfeo*. Charles Bruck (1911-1995) was born in Romania, became a pupil of Pierre Monteux (who had conducted the original production with Kathleen in 1949) and was principal conductor of the former Netherlands Opera during the early 1950s; a further recording of him conducting *Orfeo*, made several years after this with the Belgian mezzo Rita Gorr, has also been issued commercially.

Much has been written about the different performing versions of *Orfeo ed Euridice*; suffice it to say that this performance is quoted in EMI's booklet as being the '1889 Ricordi Edition' and of course contains considerably more music than the 'concise' set from Glyndebourne. Four excerpts were issued by EMI on CD in excellent sound (particularly bearing in mind its live performance origin) and in 2004 that company's first complete CD issue of the performance was released – a most

Orfeo, *Amsterdam, with Greet Koeman*

The Dutch Orfeo *on HMV, 1978*

welcome addition to the catalogue. No libretto or translations are included with this issue, but purchasers are informed that they may be downloaded from EMI Classics' website. The booklet notes continue their advocacy of a performance in January 1951 as the source of this recording – perhaps unaware of the further series of stagings and the delayed broadcast from the Holland Festival six months later. The complete performance has also been available for several years on a Verona Record Company two-CD set, in rather less vivid sound, but with Italian (only) libretto included. The producer for the original EMI issue of this recording was Klaas A Posthuma, and the transfer engineer Maarten Proost.

8.15pm on 12.7.51
Concertgebouw, Amsterdam

KF 172 **MAHLER**/Rückert
Kindertotenlieder/German
Conductor: Otto Klemperer, Concertgebouw Orchestra Amsterdam
A recording in the archives of Katholieke Radio Omroep

KF 173 **MAHLER**/Klopstock and Mahler
Symphony No. 2 in C Minor, The Resurrection/German
Soprano: Jo Vincent, Conductor: Otto Klemperer,
Concertgebouw Orchestra, Amsterdam Toonkunstkoor
A recording made available by courtesy of Nederlandse Omroep
Stichting and Katholieke Radio Omroep
Dutch Radio Sound Archives NOB References: EM-HM-0753,
EM-HM-0878 and EM-HM-0908
KF 173a Urlicht/Fourth movement

The second of Kathleen's Holland Festival performances to be recorded,
which remained for years in Dutch Radio archives, was a concert in the
Concertgebouw, Amsterdam, given on 12 July, though not broadcast until
the following week. It commemorated the death forty years earlier (on 18
May 1911) of Gustav Mahler, and was conducted by Dr Otto Klemperer
(1885-1973), whom the composer had known well, and as a young man

Decca's
Resurrection Symphony
CD, 1990

138

Concertgebouw, Amsterdam

Jo Vincent

had encouraged in his musical career. Working with Klemperer was a very different experience from performing with Walter, as Kathleen made clear in a letter to John Newmark on 24 September 1951: 'I hate to work with Klemperer. I find him gross, bullying, unmoving and conducting insecurely from memory, because – to quote his words – "that snot Toscanini does!" I find he shouts like a madman – not at me, not bluidy likely – just to try and impress – though why he should think it impresses I can't think. Perhaps his Mahler comes off sometimes, because he wastes no time nor sentiment – but ohh!!! Whattaman!' On 12 July 1951 Klemperer's Mahler certainly did come off, and Kathleen, the other singers and the Concertgebouw Orchestra gave their best for him.

The programme that evening opened with Mozart's *Masonic Funeral Music*, after which Kathleen sang *Kindertotenlieder*. Following the interval the *Resurrection Symphony* was performed, with Kathleen and the Dutch soprano Jo Vincent (1898-1989) as soloists. The two Mahler works (and maybe the Mozart too) were recorded and the delayed broadcast of the symphony took place on 17 July 1951.

The symphony was first issued by Decca in September 1982 on two LPs and equivalent cassettes. The sound on this issue is clear, with a wide dynamic range, everything from solo singing to the loudest orchestral tuttis being admirably recorded; there is a small amount of surface noise from the original discs, to which the ears soon become attuned, and easily 'listen through' to the music. For some years before Decca's issue, the symphony was available on an Educ Media LP set, together with two extracts from Kathleen's 1948 New York performance of *Das Lied von der Erde*. More recently, the fourth movement, *Urlicht*, the short solo for contralto also included by Mahler in *Des Knaben Wunderhorn*, has been issued on a Verona CD, together with excerpts from the Vienna Festival performances of Bach recorded in 1950; and Verona have issued the symphony complete on one CD, but sold together with another, of Dietrich Fischer-Dieskau singing Mahler's *Lieder eines fahrenden Gesellen* under Wilhelm Furtwängler. Guild, Archipel and Aura, among others, have released the symphony on CD. Decca's own CD version was issued in 1990, on a single disc, and whilst its sound quality is far truer than Verona's, it has had the concert hall atmosphere removed between the first and second, and second and third movements. On Verona, the feel of a live performance is maintained; the strings re-tune, and the audience shuffles, but not distractingly. It all sounds more natural. Perhaps the two versions were based on different tapes (made from the same master discs), one of which had been 'tidied up'. Guild intends to release in May 2005 a re-mastered edition claiming significantly improved sonics derived from a new Dutch source. The album will include the original broadcast commentary, photos, articles on the composer, the symphony and Ferrier's vocal art and life.

Kindertotenlieder was issued as one side of a Decca LP and cassette in November 1987, but its sound quality is decidedly inferior to the symphony. The original discs have become worn and scratched over the years, and whilst this is a valuable performance to hear – a very different reading from Bruno Walter in 1949 – and enjoys the benefit of being a public performance, in clarity of orchestral detail it leaves a good deal to be desired. On its 1992 Decca CD release it retained the original LP coupling of the 1952 *Liebeslieder Walzer*. There are no plans at present to reconstruct the original concert and issue both Mahler works together on CD.

7.55pm-10.35pm on 17.7.51
The Concert Hall, Broadcasting House, London

KF 174 BACH

Mass in B Minor, BWV 232/Latin
Soprano: Suzanne Danco, Tenor: Peter Pears, Baritone: Bruce Boyce,
Bass: Norman Walker, Conductor: Georges Enesco, Boyd Neel Orchestra,
BBC Chorus, Harpsichord: George Malcolm,
Chorus Master: Leslie Woodgate
BBC Sound Archives Reference: T 80775
BBC Transcription side nos: 67625-36 (six discs)
NSA Reference: NSA Tape B 6063

KF 174a	*Christe eleison*
KF 174b	*Laudamus Te*
KF 174c	*Qui sedes*
KF 174d	*Et in unum Dominum*
KF 174e	*Agnus Dei*

Whilst still in Holland, Kathleen sang the *B Minor Mass* with Georges Enesco conducting, and almost immediately after her return to London sang the same work twice more with him for the BBC. The performance on 17 July was broadcast at 7.55pm on the Third Programme, and the following evening the same forces gave another on the Home Service at 7.50pm, both from the Concert Hall at Broadcasting House, London. By chance, at least three complete transcription sets of the earlier performance appear to have survived; one was discovered (it was reported at the time) in the late 1980s, lying in a box with some other discs, in a corner of Bush House, London, home of the BBC World Service. On 6 July 1990 the BBC broadcast the performance again in their Radio 3 series *Mining the Archive*, probably the first time for almost thirty-eight years that it had been heard on air in the UK. Its first commercial release was on the BBC Legends label in 1998. Five extracts have also been issued on the WISP label.

Enesco, born in 1881, is perhaps best remembered as the teacher of Yehudi Menuhin, Christian Ferras and Arthur Grumiaux; but his reputation as Romania's foremost classical musician of the 20th century is entirely justified, as violinist, conductor and composer of predominantly orchestral and chamber works, though his masterpiece is considered to be the opera *Oedipe*. At the time of this *B Minor Mass* performance he had left his native country and established his home in Paris, where he died in 1955.

Comparisons with Karajan's performance in Vienna in 1950 show how much more 'traditionally' Enesco took his Bach. His tempi are slower, the pulse of the work less marked. His *Et in unum Dominum* takes 5' 19" compared with Karajan's 4' 37", and *Qui sedes* is 5' 53", where Karajan takes 5' 13" and Boult 5' 25". But the recording provides an illustration of the approach to Bach's music prevalent in the 1950s, before authentic styles of performance had gained popularity. It shows, too, how Kathleen sang *Laudamus Te*, of which no other recording exists. Schwarzkopf had sung it in Vienna, and it was not included in Kathleen's recital of Bach arias recorded under Boult in 1952, although two other numbers from this Mass were; and, despite a plan to record it at her first session for Decca back in 1946, it was not, after all, made on that occasion.

Michael Letchford, formerly General Manager of Decca UK, recalls his friendship with the soprano Suzanne Danco (1911-2000): 'In 1984 I had the opportunity to make some cassette copies of a tape of the BBC broadcast of Bach's *Mass in B Minor* lent to me by Maurice Leonard. I sent a copy to Suzanne Danco in Florence and in a letter dated October 21st 1984 she wrote "Yesterday we heard religiously the Bach Mass. It was a great emotion to hear Kathleen Ferrier and Peter Pears. The chorus is also marvellous. If I can tell you the truth, I felt that Enesco's tempi very slow." She also told me that she asked Ferrier to sing *Laudamus Te* instead of herself as it lay rather low for her.'

Letchford himself owns a set of six 14-inch transcription discs, which reveal a curious anomaly about the singers in this performance. Bruce Boyce (1910-1996) was publicised in advance as participating in the broadcast, and his name appears on the transcription discs' labels, but neither the announcer's introduction (preserved on the discs), nor the original continuity sheets that have survived, make any mention of him.

BBC Transcription disc of the
Mass in B Minor, *17 July 1951*

BBC B Minor Mass conducted by Enesco
– BBC Legends, 1998

Moreover, notes which accompanied the tape lent to Letchford by Maurice Leonard in 1984 also omit any reference to Boyce, and refer instead to Scott Joynt, a well-known British baritone of the 1950s. Might Boyce have been unable to take part in the broadcast? Might Joynt have replaced him? Might the BBC not have wished for the change to be made public? Or is Joynt's name simply an error, or a misunderstanding? The singer – whichever he was – had only one aria in the *Mass*, and collectors with a knowledge of these two gentlemen's voices might like to identify which is the correct one.

The Listener's critic commented on Enesco's 'careful regard for Bach's orchestration, which showed how unpleasant it can sound to modern ears'. How much more unpleasant might that critic find a performance in the twenty-first century! Alan Blyth, the eminent music critic, believes that this recording, together with the Dutch *Rape of Lucretia* and *Orfeo ed Euridice*, represents most faithfully the sound of Kathleen's voice as he recalls hearing it in the 1940s and 1950s. Because they were all live performances, they reproduce the directness and spontaneity that did not come naturally to her in the cold atmosphere of the recording studio.

BBC archives have revealed the fees paid to the artists on this occasion. Danco received 120 guineas (£126), Kathleen 80 guineas (£84) and Peter Pears 25 (£26.25).

7.30pm–9.00pm on 3.9.51
BBC Studio 1, 5 Queen St, Edinburgh

KF 175 SCHUBERT/Rückert
Lachen und Weinen, D 777, Op. 59, No. 4/German

KF 176 SCHUBERT/Willemer adapted by Goethe
Suleika I, D 776, Op. 59, No. 3/German
(Incomplete)

KF 177 SCHUBERT/Willemer adapted by Goethe
Suleika II, D 717, Op. 31/German

KF 178 BRAHMS/Tieck
Ruhe Süssliebchen in Schatten (from *Die schöne Magelone*) *Op. 33, No. 9*/German

KF 179 BRAHMS/Hungarian poem, German translation by Daumer
Wir wandelten, Op. 96, No. 2
(Incomplete)

KF 180 **BRAHMS**/Daumer
Botschaft, Op. 47, No. 1/German

KF 181 **SCHUMANN**/Chamisso
Frauenliebe und Leben, Op. 42 (Eight songs)/German
(Incomplete)

All items, Piano: Bruno Walter
Never commercially issued /NSA Reference:
NSA Tapes T11540WR and T11544WR

BBC radio audiences in September 1951 were able to enjoy an extraordinarily rich – and somewhat repetitive – feast of Lieder performances by Kathleen, accompanied by Bruno Walter, from the Edinburgh Festival.

The success of their recital together in September 1949 led to great expectations from a further Usher Hall Liederabend on 6 September 1951. Part of the performance was broadcast live on the BBC Home Service from 7.30pm-8.00pm and during those thirty minutes Kathleen sang six Schubert Lieder; alas, nothing from that occasion seems to have survived.

However, on 3 September, in their Edinburgh studios, the BBC had pre-recorded a joint recital, including several items which were repeated at the public performance three days later; *Ganymed*, *Lachen und Weinen*, *Suleika I* and *Suleika II* were all sung on both occasions. In addition, the BBC studio recording offered *Ruhe Süssliebchen in Schatten*, *Wir wandelten* and *Botschaft* by Brahms, and a complete performance of Schumann's *Frauenliebe und Leben*, all in all somewhat reminiscent of the programme performed at the Usher Hall on 7 September 1949 and subsequently released commercially by Decca. (*KF 87-KF 97*)

The 1951 BBC studio recording was first transmitted on the Third Programme on 16 September, being repeated in full exactly a week later; it was from the earlier of these two broadcasts that seven items in the K H Leech collection originated, thus preserving almost the entire programme. Only *Ganymed* and one song from *Frauenliebe und Leben* are missing.

Suleika I is incomplete here – it suffers a side turn towards the close of the performance – but *Suleika II* is complete, and no other version by Kathleen is known to exist. *Wir wandelten* is again missing part of its piano introduction – all three of Kathleen's recordings of this song are similarly afflicted!

The performance of *Frauenliebe und Leben* is incomplete, but the documentation accompanying the tape dubbing at the NSA is ambiguous. It notes that 'Songs No. 1 and 5 not found. These sides could be from commercial releases?' In fact, the first song *is* included – only the fifth song, *Helft mir, ihr Schwestern* is missing, but does the appended note imply that one or more of the songs in this collection were taken from a commercial recording? Kathleen's Decca version, accompanied by John Newmark, had been issued eight months before these Leech acetates were recorded, but Leech's recording date is clearly marked 16.9.51 – exactly right. On balance it seems likely that the seven surviving songs are all from this 1951 recital; fortunately they are all individually complete, though the sound quality of this recording is far below that of the same work from the Usher Hall in September 1949.

A memo dated 25 September 1951, written by Kenneth Wright, Assistant Head of Music – Television, which refers to the live Usher Hall recital, is revealing. 'Bruno Walter played much better than two years ago; with more accuracy and control. The anticipation by the left hand of the right, so noticeable 'on the air' seems to matter less in the hall, when the whole effect is rather the genius he has for creating a sort of orchestral background for the voice. He was at his very best in Mahler, which was not used by TP [the Third Programme] and his great belief in Mahler's songs inspired Ferrier to a much greater vitality and this group in the public recital was 100% enjoyable … Nevertheless, I found, in spite of Walter's authority and understanding, much of the Schubert, Brahms and Schumann a bit dull, and this I think is due to the monotony of her rich vocal colour. All Walter had taught her – line, shape etc became less effective on this account …'

These home-recorded discs extend our knowledge of the Ferrier/Walter partnership and add four new songs to the precious legacy that they left. They are the last of Kathleen's recordings in this particular collection, now held at the NSA; but, whilst the enthusiastic Mr Leech seems to have been active well into the 1950s recording a wide variety of speech and music programmes, he seems not to have preserved any of Kathleen's later broadcasts.

3.00pm-4.30pm on 16.11.1951
Free Trade Hall, Manchester

KF 182 **ELGAR**/A C Benson
    Land of Hope and Glory/English
    Conductor: Sir John Barbirolli
    Hallé Orchestra, Leader: Laurance Turner
    Hallé Choir, Chorus Master: Herbert Bardgett
    (Incomplete)
    From a record owned by the Barbirolli Society

KF with Sir John Barbirolli

'Opening of the Free Trade Hall. Sang *Land of Hope and Glory*. The Queen [later Queen Elizabeth, the Queen Mother] there. Memorable day' reads Kathleen's diary for 16 November 1951; eight days later she wrote to her friend Benita Cress in the USA: '... I'm just back from the frozen north, where I sang – in Manchester – at the opening of the new hall which was bombed in the war. The Queen was there to open it – looking delicious – and it was all very exciting. Sang *Land of Hope and Glory* with orch and choir and made 'em all cry – luvly!'.

A BBC Home Service broadcast of the concert was probably the source of a unique recording of Kathleen's contribution, commercially issued for the first time on a BBC Legends CD in 2002.

The concert was the occasion of much rejoicing, both locally and nationally. Sir John Barbirolli and Herbert Bardgett conducted the Hallé Orchestra and its Choir in a selection of British music. Maurice Johnstone's *Celebration Overture – Banners* opened the proceedings, followed by Barbirolli's own *Elizabethan Suite*. Bardgett then conducted (presumably the choral arrangement of) Vaughan Williams' *Serenade to Music*, with Sir John returning for Sir Hamilton Harty's arrangement of Handel's *Water Music* – an appropriate choice, as Harty had been permanent conductor of the Hallé from 1920 until 1933. To conclude, Kathleen sang Elgar's *Land of Hope and Glory* – a final paean of praise and celebration. Did she sing the work on any other occasion? No evidence of that has been found.

Lady Barbirolli, who was present at the re-opening, recalls: 'The Hallé Orchestra was reformed by my husband in 1943 on his return to England after seven years with the New York Philharmonic Orchestra. The only concert hall in Manchester at the time was the Free Trade Hall which was badly bombed and in need of massive repair. So many buildings were damaged or destroyed during the war that there had to be a waiting list for attention. The Free Trade Hall was finally rebuilt and was opened in November 1951. During the waiting years (1943-1951) concerts had to be held anywhere available; at the Bellevue Circus, whose building was suitable for large audiences of about 4,000 or, on Sundays only, in cinemas which were unsatisfactory acoustically and inconvenient for transport. So the opening of the Free Trade Hall after a wait of some years was a great longed-for welcome occasion.

'I remember the opening very vividly. Obviously many officials were there in the packed audience and during the concert the great and much-loved Kathleen Ferrier sang *Land of Hope and Glory*. The performance was deeply moving and most memorable. She sang it rather slowly, like a wonderful solemn hymn, with deep intensity and heartfelt beauty.'

The rebuilt hall was to remain the Hallé's base until 1997, when the orchestra moved to the splendid new Bridgewater Hall close by. Now converted to a hotel and conference centre, the Free Trade Hall shared its fate with three of London's finest concert venues of bygone days: St James's Hall on Piccadilly, Queen's Hall in Langham Place and Kingsway Hall, all of which have also provided the sites for smart hotels.

The origins of *Land of Hope and Glory* lie in Elgar's *Coronation Ode*, set to words by Arthur Benson, and first performed to celebrate the coronation of King Edward VII; but so attached was Elgar to the finale that he asked Benson to provide alternative words for a new arrangement of the tune, as a self-standing song for solo voice. This setting was first sung by Clara Butt in London in June 1902, and it is this version, too, that Kathleen and the choir sang during the Manchester concert on 16 November 1951.

A recording of parts of the concert was made privately on discs and remained in a personal collection for many years. It seems almost miraculous that the discs should have survived at all, and gratifying that some years ago they were presented to the Barbirolli Society (as part of a larger collection of 'off-air' broadcasts), which made the Elgar item available for commercial issue. This four-minute fragment is the only section of the 1951 concert to have been issued commercially so far and it shares the CD with other broadcast Barbirolli performances of Bax, Delius, Walton, Rawsthorne and Vaughan Williams dating from the 1960s; all in all, a fine tribute to a much-loved English conductor.

As issued on the CD, the song is incomplete. Kathleen sings the final verse *Thy fame is ancient as the days ...* and final chorus *Land of Hope and Glory*, (which is then repeated by the choir). It is surely likely that she sang the whole piece, including the first verse *Dear land of hope ...* and the succeeding chorus, but it is impossible to be sure how much else of the song has survived without examining the original unique disc.

Kathleen wrote to Barbirolli a few days after the concert: '... It has been a memorable and very moving [experience] for me, and I have never been so proud to take a small part in your concert and triumph and to see, although I know it already, the love and respect Mancunians have for you – they BETTER HAD! ...'

Whilst sonically imperfect, with a prominent swish marring the opening bars, this *Land of Hope and Glory* is both a piece of musical history and an invaluable souvenir. The words of Paul Conway from the online *Music Web UK* review sum up the performance:

'It is sung with simple dignity by Kathleen Ferrier as a welcome antidote to the empty spectacle of the Last Night of the Proms. Here, in its post-war context, you feel the words actually meant something and only the hardest of hearts would remain unmoved by this emotionally charged rendering.'

2.00pm-5.00pm on 10.12.51
Decca studios, Broadhurst Gardens

All titles, Piano: Phyllis Spurr

KF 183 TRAD. (collected Sharp, arr. Britten)/Traditional
O waly, waly/English
Matrix DR 16592-1

KF 184 TRAD. (arr. Hughes)/Traditional
I have a bonnet trimmed with blue/English
Matrix DR 16593-1

KF 185 TRAD. (arr. Sharp)/Traditional
My boy Willie/English
Matrix DR 16593-1

KF 186 TRAD. (arr. Hughes)/Traditional
I will walk with my love/English
Matrix DR 16594-1

KF 187 TRAD. (arr. Hughes)/Traditional
The stuttering lovers/English
Matrix DR 16594-1

KF 188 QUILTER/Tennyson
Now sleeps the crimson petal, Op. 3, No. 2/English
Matrix DR 16595-1

2.00pm-5.00pm on 11.12.51
Decca studios, Broadhurst Gardens

KF 189 HUGHES (adapted Gray)/Traditional
I know where I'm going/English
Matrix DR 16601-1

KF 190 **QUILTER**/Anon
The fair house of joy, *Op. 12, No. 7*/English
Matrix DR 16602-<u>1</u>

KF 191 **QUILTER**/Herrick
To daisies, *Op. 8, No. 3*/English
Matrix DR 16603-<u>1</u>

2.00pm-5.00pm on 12.12.51
Decca studios, Broadhurst Gardens

KF 192 **TRAD.** (arr. Quilter)/Percy's Reliques
Over the mountains/English
Matrix DR 16604-<u>1</u>

KF 193 **TRAD.** (arr. Quilter)/Burns
Ye banks and braes/Scottish
Matrix DR 16605-<u>1</u>

KF 194 **TRAD.** (arr. Quilter)/Jonson
Drink to me only with thine eyes/English
Matrix DR 16606-<u>1</u>

In December 1951 Kathleen paid her first visits to Decca's studios for almost seventeen months, there to record twelve British songs, including six either composed or arranged by Roger Quilter. She had particular cause to remember with affection one song from those six – *To Daisies* – with which she had won the Silver Bowl in the 1937 Carlisle Festival; having accepted a shilling bet that she would not enter the Voice Class as well as that for Piano she delighted herself, and surprised most of her friends, by winning both! The judges of the Voice Class were Yeoman Dodds and Maurice Jacobson; the latter became a good friend and colleague, who worked with Kathleen on CEMA tours during the early days of the Second World War.

These 1951 sessions were undoubtedly recorded on tape – although it is not possible to ascertain when Decca began to use this technology at Broadhurst Gardens – but waxes were created at some stage of all twelve songs, including those which never appeared as 78s. Only seven songs were issued in that format, on six 10" sides (one side of M 681 contains both *The stuttering lovers* and *I will walk with my love*), the remainder appearing first on a 10" 33rpm record in 1952; paradoxically, whilst *To Daisies* was issued as a 78, it was the only one of the twelve songs not to be published on that early 33rpm disc.

KF with Phyllis Spurr

Peter Land, a perceptive Ferrier record collector, has established that the takes used for 33rpm (and later) issues differ from the published 78s of *Now sleeps the crimson petal* and *I know where I'm going*; just one take of each song is indicated in Decca's archives, which must lead to the conclusion that Kathleen recorded each piece more than once, but only the preferred versions were transferred from tape to wax for 78 release. For either technical or artistic reasons Decca subsequently used alternative takes, and it is those which are best known today, from their many LP, cassette and CD issues.

The output of these three December 1951 sessions can be seen as a sequel to the 1949 recordings of folk-songs, and on Decca's April 1988 CD all nineteen were presented, together with the two Scottish songs accompanied in 1950 by John Newmark.

A March 2005 release on Naxos brings together all twelve of these songs, as well as the seven from 1949, the two Scottish songs accompanied by Newmark in 1950 and an improved dubbing of the June 1952 BBC recital (excepting only **KF 218**) – a worthwhile and well-filled CD.

These were the last recording sessions at which Kathleen's friend Phyllis Spurr played for her – indeed, the last piano-accompanied sessions that Kathleen attended for Decca. With the sole exception of *O waly, waly,* none of these songs survive in other versions by Kathleen; they are all sung with a direct simplicity that defies the word 'interpretation', and both serious and humorous pieces reveal something of those qualities that she herself possessed. Kathleen's diary confirms the times and dates above and Decca's archives show how the songs were divided up over the sessions.

3.30pm-5.00pm on 4.2.52
BBC Maida Vale Studio 2, West London

KF 196 **SCHUBERT**/Goethe
Ganymed, D 544, Op, 19, No. 3/German
Piano: Benjamin Britten

KF 197 **SCHUBERT**/Platen
Du liebst mich nicht, D 756, Op. 59, No. I/German
Piano: Benjamin Britten
(Incomplete)

KF 198 **SCHUBERT**/Rückert
Lachen und Weinen, D 777, Op. 59, No. 4/German
Piano: Benjamin Britten

After a gap of three months, during which she had appeared very little in public, Kathleen embarked on a series of recitals with her friends Benjamin Britten and Peter Pears. The Victoria and Albert Museum in South Kensington was the setting for the first London performance of Britten's canticle *Abraham and Isaac*, which he had composed for, and dedicated to, Kathleen and Pears. Following a tour organised in aid of the English Opera Group (which had been founded early in 1947 by Britten, Eric Crozier and John Piper, respectively the composer, producer and designer of the first production of *The Rape of Lucretia*), Britten, Ferrier and Pears came to London to give what the composer later described as 'the happiest of concerts', and to record a broadcast for the BBC. That recording contained most of the items that had been performed on tour, including Lieder by Schubert, duets by Purcell and Morley, arias by Handel and Lotti and the first broadcast performance of *Abraham and Isaac*. The sixty-minute recital was due to be transmitted on the Third Programme between 8.25pm and 9.25pm on 6 February, two days after it had been pre-recorded at the BBC's Maida Vale Studios; but on that day the country was grieving at the passing of King George the Sixth, who had died in the morning's early hours. Radio schedules were altered, and

*KF with Benjamin Britten and Peter Pears at the Albert Hall in Nottingham,
at the start of their tour in aid of the English Opera Group, 21 January 1952*

solemn music was played as a mark of mourning. *Abraham and Isaac* did
not receive its first broadcast after all.

An abridged version of the recorded recital was transmitted on the BBC
Midland Region Home Service on 18 February, and it was not until 13
May 1952 that it was broadcast complete on the Third Programme; some
months afterwards, the BBC's copy of the recording disappeared,
seemingly destroyed. Despite continuing rumours that *Abraham and Isaac*
has survived, so far nothing has come to light; it seems very sad that her
performance of this 'sweet piece – simple and very moving', as Kathleen
described it, should have gone for ever. Despite that loss, six items from
the recital have survived, recorded at home on acetate discs by Geoff
Pollock, an avid collector of 'off the air' recordings, then living in north-
west London; by Schubert, three of the Lieder are sung by Pears and
three by Kathleen, and all are accompanied by Britten, making these

probably the only extant recordings of Britten and Kathleen performing together (but see Chapter Six, **KF 34**). *Ganymed* does not exist in any other performance of Kathleen's, and was thus a particularly exciting discovery; both *Du liebst mich nicht* and *Lachen und Weinen* have survived in other versions, but it is the special combination of accompanist and singer that makes these performances so important. Regrettably, *Du liebst mich nicht* is incomplete, shorn of its last twelve bars. Despite that, these three Lieder have been issued by Decca on cassette and CD, in a compilation first released in 1992, although those sung by Pears were not included.

At the end of their short British tour Kathleen wrote to Britten with her customary charm and humour; her affection for the composer and his partner was very clear: 'It was so lovely having concerts with you and Peter, and I felt renewed and refreshed by them and not a bit weary – (as I feared I might do after such a long rest, being a lady of leisure instead of a busy 'low singer'!) Thank you so much for everything, and for spoiling me so – I <u>did</u> love it.'

10.00pm-11.25pm on 2.4.52
The Concert Hall, Broadcasting House, London

KF 199 **BRAHMS**/Tieck

Ruhe Süssliebchen in Schatten (from *Die schöne Magelone*)
Op. 33, No. 9/German
BBC Sound Archives Reference: LP 27264
NSA Reference: NSA Tape M548W

KF 200 **BRAHMS**/Simrock

Auf dem See, *Op. 59, No. 2*/German
BBC Sound Archives Reference: LP 27264
NSA Reference: NSA Tape M548W

KF 201 **BRAHMS**/Daumer

Wir wandelten, *Op. 96, No. 2*/German
(Incomplete)
Never commercially issued/A tape in a private collection

KF 202 **BRAHMS**/Heine

Es schauen die Blumen, *Op. 96, No. 3*/German
BBC Sound Archives Reference: LP 27264
NSA Reference: NSA Tape M548W

KF 203 **BRAHMS**/Halm

Der Jäger, Op. 95, No. 4/German
All items Piano: Frederick Stone
BBC Sound Archives Reference: LP 27264
NSA Reference: NSA Tape M548W

Kathleen's surviving recordings include more works by Brahms than any other composer. She was constantly adding to her repertoire, largely on the advice of Bruno Walter, and continued to develop her interpretive powers throughout her career. The BBC recital broadcast on 2 April 1952 is the last surviving example of her singing solo Lieder by Brahms – the *Liebeslieder-Walzer* and *Vocal Quartets* were still to follow in September – and she otherwise recorded two of the five extant items.

The Third Programme recital, which was given live from the Concert Hall at Broadcasting House, consisted of six Brahms Lieder and chamber music by Dvorák. Private discs (some of which have since been placed in the BBC's archives), were made by, among others, Geoff Pollock, who recorded four of the Lieder complete. The fifth, *Wir wandelten*, lacks its first sixteen bars; this was one of the pieces that Kathleen gave as an encore in Denmark in October 1949, on the record of which the opening bars are also missing and the 1951 performance with Walter is also without part of the piano introduction, so no quite complete version of it sung by Kathleen has survived. The third work sung in the recital is missing altogether; *Radio Times* shows that *Der Tod, das ist die kühle Nacht* was scheduled to be performed, and probably it was, but it seems not to have been captured by any of the recorders that evening.

Ruhe Süssliebchen in Schatten is the ninth of fifteen romances from *Die schöne Magelone*, Op. 33; *Auf dem See* is Op. 59, No. 2, and not the Lied of the same name to words by Reinhold (*Op. 106, No. 2*) as shown on the BBC LP sleeve notes. Kathleen's diary tells of a rehearsal in the Concert Hall between 8.00 and 9.00pm, before the broadcast began at 10.00pm. Frederick Stone, for thirty years a pianist with the BBC who broadcast frequently with Kathleen, gives his reliable support. The sequence of items above is that given for the broadcast in *Radio Times*.

The four complete Lieder were originally issued on *The Singer and the Person*, the BBC's own 1979 recorded tribute to Kathleen, and have since also appeared on a Gala compilation *Songs My Father Taught Me* from 1993; the sound quality is acceptable, but not as clear as the BBC's own archive material from the same period.

9.10pm-10.25pm on 7.4.1952
BBC Maida Vale (Studio 1?) West London

KF 204 **BERKELEY**/St Teresa of Avila, translated by Arthur Symons
Four poems of St Teresa of Avila, Op. 27/English
Conductor: Hugo Rignold, London Symphony Orchestra,
Leader: George Stratton

On Sunday 6 April 1952 Kathleen sang two contemporary works from her repertoire at London's Royal Festival Hall, which had been inaugurated the previous year for the Festival of Britain and which, over fifty years later, remains one of the capital's major concert venues. The following evening she sang the same works with the same conductor and orchestra at the BBC's Maida Vale studios during the first half of a live broadcast on the Third Programme. The two pieces in question were Berkeley's *Four poems of St Teresa of Avila* and Bliss's *The Enchantress*, both of which were composed specifically for Kathleen; the English conductor Hugo Rignold was in charge of the London Symphony Orchestra. The remainder of the broadcast concert comprised orchestral works by Berlioz, Honegger and Racine Fricker and a rehearsal was held between 6.00pm and 8.30pm at Maida Vale Studio 1, which was probably also the venue for the broadcast itself.

In 1995, sound restoration engineer Ted Kendall was researching in a BBC sound archive repository when he chanced upon a boxed marked 'Kathleen Ferrier'. It contained a transcription disc of the four Berkeley songs, recorded by the BBC from the Monday evening broadcast. Keen to preserve the performance in digital format for archival purposes, Kendall was able to transfer the performance to CD before returning the disc to its shelf. The discovery remained unheralded at the time, but when BBC Radio 3 was preparing its evening-long tribute to Kathleen on 8 October 2003, Lyndon Jones, one of the programme's producers, contacted Kendall for a copy of the Berkeley recording, thus enabling the performance to be broadcast for the first time in over fifty-one years. Its reappearance was greeted with unsuppressed delight by Michael Berkeley, the composer's son, and by many thousands of other listeners that evening. This performance is in far clearer sound than the 1948 broadcast première (*KF 58*), with Kathleen in rich and resplendent voice,

Hugo Rignold

but it should not be confused with the even more recently 'discovered' version from a November 1949 BBC broadcast, conducted by Barbirolli (**KF 117**). At present there are no plans to issue this Rignold version commercially, though it certainly deserves wider circulation.

Kathleen refers to Hugo Rignold (1905-1976) three times in her diary; once in 1949, once in 1951 (on both occasions he conducted her in Mahler, with the Liverpool Philharmonic Orchestra, of which he was musical director) and finally in the context of the Festival Hall concert with the London Symphony Orchestra. After his training at the Royal Academy of Music, Rignold played for some time as a dance band musician and after the war joined Sadler's Wells Ballet as conductor. Following his six years with the Liverpool PO, and further work in the world of ballet, he became musical director of the City of Birmingham Symphony Orchestra and later held an appointment with the Cape Town Symphony Orchestra. This recording of Berkeley's *Four poems* is the only known surviving performance of him conducting a performance of Kathleen's, whose diary entry for 7 April 1952 is the last reference for either of these works; it seems likely that this was the last occasion on which she performed them. Kathleen first sang *The Enchantress* on 2 October 1951, as part of a BBC concert from Manchester conducted by Charles Groves. It is fortunate indeed that three different versions of the Berkeley have been discovered, but the apparent lack of any surviving recording of *The Enchantress* sung by its creator, despite at least two broadcasts, is very regrettable.

7.30pm-8.45pm on 22.4.52
Milton Hall, Deansgate, Manchester

KF 205 **MAHLER**/Translated from the Chinese by Bethge
Das Lied von der Erde/German
Tenor: Richard Lewis, Conductor: Sir John Barbirolli, Hallé Orchestra
A tape in a private collection

'Heavenly birthday party mit cake!' was Kathleen's diary entry on 22 April. She spent her fortieth birthday in the company of her good friends the Barbirollis; the day was memorable not only for Sir John's surprise party for her, but also for a broadcast of *Das Lied von der Erde* which she, Sir John, and the tenor Richard Lewis gave in the evening on the BBC Third Programme.

Gordon Rowley spent the evening of 22 April 1952 in his lodgings in Hertford, experimenting with a new Mark 1

Richard Lewis

Ferrograph tape recorder, and he decided to find some worthwhile music to record from the radio, as a change from the frivolous *Goon Show*. The BBC Third Programme seemed to be just what he wanted. Fortunately the tape that he made still exists, and is highly prized. Mr Rowley wrote to Maurice Leonard, Kathleen's biographer, in 1988, on reading that only one example of her singing under Barbirolli's baton had survived – Chausson's *Poème de l'amour et de la mer* – and reported the existence of another – *Das Lied von der Erde*.

Bryan Crimp, founder of Appian Publications and Recordings, relates the background to the first commercial release of this performance in 2003:

'It was Donald Dean, a connoisseur of past broadcasts of home and abroad, who provided me with an introduction to Gordon Rowley. Gordon readily parted with his precious tape – would that all collectors were so approachable and amenable! – which, I discovered, was neatly contained within its own stout leather-bound case. Despite this it was evident at first glance that the tape was in a fragile state, with the first few inches visibly crumbling and which ultimately resulted in the loss of the opening seven bars. Some have questioned why this loss was not 'patched' from a commercial recording. To be frank, experiments were made but it wasn't possible to find a performance of comparable 'instant arrest'. Small wonder; this is a truly unique interpretation. It is also a recording of immense importance; aside from being a glorious souvenir of Ferrier live in a work with which her name is inextricably linked, it also preserves for posterity Barbirolli's view of a score he failed to take into the recording studio. Nor must Richard Lewis's manfully heroic contribution be overlooked!

'Given the age and provenance of the tape (the broadcast was recorded via a standard 'wireless' on one of the first readily available domestic tape recorders), the basic sound was surprisingly good. Certainly it did not present the kind of challenge an off-air recording on acetate discs would have done. Digital technology enabled a reduction of tape hiss and invasive radio interference. Transferring the original recording to a higher tape speed facilitated hand-declicking of the heaviest electrical clicks which had proved too daunting a challenge for digital wizardry. Finally, after some elementary editing between movements and pitch adjustment, selected frequencies were boosted so that the final version had immediacy, which is not always to be found in off-air recordings of this period. Despite these "sonic adjustments", however, I trust it remains an "honest" representation of the original as recorded by Gordon Rowley, to whom we owe an incalculable debt of gratitude.'

Despite the missing start to the first song, *Das Trinklied*, and occasional aural blemishes (caused, according to Mr Rowley, by the passing of trains on the adjacent railway line), the performance has survived remarkably well, with both Kathleen and Richard Lewis in excellent voice. Certainly there is a sense of strain in parts of the sixth song, *Der Abschied*, which can also be heard on Kathleen's commercial recording under Walter made only three weeks later in Vienna, but the tension that this vocal quality adds to the performance as a whole is entirely appropriate for the music; had her voice been lighter and less rich she might more comfortably have overcome the difficulties that *Der Abschied* presents. The performance contains minor vocal imperfections – the occasional frog in the throat that Kathleen so dreaded when broadcasting – but it has a spontaneity that can sometimes be edited out of commercial issues. Now this remarkable performance is available for all to hear on an APR CD, coupled with the 1949 Norwegian *Alto Rhapsody* (**KF 103**).

Richard Lewis (1914-1990), one of Britain's foremost tenors of the century, seems first to have sung with Kathleen at Glyndebourne in 1947, where they performed together in *The Rape of Lucretia* under the auspices of the English Opera Group; both made their Covent Garden débuts in the same work in October that year. Lewis frequently partnered Kathleen in performances of *Messiah*, *The Dream of Gerontius* and *Das Lied von der Erde*, and recorded these works commercially; but as Kathleen worked for Decca and he principally for EMI, they never had the opportunity to sing together on disc. This broadcast is the only known surviving performance in which they both participated, but Lewis's EMI recording of *Gerontius*, with Janet Baker and conducted by Barbirolli, is still regarded as one of the finest available.

Rehearsals for the broadcast took place at Milton Hall in Deansgate, Manchester at 11.00am, and the live broadcast began at 7.30pm.

?15 and 16.5.52/Grosser Musikvereinssaal, Vienna

KF 206 **MAHLER**/Translated from the Chinese by Bethge
Das Lied von der Erde/German
Das Trinklied vom Jammer der Erde/Patzak/Matrix Nos. VAR 252-3
Der Einsame im Herbst/Ferrier/Matrix Nos. VAR 254-5
Von der Jugend/Patzak/Matrix No. VAR 256
Von der Schönheit/Ferrier/Matrix Nos. VAR 257-8
Der Trunkene im Frühling/Patzak/Matrix No. VAR 259
Der Abschied/Ferrier/Matrix Nos. VAR 260-66
Tenor: Julius Patzak, Conductor: Bruno Walter, Vienna Philharmonic Orchestra

The order of the works below is that in which it is believed they were recorded.

?20.5.52/Grosser Musikvereinssaal, Vienna

KF 207 **MAHLER**/Rückert
Ich bin der Welt abhanden gekommen/German
Conductor: Bruno Walter, Vienna Philharmonic Orchestra
Matrix No. VAR 269

KF 208 **MAHLER**/Rückert
Ich atmet' einen linden Duft/German
Conductor: Bruno Walter, Vienna Philharmonic Orchestra
Matrix Nos. VAR 270-1

KF 209 **MAHLER**/Rückert
Um Mitternacht/German
Conductor: Bruno Walter, Vienna Philharmonic Orchestra
Matrix Nos. VAR 267-8

Kathleen's visit to Vienna in May 1952 was far less joyful than that of June 1950. True, she was to fulfil an ambition that she had cherished for at least two years (one which seemed doomed before it had even been planned), but much of the time she was in pain, and only reluctantly did her doctor allow her to travel. Since recording *Kindertotenlieder* with Bruno Walter in 1949, her greatest ambition had been also to set down *Das Lied von der Erde* with him, but contractual agreements again threatened the project. Decca had 'lent' Kathleen to American Columbia in 1949, but the compliment was not easily returned. As early as August 1950, Walter wrote pessimistically to Kathleen about his attempts to obtain a reciprocal release to record with Decca, despite the apparent fairness of such an arrangement: 'I am afraid that my efforts to free myself for a recording of *Das Lied von der Erde* with you will not be successful. The Columbia people seem extremely reluctant to commit themselves, and although they have not given a definitely negative answer, my impression is not a very favourable one ... I made a most urgent appeal to reciprocate the courtesy of Decca having permitted you to make the *Kindertotenlieder* with us. I shall certainly continue my efforts, but I did not want to keep you waiting for an answer any longer.'

Exactly what persuaded American Columbia to relent is not clear but, had they not done so, this classic recording, which has become a standard beside which newer versions are almost inevitably compared, would never have been made. Commentators have often remarked on the tragic aspects of Kathleen's recording of *Das Lied von der Erde*, and with hindsight it is natural to impose on it more sombre overtones than it deserves. It is only fair to appreciate that at the time the recording was made, although she was clearly far from well, Kathleen was optimistic about her future. In Winifred's view, Kathleen was convinced well into 1953 that the treatment she was receiving would ensure a complete cure of her cancer. The quality of the interpretation, particularly of her third song *Der Abschied* (by far the longest of the six the work comprises), can only be fairly assessed on its musical merits, and should not be overshadowed by other unduly emotional considerations.

Details of the sessions for the recording of *Das Lied von der Erde* and the three *Rückert Lieder* have not survived in Decca's archives, so estimating the dates and schedules in Vienna necessitates a fair amount of informed guesswork. Kathleen left London by plane on 13 May, and work in the Grosser Musikvereinssaal began the next day, probably all of which was taken up with tests before the recording itself began. As tape was the medium being used, it was possible to record and hear a playback immediately, enabling the optimum balance levels between soloists and orchestra to be obtained. So the main sessions for *Das Lied* probably took place on the two days following the tests, 15 and 16 May.

Walter conducted two public performances of *Das Lied*, with Kathleen and Julius Patzak, in the Musikvereinssaal at 3.00pm on the 17th, and at 11.00am on 18 May (these are the only two dates and times noted in Kathleen's diary for the whole of her stay in Vienna); recording would surely not have continued on those days. According to Bernie Hammond, Kathleen's secretary and companion, on the day following the morning concert the participants went to the studio to hear the edited tape. As they were leaving this playback, Kathleen called to the engineers that she would see them tomorrow – 'You haven't seen the last of me yet, boys' – which leaves only 20 May, the known last day of recording, for the *Rückert Lieder*. The substantial contributions of the tenor soloist Julius Patzak were probably recorded at different sessions, but on the same days, as Kathleen's. As the two soloists never sing together, but perform alternate songs, it is quite possible that, as far as the recording was concerned, they met only at the final playback. Victor Olof of Decca, whom Kathleen had known for a number of years, was the producer in charge and naturally felt some responsibility for her while she was in Vienna.

As a young man Julius Patzak (1898-1974) established a fine operatic and concert career in Munich, and in 1945 joined the Vienna company, singing a wide range of roles. He seems first to have sung in *Das Lied von der Erde* with Kathleen at Salzburg in 1949 and, following these Viennese performances and recording sessions, they sang their final performance of it together at the Edinburgh Festival on 28 August 1952.

In his biography *Kathleen*, Maurice Leonard described the few days she spent making these recordings, together with reminiscences from Bernie:

' "I can still see Kathleen walking into the studio" remembered Bernie. "She'd be wearing a navy suit and her sensible shoes. She always gave a wave to the backroom boys, then took off her coat and got down to it. She was happy to do whatever was required and never showed signs of impatience" … The following day the tape of *Das Lied von der Erde* was spliced together and the cast assembled for the playback. Walter was calm. Julius Patzak, the tenor, was so still he seemed to be carved out of stone. Kathleen had a look of intense concentration. When the music finished there was a silence which no one seemed willing to break. "Was it all right?" Kathleen eventually asked Walter. He could not speak, but the expression on his face answered the question.'

Maurice Leonard continued with recollections of the final day's work:

'Bernie went to Kathleen's room and found her ashen faced. "I don't know if I'm going to make it," she told her. Bernie could do nothing but stand helplessly at the foot of the bed. With a visible effort, Kathleen pulled herself together.' At the last session, Victor Olof despaired of securing a complete version of *Um Mitternacht*. 'Time was running out and Olof dreaded that they might have to leave Vienna without a releasable version of the song. Kathleen tried another take but was still unhappy. A third take had to be abandoned as her voice cracked … Screwing her eyes with the pain, and with her back hunched, she dragged herself in front of the microphone. Kathleen sang that song as she had never sung it before. Bruno Walter had tears running down his face, but his beat never wavered. The take was an artistic and technical triumph. "That was hard," murmured Kathleen as Bernie helped her back to her chair.'

On 21 May Kathleen and Walter left Vienna. They parted at Zurich airport where both had to change planes, and they never met again. *Das Lied von der Erde*, the work that brought them together five years earlier, proved also to be their final collaboration.

When the two-LP set of *Das Lied von der Erde* and the *Rückert Lieder* was first released, there was some criticism of the flawed sound of the celesta towards the close of *Der Abschied*; these comments angered Olof, for the celesta was insignificant compared to Kathleen's moving and inspired singing. He felt it better to keep the take as it was, rather than try again and risk losing the interpretation. As originally issued, *Das Lied von der Erde* required three sides of 12" LP to accommodate its sixty minutes' playing time, so the three of Mahler's five Lieder to words by Friedrich Rückert were used on the fourth side. In September 1954 the Lieder were released together on a 10" 33 rpm record, and in 1969 on a Decca *Ace of Clubs* LP, as a pairing with Strauss's *Vier letzte Lieder* sung by Lisa della Casa. It would have been ideal if Kathleen had also recorded the other two *Rückert Lieder – Liebst du um Schönheit* and *Blicke mir nicht in die Lieder*

Das Lied von der Erde –
Decca, 1984

– and thus completed the set, but there is no indication that such a course was ever intended for these sessions in Vienna.

In September 2000 Decca re-issued *Das Lied*, together with the *Rückert Lieder*, on a well-filled CD in sound, superbly re-mastered at 96 kHz in 24-bit from the original analogue masters, which entirely belies its fifty-three years. Naxos has released the same works at budget price, but dubbed from Decca's commercial pressings, with somewhat less presence, though certainly offering good value. Other labels are also presenting these works in various compilations.

Although neither *Das Lied von der Erde* nor the *Rückert Lieder* were ever issued by Decca on 78s, matrices were prepared; the prefix V indicates that the recording was made in Vienna, but the sequence of matrix numbers does not necessarily indicate the order of recording.

These Mahler works are the only commercial recordings that Kathleen made outside London although, of course, Decca and other companies have since issued performances from other cities. The recording producer for all these sessions was Victor Olof and the recording engineer was Cyril Windebank.

? 3.00pm on 17.5.52 and 11.00am on 18.5.52
Grosser Musikvereinssaal, Vienna

KF 210 MAHLER/Translated from the Chinese by Bethge
Das Lied von der Erde/German
Tenor: Julius Patzak, Conductor: Bruno Walter,
Vienna Philharmonic Orchestra

For many years, various tapes and even more rumours, alleging the existence of a live recording of *Das Lied von der Erde* made during one of the public concerts of 17 and 18 May 1952 in Vienna's Musikvereinssaal, have been circulating among collectors. Then, during the spring of 2003, two recordings were issued commercially by Andante and Tahra, both of which claim the performance of 17 May as their source; but as these recordings are clearly quite different, as simple spot checks prove, considerable controversy has arisen, initially in Japan, then in the review and correspondence pages of *The Gramophone* and online, about the authenticity and recording dates of both. In an attempt to air this topic fairly, contributions from Professor Gottfried Kraus of Andante, Myriam Scherchen of Tahra and Rob Cowan, reviewer and regular contributor to *The Gramophone*, are presented here, in some cases in an edited, but hopefully balanced, version.

In May 2003 *The Gramophone* published a review by Richard Osborne of Andante's version, issued as part of a lavish four-CD set *Vienna Philharmonic – 1948-1955*, with Bruno Walter conducting Mahler's second and fourth symphonies, orchestral songs and *Das Lied von der Erde*.

Osborne commented of the performance:

'... As a reading, it is identical with that on the studio [Decca] recording. What is different can best be described as a certain airiness and ease due to the natural rhythms of the live performance and to the altogether more natural balance of the radio sound, something that benefits Patzak, Ferrier and the orchestra whose playing is superbly concentrated and sure-footed (a couple of horn stumbles in the *Abschied* are neither here nor there) ...'

Rob Cowan, who had already heard the Andante disc, was now reviewing Tahra's issue in the *Replay* section of *The Gramophone*, a few pages later:

'... The arrival of Tahra's CD convinces me beyond doubt that Andante's release is actually a rather tired-sounding transfer of the Decca recording. Various spot checks and a good deal of ear-straining confirmed my suspicions, for example the passage from 6'12" to 6'25" into the second song where squeaking chairs and what sounds like an approaching car are identical to both discs (albeit far clearer on Decca). One passage in *Der Abschied* was less conclusive, which had me wondering whether different takes were involved, Austrian radio having perhaps obtained an alternative copy master tape of the Decca at the time of release, intended for vinyl-free broadcast. Hence the understandable confusion with the genuine live performance. However, the Tahra recording is in some respects quite different to its Decca counterpart. Aside from the more closely balanced voices and less precise orchestral playing, there's the inevitable extra frisson generated in concert ... Julius Patzak makes numerous subtle changes to his interpretation, the most obvious being at the start of the third song *Von der Jugend*, where his live singing is noticeably more animated than on the Decca. Those who know the Decca recording backwards – or think they do – will be fascinated, and Tahra's transfer is extremely good.'

A customer posted the following question on Andante's website after reading the above remarks:

'I wondered whether you would care to comment on Rob Cowan's comments on your version of *Das Lied von der Erde* contained in this month's *Gramophone*. Having just bought your set I, too, listened carefully and could not distinguish it from the Decca recording, except by the inferior sound. Someone has gone to a lot of trouble inserting audience noise between the songs. I find it significant that one can hear no audience noise at all during the performance, something that is very unusual for a "live" concert.'

In response to Cowan, Professor Gottfried Kraus wrote (in his capacity as producer of Andante's series of official releases from the VPO and Salzburg archives) to James Jolly, *The Gramophone*'s editor, 'to clear up some understandable confusion …'

'… Because the world of postwar broadcast recordings is so often murky, I wish Mr. Cowan had contacted me prior to writing his column. I would have explained to him the following: In 1952, the Vienna Festival opened on 17 and 18 May with two concerts of the VPO conducted by Walter, with a program of Mozart's *Symphony K. 550* and Mahler's *Das Lied von der Erde* with Ferrier and Julius Patzak. Both of these concerts were recorded for radio broadcast: the first one by Sendergruppe Rotweißrot, the second by the RAVAG. The Sendergruppe Rotweißrot was between 1945 and 1955 the radio network sponsored by the American forces in occupied Austria; … The RAVAG was the formal successor of the pre-war Austrian Radio but administered in post-war years by the Russians, who occupied a quarter of Vienna and environs. (The British and the French forces had also their common network, with local studios in the south and the west of Austria. In 1955, when the foreign forces left Austria, these local studios were liquidated or put together to form Österreichischer Rundfunk, which in 1968 was reformed as the ORF.) When the Vienna studio Rotweißrot was liquidated in 1955, the last head of music kept privately several precious recordings; about 20 years later, he gifted these treasures to the VPO and the Vienna Symphony Orchestra for their archives.

The Rotweißrot recording of *Das Lied*, made at the 17 May concert, exists in the original format – 30 ips, 76cm/sec tapes, uncut, unedited and so far as I know never before transferred – at the VPO archive. The RAVAG recording, from 18 May, is kept in 38cm/sec copies at the ORF archive; this recording – which is not as good as the Rotweißrot recording, either in performance terms or sonically – was broadcast by the ORF at least once in the weekly program called *Phonomuseum* that was founded while I worked as head of Austrian Radio's music department and that was presented by me for more than 20 years. Although the credits on the Tahra release list the 17 May 1952 concert as its source – but with nothing given for the origin of the tape – it seems possible that the actual source of that label's live *Das Lied* is an "off the air" recording of this latter-day broadcast of the RAVAG-recorded 18 May performance (particularly as the track timings vary markedly from the Andante release). For the Andante release, we used the original tapes from the VPO archive. They were copied in the Vienna studio of Othmar Eichinger with whom I have worked since 1990 on hundreds of CDs ... Mr. Eichinger did the remastering, and beyond brief portions taken from the 18 May live recording at the ORF to correct small dropouts or distortions, he used none other than the Rotweißrot recording of *Das Lied* made at the concert of 17 May 1952.

Decca produced its "studio" recording of *Das Lied* at the Musikverein in the days around the concerts ... The similarity in interpretation, performance and sound between the Decca and Andante releases may not only stem from the same artists performing in the same venue during the same time period; it could be that Decca used portions of the live concerts to incorporate into their masters ...'

In the meantime Rob Cowan had further investigated the Andante performance:

'... what remains indisputable is that numerous portions of the two performances (Andante [A] and Decca [D]) are identical. I would invite listeners to check for themselves for extraneous noises in (for example) *Das Trinklied von Jammer der Erde* 1'10"[D]/1'08"[A], then [6'01"[D] and 5'58"[A]; *Der Einsame in Herbst* 4'09"[D]/4'08"[A] ... Whether Decca called on the live recording or Andante/Austrian radio on the studio takes, the sum effect is the same; at the very least, partial duplication. As to the Tahra alternative, I stand by my original claim that interpretive variations between Tahra and Andante/Decca are far more obvious – and in my view more significant – than any that might occur between Andante and Decca. Those differences are strictly for completists.'

In order to balance the contributions, Myriam Scherchen of Tahra prepared the following statement specifically for publication here:

'When we decided, early in 2003, to release the then still-unissued live performance of *Das Lied von der Erde* with Kathleen Ferrier and the Vienna Philharmonic, we didn't know that, almost at the same time, the Andante label had the same idea and, moreover, that it would set off a controversy on the matter of 'authenticity' in Japan, and subsequently in the pages of *The Gramophone* magazine.

According to well-authenticated information, Katheen Ferrier sang *Das*

Lied von der Erde twice in public in Vienna during May 1952: on May 17th and the following day, May 18th. Both concerts were recorded.

Keeping our sources confidential, we can report the following: the original recording was given to a producer of French Radio in Vienna, on condition that it be neither released nor broadcast, which was the case. The tape box gives the date as May 17th 1952. A copy of this tape was given some time later to a great admirer of Bruno Walter's, who kept it for almost twenty years in his personal archive. He finally agreed to put it at our disposal in 2003, with the prospect of a CD release, now that 50 years had elapsed and it was, therefore, in the public domain according to the European law of copyright.

Incidentally, the work performed before *Das Lied von der Erde*, ie Mozart's *Symphony No. 40*, released on Tahra CDs Tah 508-509, was also taken from the performance of May 17th. Sony had already released the Mozart recording of May 18th. Comparison of these two versions shows minimal differences, mainly coughs.

Therefore we affirm that, according to all the evidence we have, the recording of *Das Lied von der Erde* released by Tahra is that of May 17th 1952 and not that of May 18th. Another recording of this work, still unissued and with the same interpreters, dating back to 1949, is in the safekeeping of the ORF. The ORF also has two short interviews given by Bruno Walter and Kathleen Ferrier that were recorded on that occasion. Unfortunately, it has been impossible to obtain copies of them and to issue them. ORF gave as grounds for its refusal to release them the fact that these recordings were "reserved" for the Vienna Philharmonic Orchestra.'

The hint of yet another recording of *Das Lied von der Erde*, to which Mme Scherchen alludes, still lying in a Viennese archive is tantalising; it surely relates to one of the two performances that Kathleen gave during the Salzburg Festival, together with Bruno Walter and Julius Patzak, at the Festspielhaus on 21 and 22 August 1949. The reference to short recorded interviews perhaps links to a note in Kathleen's diary on Saturday 20 August – 'Radio 4pm'. Whilst such sketchy information precludes a fuller entry for these recordings in the current edition of this book, it is nevertheless important that mention be made here, in the hope that they will become openly available at some time in the future.

A tantalising programme entry in *Radio Times* for 18 December 1949 announces a broadcast from Hilversum of 'a recording of *Das Lied von der Erde* conducted by Bruno Walter, with Kathleen Ferrier, Julius Patzak and the Vienna Philharmonic Orchestra'. Might this be the very recording allegedly still held in the private vaults of ORF? Up to the time of writing, a number of enquiries to ORF about these 1949 recordings have remained unanswered.

7.30pm-8.00pm on 5.6.52
The Concert Hall, Broadcasting House, London

KF 211 **STANFORD**/M. O'Neill
The fairy lough, Op. 77, No. 2/English

KF 212 **STANFORD**/W.M. Letts
A soft day, Op. 140, No. 3/English

KF 213 **PARRY**/Anon
Love is a bable, Op. 152, No. 3/English

KF 214 **VAUGHAN WILLIAMS**/D.G. Rossetti
Silent Noon/English

KF 215 **BRIDGE**/Tennyson
Go not, happy day/English

KF 216 **WARLOCK**/J. Fletcher
Sleep/English

KF 217 **WARLOCK**/Shakespeare
Pretty ring time (From *As You Like it*)/English

KF 218 **TRAD.** (coll. Sharp, arr. Britten)/Traditional
O waly, waly/English

KF 219 **TRAD.** (arr. Britten)/Traditional
Come you not from Newcastle?/English

KF 220 **TRAD.** (arr. Hughes)/Traditional
Kitty my love/English

All items Piano: Frederick Stone
For the entire recital: BBC Sound Archives Reference: T 29656
NSA Reference: NSA Tape T 9188R

This song recital, broadcast on 5 June 1952, was the first non-commercial recording of Kathleen's issued by Decca. It was also the first from which the royalties were given to the Cancer Fund at University College Hospital, which had been opened in her name. The recital was originally released complete (ten songs) in June 1954 on a 10" 33rpm record, and was reissued in the same format, but with a different record number, in October 1959. Kathleen recorded only one of the songs from the recital, *O waly, waly*, commercially, but two others (*The Fairy Lough* and *Love is a bable*) survive from other radio broadcasts. *O waly, waly* was part of Decca's own recital recording made in December 1951. This June 1952 version was included on only the first two commercial issues of the broadcast; subsequently it was omitted, perhaps as it was felt that Decca's own was a better recorded performance. On more recent Decca cassette and CD issues it has at last been reinstated, once more completing this attractive recital as originally broadcast.

In 2003, as part of a four-CD set, Guild also issued the broadcast, which 'was acquired from Dr. Elkins … Some portions … have been previously released'. This curious comment in their booklet ignores the fact that the *whole* recital has been released by Decca and does not acknowledge that their own issue omits *O waly, waly*. Is that simply coincidence? Whatever Guild's source, it has to be said that their version makes uncomfortable listening, the piano suffering from distressingly high 'wow' levels. In an ideal world, the original BBC recording would be carefully re-mastered, which would surely realise a better sound even than Decca's current reasonably acceptable offering.

Some major British composers and folk-song arrangers are represented. Kathleen's only recordings of Vaughan Williams (who, it is known, was a great admirer), and Frank Bridge (a teacher of Benjamin Britten), are included, as well as two songs composed (rather than arranged) by Peter Warlock. (Vaughan Williams may have been present when Kathleen sang the role of Maurya in a concert performance of his rarely-performed *Riders to the Sea* in the Central Hall, Westminster on 26 November 1948, conducted by Walter Goehr.)

Two of Britten's arrangements of folk-songs are listed in *Radio Times* as being the final items of this broadcast recital, but time was obviously found to add *Kitty my love*, arranged by Hughes, as a delightful conclusion. Perhaps the broadcast was under-running by one minute fifteen seconds. Kathleen would remember with affection *Silent Noon*, as it was with that song that she won the Gold Cup at the Workington Festival in 1938. The adjudicator on that occasion was Dr J E Hutchinson who, the following year, became her first professional singing teacher, provided her with a really sound vocal technique and introduced her to the repertoire that was the basis of her initial success in the early days of the Second World War.

This short recital was broadcast live from the BBC Concert Hall on the Home Service.

8.00pm-8.55pm and 9.10pm-9.40pm on 2.9.52
Usher Hall, Edinburgh

KF 221 **BRAHMS**

Three Vocal Quartets, *Op. 64*/German
An die Heimat/Sternau
Der Abend/Schiller
Fragen/Daumer
Soprano: Irmgard Seefried, Tenor: Julius Patzak,
Baritone: Horst Günther, Piano: Hans Gal

KF 222 **BRAHMS**/Polydora

Liebeslieder-Walzer (18 vocal waltzes), *Op. 52*/German
Soprano: Irmgard Seefried, Tenor: Julius Patzak, Baritone: Horst Günther,
Piano Duet: Clifford Curzon and Hans Gal

KF 223 **BRAHMS**/Polydora

Zum Schluss, No. 15 from *Neue Liebeslieder, Op. 65*/German
Soprano: Irmgard Seefried, Tenor: Julius Patzak, Baritone: Horst Günther,
Piano Duet: Clifford Curzon and Hans Gal

Kathleen was booked to sing in four concerts at the 1952 Edinburgh International Festival; she had not appeared in public since early June, and was looking forward to performing again with Barbirolli and van Beinum in three familiar works – *The Dream of Gerontius, Messiah* and *Das Lied von der Erde*. However, one evening at the Usher Hall was being devoted to music that she had not sung before – and would never sing again: Brahms' *Three Vocal Quartets*, and his more popular *Liebeslieder-Walzer*. In both of these works she was joined by soprano Irmgard Seefried, tenor Julius Patzak, and baritone Horst Günther (who substituted at short notice for the indisposed Frederick Dalberg). Pianists Clifford Curzon and Hans Gal were the accompanists, with the programme being completed by Curzon and Gal playing Schubert piano pieces. The concert was a terrific success and fortunately parts of the broadcast were recorded privately by at least three listeners to the BBC

Liebeslieder-Walzer *at the Edinburgh Festival, 2 September 1952,*
l to r: Irmgard Seefried, KF, Julius Patzak and Horst Günther,
with Clifford Curzon and Hans Gal accompanying

Third Programme; one of them was Alan Blyth, the author and music critic, and another Geoff Pollock, who had already recorded Schubert and Brahms Lieder 'off the air' earlier in the year. When Decca were planning to release the public performance of *Kindertotenlieder* conducted by Klemperer, recorded in the Concertgebouw, Amsterdam in July 1951, they hoped to find a pairing for the LP and tape in which no other conductor had participated. This meant either searching for another Klemperer performance (and as he was contracted to EMI that itself might cause further complications), or finding a work in which no conductor took part. It was then that the tapes of *Liebeslieder Walzer* were traced, and one in particular was selected as the source for the issued recording. As the work needs no conductor, simply four singers and two pianists, it admirably filled the requirements as partner to *Kindertotenlieder*, and its lilting charm contrasts delightfully with the gravity of the Mahler. In addition, Number 15 from a later set of vocal waltzes – *Neue Liebeslieder* – was also performed and has been included with the Opus 52 on the issued recording. Permission to publish the recording had to be obtained from the performers, or their estates, and their royalty payments went to assist the Kathleen Ferrier Cancer Fund at University College Hospital.

UNDER THE PATRONAGE OF
HER MAJESTY THE QUEEN AND HER MAJESTY
QUEEN ELIZABETH THE QUEEN MOTHER

EDINBURGH
INTERNATIONAL
FESTIVAL
OF MUSIC & DRAMA

IN ASSOCIATION WITH THE ARTS COUNCIL OF GREAT BR
BRITISH COUNCIL, AND THE CORPORATION OF THE CITY OF

Usher Hall, Edinburgh
Tuesday, 2nd September 1952
at 8 p.m.

USHER HALL

Tuesday, 2nd September 1952

at 8 p.m.

SCHUBERT & BRAHMS
RECITAL

IRMGARD SEEFRIED (*Soprano*)
KATHLEEN FERRIER (*Contralto*)
JULIUS PATZAK (*Tenor*)
FREDERICK DALBERG (*Bass*)

CLIFFORD CURZON (*Piano*)
HANS GAL (*Piano*)

Of the distinguished artists in this joint recital, Irmgard Seefried was born in Bavaria and has been a member of the Vienna State Opera for nine years; Julius Patzak, Viennese by birth, spent seventeen years in Munich and at present is also a member of the Vienna State Opera Company; Kathleen Ferrier and Clifford Curzon are both British artists of international reputation; Frederick Dalberg has spent roughly equal thirds of his life in his native England, in South Africa and in Germany, where he sang at the Leipzig, Berlin and Munich opera houses; and Hans Gal, an Austrian composer, came to this country in 1938 and is a lecturer in music at Edinburgh University.

KF sings Brahms at her last Edinburgh Festival, 2 September 1952

Kathleen's role in these recordings is, it must be said, fairly modest. The other singers generally take prominence, with Seefried's and Patzak's contributions covering Kathleen's lower musical line. She has no solo, as does Seefried in the seventh waltz, but nevertheless the performance is delightfully produced in good sound for its vintage – and provides an apparently unique souvenir of Kathleen's final Edinburgh Festival season. As Maurice Leonard wrote in his biography, 'Audience members on the extreme left of the auditorium had a bonus with a view of Kathleen and Seefried dancing with each other, believing they were out of sight in the wings' – it was clearly a very happy concert for all concerned.

Apart from the issued *Liebeslieder-Walzer*, at least one recording has survived of the lesser-known *Three Vocal Quartets*, which were performed in the first half of the programme. Brahms set words by three German writers for his Opus 64; this Edinburgh version is to be released for the first time by Pearl in October 2005.

10.25pm-11.15pm on 29.9.52
BBC Maida Vale Studio 2, West London

KF 224 **SCHUBERT**/Willemer adapted by Goethe
Suleika 1, D 720, Op. 14, No. 1/German
Never commercially issued

KF 225 **SCHUBERT**/Von Chézy
Der Vollmond strahlt (Romance from *Rosamunde*), D 797, Op. 26/German
Never commercially issued

KF 226 **SCHUBERT**/Goethe
Rastlose Liebe, D 138, Op. 5, No. I/German

KF 227 **SCHUBERT**/Müller
Wasserfluth (from *Winterreise*), D 911, Op. 89, No. 6/German

KF 228 **SCHUBERT**/Craigher
Die junge Nonne, D 828, Op. 43, No. I/German
Never commercially issued
BBC Sound Archives Reference: LP 27264
NSA Reference: NSA Tape T9188W

All with Frederick Stone: Piano

Kathleen and Dame Myra Hess had been friends for almost ten years – since Kathleen's first London concert at the National Gallery – and although they never recorded together, on 29 September 1952 they shared a BBC Third Programme recital, broadcast live from Maida Vale Studios. Accompanied by Frederick Stone, Kathleen sang five Schubert Lieder; interspersed with them, Dame Myra played solo piano music by Schubert and Schumann. Two of Kathleen's contributions have been issued by the BBC, on *The Singer and the Person* album in 1979, and by Gala on their CD and cassette release *Songs My Father Taught Me* (which extensively copied material from the earlier BBC issue); but the remaining three songs (other versions of which had, by 1979, already been issued by Decca) remain unpublished, and probably unheard on the air since the original broadcast. Kathleen repeated three items which were recorded at the 1949 Edinburgh Festival recital with Bruno Walter, *Suleika 1*, *Der Vollmond strahlt* and *Die junge Nonne*. She had also made this last title for Decca in 1947. The two otherwise unrecorded items that *were* released are *Rastlose Liebe, Op. 5, No. 1*, and *Wasserfluth*, the sixth of the twenty-four songs that comprise *Winterreise, Op. 89*. Kathleen never sang complete performances of *Winterreise*; indeed, until the 1980s women very seldom sang it at all, but it is interesting that she chose to perform this extract from it. Was she, perhaps, considering the whole work as a recital piece? These performances were recorded by the BBC and retained in their own archives; the sound quality is good, which makes their inaccessibility all the more regrettable.

Rehearsals were held at Maida Vale at 8.15pm, before the broadcast began at 10.25pm.

2.00pm-5.00pm and 6.00pm-9.00pm on 7.10.52
Kingsway Hall, London

KF 229 BACH (Revised by Elgar and Atkins)/The Bible, translated from the German by Troutbeck and Johnson
Grief for sin (St Matthew Passion, BWV 244)/English
Matrices AR 17234/5

KF 230 BACH/Translated from the German
All is fulfilled (St John Passion, BWV 245)/English
Viola da gamba: Ambrose Gauntlet
Matrix AR 17236

KF 231 BACH
Qui sedes (Mass in B Minor, BWV 232)/Latin
Oboe d'amore: Michael Dobson
Matrix AR 17237

KF 232 BACH

Agnus Dei (*Mass in B Minor, BWV 232*)/Latin
Matrix AR 17238

10.00am-1.00pm and 2.00pm-5.00pm on 8.10.52
Kingsway Hall, London

KF 233 HANDEL/The Bible – Isaiah XL, verse 9

and Isaiah LX, verse 1, arranged Jennens
O Thou, that tellest good tidings to Zion (*Messiah*)/English
Matrix AR 17228

KF 234 HANDEL/The Bible, arranged Morell after *I Maccabees* etc

Father of Heaven (*Judas Maccabaeus*)/English
Matrices AR 17231/2

KF 235 HANDEL/The Bible – Isaiah LIII, verse 3, arranged Jennens

He was despised (*Messiah*)/English
Matrices AR 17229/30

KF 236 HANDEL/Hamilton, after Milton's *Samson Agonistes* and others

Return, O God of Hosts (*Samson*)/English
Matrix AR 17233

All with Conductor: Sir Adrian Boult
and the London Philharmonic Orchestra
Harpsichord continuo: Basil Lam.

19.2.60 and 13.5.60
Kingsway Hall, London

Re-created versions of the above works,
with stereophonically recorded accompaniments
Conductor: Sir Adrian Boult, London Philharmonic Orchestra

KF 237 BACH

Grief for sin

KF 238 BACH

All is fulfilled

KF 239 BACH
Qui sedes

KF 240 BACH
Agnus Dei

KF 241 HANDEL
O Thou, that tellest good tidings to Zion

KF 242 HANDEL
Father of Heaven

KF 243 HANDEL
He was despised

KF 244 HANDEL
Return, O God of Hosts

Kathleen's last commercial sessions took place on 7 and 8 October 1952 in Kingsway Hall, London, the venue for her first Decca recording almost seven years earlier. With the London Philharmonic Orchestra under Sir Adrian Boult, she recorded four arias by Bach and four by Handel.

The Bach arias were taped on 7 October. Kathleen's diary shows that there were originally plans to record the short Cantata No. 53 – *Schlage doch gewünschte Stunde* (sometimes attributed to Bach, but now believed to be by G M Hoffmann) on this day. That diary entry was then crossed through, leaving two arias from the *Mass in B Minor*, *Grief for sin* from *St Matthew Passion*, and *It is finished* (but performed under the title *All is fulfilled*) from *St John Passion*. For many years these excerpts from the *Mass* were believed to be the sole surviving examples of Kathleen singing from the work, and they still remain the only ones published by Decca.

Grief for sin was sung in its full version, with da capo repeat; the same aria performed in Decca's 1947/1948 set under Dr Jacques was given without repeat, and its re-recording at this 1952 session may have been due to Kathleen's wish to make a complete version. Unfortunately, the recitative *My Master and my Lord*, which precedes it, was not taped. Kathleen recorded no other music from *St John Passion*; she sang the complete work occasionally during her career, but less frequently than either the *B Minor Mass* or *St Matthew Passion*. In this performance she uses the words 'All is fulfilled' throughout the aria, reverting only for the final two phrases to 'It is finished', the title she gave it in her diary.

During two sessions on 8 October Kathleen recorded four pieces by Handel, none of which survives in other versions. *Messiah* is represented by the two principal alto arias. Since signing her first contract with Decca, Kathleen had hoped to record a complete version of the work. Indeed, they had promised such a recording as an incentive to her in 1946, but it never took place, much to her disappointment; as a final irony, Decca *did* record a complete version in January 1954, also conducted by Sir Adrian Boult, with the young Norma Procter singing the alto part.

Although Kathleen recorded Bach's *Grief for sin* in its full version the previous day, *He was despised* was sung with both the preceding recitative and, more importantly, its powerful middle section *He gave His back to the smiters*, omitted. This robs the aria of much of its dramatic impact, and the contrast of moods is entirely lost. It was clearly unusual to include the middle section in public performances at the time, as a diary note for 15 December 1947, referring to an evening at the Civic Hall, Wolverhampton, mentions: ' "Despised" – all of it. 18th century score', perhaps an early concession to the progress of authentic performance style. Certainly the recording would have been more effective had it been sung complete. The other two arias by Handel, *Father of Heaven* from *Judas Maccabaeus* and *Return, O God of Hosts!* from *Samson* are less familiar than those from *Messiah*, and demonstrate Kathleen's undoubted skill at sculpting an elegant musical line. Apart from *O Thou that tellest*, the overall impression that this recital leaves on the listener is of somewhat sombre interpretations of baroque music, sung in the then-customary undecorated style.

Decca hoped that Sir John Barbirolli would be available to conduct these sessions; he was at the time contracted to EMI, and correspondence about his possible release survives in record company archives but clearly the decision-makers at EMI did not feel in any way inclined to lend him. Ironically, at about the same time, the possibility of Kathleen's being lent to EMI was under discussion, for new recordings of Beethoven's *Ninth Symphony*, probably with Toscanini, and the *Mass in B Minor* with Karajan. Even had her final illness not prevented it, it seems unlikely that Decca would have released her, albeit in exchange for Sir John Barbirolli.

So it was, then, that Sir Adrian Boult (1889-1983) took charge of these sessions, for the only commercial recordings that he made with Kathleen. They seem seldom to have worked together – he achieves few mentions in her diary or correspondence – but one diary comment noted beside a performance in October 1950 perhaps reveals Kathleen's private opinion: 'R[oyal] A[lbert] H[all] London Phil. *Gerontius*. 7.30. Sir Adrian. Dull in the extreme'. Perhaps for her he was 'a safe pair of hands' without being able to offer any of the appealing showmanship of Sargent or the warm musical affection of Barbirolli; but it should not be forgotten that Boult conducted the first British performance of Mahler's *Third Symphony*, with Kathleen as soloist, in 1947 (**KF 52**).

John Culshaw, who had supervised some of Kathleen's previous recordings, was producer, and wrote most movingly in the notes to the original stereo version of this recital in 1960: '... During the afternoon session on the 8th [October] a telephone message came through from the hospital where Kathleen had recently undergone examination. I had never seen her look more radiant than when she returned to the platform a few moments later, "They say I'm alright, luv" she said, reverting to the Lancashire accent which always came out in moments of great joy or humour. A few minutes later she sang *He was despised* with a beauty and simplicity that I cannot think has been, or will be surpassed. On October 8th 1953, one year to the day after the last session, she died in University College Hospital.'

Sir Adrian Boult, in his companion sleeve note to the same LP release, recalled: 'The recording was in the charge of my old friends John Culshaw, and 'Wilkie' (Kenneth Wilkinson) who has long been the presiding genius of Decca engineering. The sessions went smoothly and happily. The great artist appeared to be in splendid form, and eagerly ran into the recording room to check every point, and make sure that the results were as near perfection as possible.'

As keen as ever to continue her round of performances countrywide, at the close of the two testing sessions on 8 October Kathleen had dinner with Sir John Barbirolli and then took the night sleeper to Bridge of Allan, near Stirling, to give a recital the following day. The day after that, it was back home again, with further appearances in London, Dublin and Manchester before the month's end.

78rpm matrices were made of every item from these original Bach/Handel Kingsway Hall sessions, although none of the arias was ever issued as a 78 record. Their first appearance in the UK was on a 12" LP, issued in February 1953, the month of Kathleen's last public appearance.

Kathleen's career ended too soon for any of her recordings to have been made in genuine stereophonic sound; but in the late 1950s almost every new LP issue was available in both mono and stereo versions, and Decca decided to release these eight arias in a new stereophonic format. Adding fresh orchestral backgrounds to existing recordings was not a new technique. It had been tried in the 1920s and 1930s when several pre-electric performances of Caruso and Tetrazzini had been enhanced by the addition of an electrically recorded orchestral or organ accompaniment; but Decca's plan was subtler, and somewhat more effective, than those early attempts.

In the October 1960 issue of *The Gramophone,* James Walker, 'a member of the recording staff of the Decca Record Co.', wrote about the creation of this stereo enhancement during sessions with the London Philharmonic Orchestra at Kingsway Hall, in February and May of that year:

'What we planned to do was this. The original tapes were to be played back at the same time that the new accompaniment was being performed, and the two fed simultaneously on to a new master tape. "Wilkie" (Mr Kenneth Wilkinson) had suggested an ingenious gadget that took out a lot of the bass and cut back the top, thus eliminating as far as possible the original orchestral accompaniment, and yet miraculously preserving the quality of Kathleen's voice. We had to take into consideration the enormous strides that have been made in recording techniques since 1952, and that the characteristics of the old tapes were entirely different from those now in use. This all had to be compensated for when playing them back. Assuming that problems of balance could be satisfactorily solved and the new accompaniment perfectly synchronised with the old, we were all set ... . I find listening to this record a very moving experience. Somehow the voice itself has taken on a new dimension and also an added lustre, so that, as it floats freely out above the orchestra, for a moment one is convinced that Kathleen herself is actually standing there.'

Boult was on the podium beside a loudspeaker relaying the original recording at a very low volume, enabling him to maintain exactly the right speeds, and after what must have been very much trial and error, completely new, fully synchronized accompaniments were successfully taped.

Two of the arias have important parts for solo instrumental accompaniments. Ambrose Gauntlet, who played the viola de gamba in *All is fulfilled,* suffers less from the new format than Michael Dobson, player of the oboe d'amore in *Qui sedes.* While the soloist is playing with the orchestra only, he seems to be performing in the remake, but while he is supporting Kathleen's voice, the original accompaniment appears to have been retained; this leads to a change in prominence of the instrument, exaggerated by the different aural qualities of the two recordings. It is not clear whether these instrumentalists participated in both the original sessions and the re-make, but there would certainly have been many players in the LPO who were present in 1952 and again in 1960. Heard today, the effect of this stereophonic enhancement is perhaps less impressive than it was at the time, when stereo records were still something of a novelty, and the technical skill that went to creating these versions was greatly admired.

The new performances were released by Decca in September 1960, and most subsequent reissues were in the stereo format until December 1985, when the arias made their first appearance on CD. For that version, and

Decca's stereo CD
including the re-created
accompaniment, 2004

its companion issues on LP and cassette released in 1986, the original mono tapes were used. The first international release of the stereo versions on a Decca CD was in December 2004, when they were issued in the *Classic Recitals* series, incorporating in their presentation the original artwork and sleeve notes from almost 45 years earlier.

These are the only recordings of Kathleen's to have been re-created in real stereo: indeed, there appear not to have been any other attempts at all to enhance mono originals in this way. This method of genuine stereophonic re-recording should not be confused with the electronic enhancement, which was used on some issues of Kathleen's recordings (and many others as well), originally made monophonically. Electronic stereo gives a broader spread to the sound of a recording, but not the directional quality that is a feature of true stereo.

The recording producer for the original sessions was John Culshaw and, for the stereo re-make, James Walker; the engineer on both occasions was the legendary 'Wilkie', so beloved of generations of Decca recording artists. The order above is that in which it is believed the recordings were made.

Howard Ferguson

William Wordsworth

Edmund Rubbra

Chapter Nineteen
January–June 1953

3.00pm-4.00pm on 12.1.53
BBC Maida Vale Studio V, West London

KF 246 **FERGUSON**/Denton Welch (from *A Last Sheaf*)
Discovery, Op. 13/English
Dreams melting
The Freedom of the City
Babylon
Jane Allen
Discovery
Piano: Ernest Lush

KF 247 **WORDSWORTH**
Three Songs, Op. 5/English
Red Skies   Stephen Phillips
Clouds   Rupert Brooke
The Wind   Wilfred Gibson
Piano: Ernest Lush

KF 248 **RUBBRA**/The Bible
Three Psalms, *Nos 6, 23 and 150, Op. 61*
O Lord, rebuke me not
The Lord is my Shepherd
Praise ye The Lord
Piano: Ernest Lush

For the entire recital: BBC Sound Archives Reference: Tape T 20487-9
NSA Reference: NSA Tape M4420W

In January 1953 Kathleen began rehearsing the new production in
English of *Orpheus* which, at Sir John Barbirolli's instigation, was being
mounted specially for her at Covent Garden. The two performances she
gave, of the four that were planned, were her last public appearances.
Her last new recital for the BBC also dates from January, although it was
not broadcast until 4 April on the Third Programme. The recording was

saved in the BBC Sound Archives, and was first issued commercially by Decca in November 1975. It provided the fourth side of the double LP set of which the first three sides were the 1949 Edinburgh Festival recital. The twenty-four minute broadcast consisted of music by contemporary British composers: Howard Ferguson, Edmund Rubbra and William Wordsworth.

Ferguson's *Discovery*, composed in 1951, consists of five songs to texts by Denton Welch, from his anthology *A Last Sheaf*; Wordsworth's *Three Songs, Op. 5*, were composed in 1935; and Rubbra's *Three Psalms, Op. 61* in 1946. Kathleen's first broadcast of *Three Psalms* was recorded off the air in 1947 (**KF 50**), but this later performance enjoys far better sound, and a more sympathetically caught, if not ideal, piano accompaniment. It seems fitting that Kathleen should have been the dedicatee of the last music she recorded.

Rubbra's youngest son, Adrian Yardley, relates these songs to other works of his father's ouput:

'*Three Psalms, Op. 61* were written for Kathleen Ferrier and first performed by her in 1947. They were composed after a long period of wartime creative silence and are closely related to the *Missa Cantuariensis* of 1945, written for Canterbury Cathedral, and the *Cello sonata* of 1946, inspired by the playing of William Pleeth. Of all Rubbra's works, however, the *Three Psalms* were most closely written with a particular artist in mind and Kathleen Ferrier's unique contralto voice provided an inspiration for one of the composer's most searching pieces. More a triptych than a true cycle, the texts chosen reflect Rubbra's post-war deepening religious faith but are especially poignant in relation to Kathleen Ferrier's recording, which was to be her last. There is no sign of a lessening of vocal powers however, and the central song, *The Lord is my Shepherd* (Psalm XXIII) reminds the listener of Ferrier's magnificent Decca *Das Lied von der Erde* recording, so deeply felt is her response to the text.'

In a letter to the author written in 1990, Howard Ferguson recalled working with Kathleen on his songs: 'She sang my *Discovery* most beautifully, with all the warmth, understanding and musicality that was so typical of her performances. One very poignant memory remains of the rehearsal at which I played through the cycle with Kathleen at her Frognal flat. The macabre third song, *Jane Allen*, is about a mad housemaid who, after finishing her work, drank a cup of Indian tea, then dropped a letter in a tree. It ends, "And this is what the letter said: When you get this, I'll be dead." I knew only too well how ill Kathleen then was; and when she turned to me at the end of the song and said very simply, "Poor soul," I had the greatest difficulty in not bursting into tears.'

Kathleen and Ferguson must have known each other for several years at the time of this performance. He had been an organiser of, and participant in, the wartime National Gallery concerts devised by Dame Myra Hess, in a number of which Kathleen took part. A diary note for 7 November 1951, indicating that Kathleen had an appointment to meet Ferguson, may have been in preparation for her study of this short song cycle.

In Ferguson's view, Ernest Lush, for many years one of the BBC's highly regarded in-house pianists, suffered from a poorly balanced recording, to the detriment of the accompaniment; in fact, it seems fairly typical of the fashion of the time, and does no undue disservice to the performance as a whole. Lush offers good support to Kathleen's singing of the music of all three composers. *Radio Times* lists the songs in *Discovery* in a different sequence from Decca's issue; the apparent order of the broadcast puts *Dreams Melting* at the beginning, leaving the title song to the end.

Wordsworth's three songs are set to poems by Stephen Phillips, Rupert Brooke and Wilfred Gibson; whilst that is the order in which *Radio Times* lists their performance, it is not the sequence in which Decca have issued them. The Brooke and Gibson songs' positions are exchanged. Kathleen wrote a note to Wordsworth after this broadcast, in response to a message from him; 'Thank you for your postcard. I was in hospital when it arrived, and had already recorded the songs. I hope my F sharp [a misprint in the score of *Clouds*] didn't offend your ears too much, and that my interpretation did not cause you too much agony ...' but he later generously acknowledged that 'It sounds quite good as sung!'

None of the works from this recital has achieved great popularity since this recording was made, but it is typical of Kathleen that she sang them with the same conviction and perception as anything grander or better loved from her repertoire. Her diary reveals that she and Ernest Lush rehearsed at Maida Vale Studios between 2.00pm and 3.00pm on 12 January, and that the recording was made between 3.00pm and 4.00pm. Its first broadcast was at 6.50pm on 4 April, almost twelve weeks later. The order above is that indicated for the broadcast in *Radio Times*.

Psalm 150

Praise ye the Lord.
Praise God in His sanctuary:
Praise Him in the firmament of His power.
Praise Him for His mighty acts:
Praise Him according to His excellent greatness.
Praise Him with the sound of the trumpet:
Praise Him with the psaltery and harp.
Praise Him with the timbrel and dance:
Praise Him with stringed instruments and organs.
Praise Him upon the loud cymbals:
Praise Him upon the high sounding cymbals.
Let ev'ry thing that hath breath praise the Lord.
Praise ye the Lord.

Chapter Twenty
Recordings that might have been

THE RECORDINGS OF KATHLEEN FERRIER that 'might have been' fall into three distinct categories:

I Those which are known to have been made, commercially, by broadcasting organisations or privately, but which seem not to have survived.

II Those planned to be made, but which never were.

III Those of works which were particularly important in her repertoire, but which were apparently never even contemplated.

I The main text includes commercial recordings for EMI and Decca which were made, but which were destroyed before issue. These are:

KF 21   *O wert thou in the cauld blast?*/Mendelssohn

KF 22   *Turn ye to me*/Traditional

KF 48   *Vier ernste Gesänge*/Brahms

KF 53   *Gestillte Sehnsucht*/Brahms

KF 54   *Geistliches Wiegenlied*/Brahms

KF 61   *Frondi tenere ... Ombra mai fu*/Handel
         (One test pressing of take 3 survives)

KF 62   *Gestillte Sehnsucht*/Brahms

KF 63   *Geistliches Wiegenlied*/Brahms

KF 79   *Der Musensohn*/Schubert

and presumably all takes, other than those which were used for commercial issue, recorded between 1944 and 1952.

Many of Kathleen's broadcasts were pre-recorded by the BBC for later transmission, or were recorded by them 'live' at the time for a subsequent repeat; only a few of these have survived, (notably Bach's *B Minor Mass* **KF 174**), a large quantity having been later destroyed 'in the usual course of events'. In the Netherlands the complete *Orfeo* **KF 171**, Mahler's *Second Symphony* and *Kindertotenlieder* **KF 172-173** were recorded at public performances in advance of their broadcast date. Perhaps the greatest loss in this category is the BBC broadcast that included Britten's *Abraham and Isaac* from 4 February 1952, in which Kathleen was joined by Peter Pears and accompanied by the composer. Rumours of a copy surviving into the 1970s still circulate, but they remain rumours. The complete programme for that broadcast was:

1. Tenor   Recit. *Ah! che pur troppo e vero*/Handel, realised Britten

               Aria *Col partir la bella Chlori*

2. Contralto   Aria *Pur dicesti*/Lotti, realised Britten

3. Duets   *Sweet nymph, come to thy lover*

               I go before, my darling/Morley

4. Duet   *Corydon and Mopsa's Dialogue*/Purcell, realised Britten
               (*The Fairy Queen*)

5. Lieder (contralto)   *Ganymed*/Schubert

                         Du liebst mich nicht/Schubert

                         Lachen und Weinen/Schubert

   Lieder (tenor)   *Vom Mitleiden Maria*/Schubert

                         Der zürnenden Diana/Schubert

                         Liebesbotschaft/Schubert

6. Duet   *Abraham and Isaac* – a canticle/Britten
               (from the *Chester Miracle Play* for contralto, tenor and piano Op. 51)

As is known, several radio enthusiasts recorded some of Kathleen's broadcasts, either on acetate discs, or, from the early 1950s, on tape. A number of surviving recordings have, of course, been preserved in this way, such as **KF 122-124**, **KF 205** and the K H Leech collection, now at the NSA.

A set of amateur recordings of Kathleen was made in the 1940s by a pupil at Rugby School, on the occasion of a recital there (perhaps during her visit on either 1 July 1945 or 13 April 1946); when she heard the results later, she declared that they sounded better than her commercial versions of the same pieces; these have not been traced, and it is not known whether they have survived.

II Several references are made in the text to recordings which either a record company, or Kathleen herself, hoped, expected, or was asked to make. Some others, not mentioned, have also been traced, and are included in the list below: some details are taken from the diary.

1.	*Sapphic Ode*/Brahms	6.3.45	Abbey Road
2.	*May Night*/Brahms	6.3.45	Abbey Road

3.	*Sapphic Ode*/Brahms	20.4.45	Abbey Road
4.	*May Night*/Brahms	20.4.45	Abbey Road
5.	*Laudamus Te*/Bach	6.2.46	Kingsway Hall
6.	*Schlage doch gewünschte Stunde*/Bach or Hoffmann?		
		7.10.52	Kingsway Hall
7.	*Mass in B Minor*/Bach	.11.52	Vienna and London
8.	*Symphony No. 9*/Beethoven	.53?	New York?
9.	*Four Serious Songs*/Brahms	5-7.1.53	Kingsway Hall
10.	*Rhapsody for alto, male chorus and orchestra*/Brahms		
		5-7.1.53	Kingsway Hall
11.	*Abraham and Isaac*/Britten	28-29.5.53	Hamilton Terrace, St John's Wood
12.	*Corydon and Mopsa's Dialogue*/Purcell	28-29.5.53	Hamilton Terrace, St John's Wood
13.	*Canzonets*/Morley	28-29.5.53	Hamilton Terrace, St John's Wood

The two sets of sessions for 1953 are particularly interesting. No doubt Kathleen and Decca were keen to record two of her favourite works for issue on LP, and arranged four three-hour sessions at Kingsway Hall on 5, 6 and 7 January, just before rehearsals began for *Orpheus* at Covent Garden. *Four Serious Songs* was surely planned in Sargent's orchestral version, as the performance recorded with John Newmark's piano accompaniment was not yet three years old; and Kingsway Hall would be an unlikely venue for a piano accompanied session.

Kathleen's recording of *Alto Rhapsody* with Krauss had been made five years earlier and suffered from three side changes in its 78 format. A new version, recorded on tape rather than wax, would probably be an improvement on it. No conductor or orchestra is mentioned in connection with these sessions, which are all marked 'Cancelled' in Kathleen's diary.

A bizarre newspaper cutting from October 1953 has been found which, whilst deeply regretting Kathleen's death, also announces that '... the last two recordings she made will be in the shops in about two weeks' time. They are four of Brahms's songs, and his *Alto Rhapsody*'. Odd indeed, as it was already over nine months since they had *not* been recorded at Kingsway Hall. What *was* issued in November 1953 was the first LP version of the Krauss *Rhapsody*, coupled with the two *Songs with Viola, Op. 91*, *Sapphische Ode* and *Botschaft* – the first release of the latter two in any format.

The more famous, and more deeply regretted, instance of pre-advertising was the announcement, in *The Gramophone*'s May 1953 edition, of the release of a 12" LP, number LXT 2789, which contained duets by Purcell, Morley and Britten. The dates of 28 and 29 May marked 'Recording' in Kathleen's diary were surely those booked to tape the duets, which included *Abraham and Isaac*. After Kathleen was taken ill at Covent Garden in February, Decca arranged to record at her new flat in Hamilton Terrace, St John's Wood. Arthur Bannister, Decca's recording engineer, remembered being sent there in advance to test the acoustics of Kathleen's room; it seemed to promise well. Before the recording could be started, however, she suffered a serious relapse, and was rushed back into hospital. The record was never made and, in November's issue of *The Gramophone*, Decca had to publish a notice of regret that it would not after all be possible to issue it. Then Britten remembered the recording that had been made for the BBC broadcast in February 1952; that could be used for commercial release instead. But on investigation it was found that it had disappeared, presumably destroyed in the normal course of events, after being broadcast once or twice again. Perhaps, somewhere, a copy of *Abraham and Isaac* is still in a collection, waiting to be found and enjoyed. This, surely, of all the recordings 'that might have been' is the most keenly missed.

There is no evidence that Kathleen was ever actually invited to take part in Decca's complete *Messiah*, eventually recorded in January 1954; she was probably already in hospital when arrangements were being made for the sessions, and it may have been thought better not to refer to it at that stage, after she had waited over seven years to participate in it.

III Of the many works in Kathleen's repertoire that she did not record, nor ever planned to, a handful stand out that really should have been made. Apart from the incomplete *Land of Hope and Glory* (**KF 182**) and the two fragments from *The Dream of Gerontius* (**KF 4**), nothing by Elgar was ever recorded. A complete version of the oratorio, preferably with Barbirolli conducting, would have preserved her moving interpretation of the Angel; but, as in the case of Bruno Walter, borrowing and lending musicians between companies was an almost insuperable problem, and Barbirolli was contracted at that time to EMI. Although Kathleen never cared for Elgar's *Sea Pictures*, that, too, could have made a fine recording. She occasionally sang *The Apostles* and *The Kingdom*, from which she left nothing. Kathleen sang songs by twentieth-century British composers, such as Holst, Moeran, Michael Head, Bax, Scott, and Delius, of which not a note was recorded; and others by Vaughan Williams and Stanford, who are represented by only one and three surviving pieces respectively. She also performed music from earlier centuries, by Boyce, Byrd and Carey, of which we have nothing. During 1951 and 1952 Kathleen was studying songs by Fauré and performed them in public (it would appear from her diary) on two occasions. She never recorded them.

Although three major Bach recordings have come to light in the last fifteen years, (**KF 136**, **KF 142** and **KF 174**) nothing survives of Kathleen's interpretations of his *Christmas Oratorio* or *Magnificat*, and but one aria from *St John Passion*. We can hear a small handful of arias from operas by Handel; she sang others in her recitals. She recorded none of his oratorios or operas in complete performances, although an excerpt each from *Judas Maccabaeus* and *Samson* was made in October 1952.

Kathleen's repertoire of German Lieder was growing year by year, especially those by Brahms and Schubert; some of the more popular ones that she never recorded were *Mainacht*, *Minnelied*, *Heimkehr*, *Heidenröslein*, *Erlkönig*, and *An Sylvia*. The list could be longer.

After the exciting discoveries of some of Kathleen's broadcasts in recent years, including *Land of Hope and Glory* from Manchester in 1951, *Das Lied von der Erde* from Vienna in 1952, two versions of Berkeley's *Four poems of St Teresa of Avila* (1949 and 1952) and fragments from the first Edinburgh Festival in 1947, it is hoped that others will still be found, and issued commercially; there is still so much that might have been.

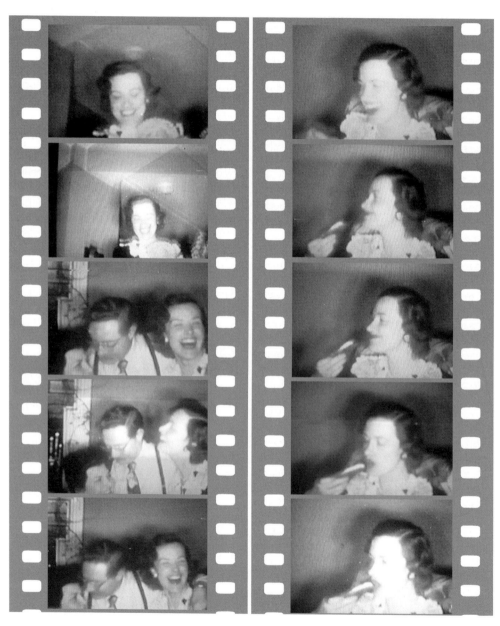

KF on film: representative frames from the first sequence of the first film, with William Griffis

Chapter Twenty-One

Kathleen Ferrier on film

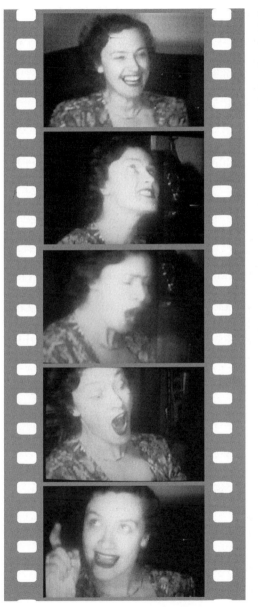

ONLY TWO FILMS of Kathleen have been traced during research, both of which are without soundtrack.

The earlier film, which cannot be accurately dated, comprises footage taken on two separate occasions – a situation made particularly clear on seeing it in colour, as Kathleen is shown in different dresses and sporting different coiffures. The first section lasts one minute thirty seconds and shows her in a dark blue dress with broad white lacy collar, following soprano Ann Ayars and an unidentified woman (perhaps Ann's friend Dottie), carrying vases of spring flowers down a short flight of stairs. Further general shots show Kathleen's evident enjoyment of a chocolate éclair and William Griffis (at whose New York apartment the film is believed to have been taken) with other unidentified companions. Kathleen's distinctive longer hairstyle seems to match that in other photographs of her 1949 transatlantic visit.

In the second section, of one minute forty-four seconds, and probably also taken in New York, Kathleen is seen alone, with a shorter hairstyle, wearing a blue patterned dress, and reciting one of her favourite little rhymes, with hand and arm movements to match. Lip-readers believe it may be:

I wish I were a fascinating bitch
I'd never be poor, I'd always be rich.
I'd live in a house with a little red light
And sleep all day and work all night …

The first film, from the second sequence

She then accompanies herself on the piano, guying the interpretations of other singers who take simple songs too seriously; the numbers being performed here have been identified as part of *The Floral Dance*, up to the penultimate line of the first verse, and an extract from *Sing, joyous bird*. The choice of these two pieces surely links it with the occasion at which the sound recording of *Kathleen Ferrier at a Party* (**KF 83**) was made, possibly early in 1949, but sound and film are not synchronised. From a remark heard on the tape it could be assumed that someone had forgotten to start the recorder while the film was running and instead of acting as a true soundtrack to the film, it is another performance of probably the same material. In the BBC film *Blow the wind southerly*, first shown in 1968, the 'soundtrack' was put to the film, and conveyed an impression of Kathleen performing her 'cabaret' repertoire; the 2003 television tribute *An Ordinary Diva* also included sections of this scene. These fragments are the only known extant true colour images of Kathleen (either stills or movies) although in the past many record covers and CD booklets have utilised artificially coloured monochrome photographs.

The second surviving film of Kathleen originated in the Netherlands. On 1 July 1951 she flew to Schiphol Airport, near Amsterdam, at the start of her visit to the Holland Festival. The newsreel camera filmed the arrival of three celebrities: Tamara Toumanova, the ballerina, Walt Disney, who also gave a short interview, and Kathleen. She is seen descending the steps from the plane, smiling broadly, and talking to Peter Diamand, Director of the Holland Festival; following her is Bernadine Hammond, her companion, who had accompanied her since the onset of her illness the previous March. The film of Kathleen lasts just twelve seconds. On a postcard to Win, Kathleen wrote: 'Here safely once more – good flight. Met by news cameras – five ordinary cameras and Peter D armed with carnations! Bernie very impressed! ... Going to flix as often as possible to see how photogenic I am!' In the biography of her sister, Win wrote: '... Kathleen wanted to see the newsreel which included this arrival, but she was too busy, so Bernie went. Just as the newsreel

began some people stood up to let others in, and by the time they sat down the incident was over. Bernie had to sit through the whole programme again, in order to see the part of the film showing their arrival ...'

Nothing seems to survive of Kathleen performing on stage or in the concert hall, and no trace of any recorded television appearances has been found.

Schiphol airport, July 1951

192

Chapter Twenty-Two
Some commemorative UK broadcasts and a DVD

1968 *Blow the wind southerly*

On 6 October 1968, BBC1 TV broadcast a specially made film in the *Omnibus* series, *Blow the wind southerly*, directed by John Drummond, to mark the 15th anniversary of Kathleen's death; the executive producer was Kathleen's erstwhile recording producer at Decca, John Culshaw.

This hour-long black and white feature included contributions from several of Kathleen's friends from her childhood and early-married life, members of her family and colleagues, and it combined them with contemporary (1968) footage of significant places in her life. Still photographs – many of them now familiar to Ferrier enthusiasts – were evocatively used to enhance this most moving portrait, with the narration written and spoken by John Drummond himself.

The film was notable for including many of Kathleen's recordings, perhaps most importantly excerpts from the then recently re-discovered *Rape of Lucretia* of 1946 and the New York Party scene, which was used as a *faux* soundtrack to the short film of the same occasion.

Blow the wind southerly was shown again, on BBC2 TV, on 30 September 1978, but the programme has never been commercially available and further broadcasts now seem unlikely. Extracts from it were used again in the 2003 presentation *An Ordinary Diva*.

Those who took part in the film were: Helen Anderson, Sir John Barbirolli, Tom Barker, Edith Bolton, Benjamin Britten, Annie Chadwick, Stella Cooper, Bill and Eleanor Coyd, Winifred Fee, Winifred Ferrier, John Francis, Bernie Hammond, Elsie Haworth, Roy Henderson, Dr J E Hutchinson, Maurice Jacobson, Elsie Livesey, Laura Lowes, Ena Mitchell, Gerald Moore, John Newmark, Peter Pears, and Dorothy Watson.

1978 *A Voice is a Person*

A Voice is a Person, introduced by Sir Peter Pears, was broadcast on BBC Radio 4 on 4 October 1978. This hour-long tribute provided the basis for the *BBC Artium* LP/cassette *Kathleen Ferrier – The Singer and the Person* (and subsequent unofficial CD issues, which used some of the same material). The producer of the original radio programme was Patricia Brent. Contributions were included from Sir John Barbirolli, Benjamin Britten, Roy Henderson and Gerald Moore and were largely taken from the film *Blow the wind southerly* of 1968.

2003 During 2003 the BBC broadcast three important tributes to Kathleen, to commemorate her death on 8 October 1953.

Our Kath

One 15-minute episode from this ten-part serial was broadcast twice each weekday on Radio 4, between 29 September and 10 October. Entitled *Our Kath*, its script was written by Claire Luckham and the producer/director was Janet Whitaker.

As linking narrator of Kathleen's life story, Shirley Dixon took the role of Winifred; Daniel Ryan was Bert Wilson, Kathleen's husband and Nicholas Boulton Benjamin Britten; Robert Rietti played Bruno Walter, John Carlisle Sir John Barbirolli, and Beckley Hindley was the adult Kathleen herself.

Listeners familiar with the Ferrier sisters' speaking voices may have found credibility somewhat stretched by their new radio *personae*, but the serial gave a touching and mostly accurate account of Kathleen's childhood in Blackburn through to her amazing rise to success and celebrity; and it surely introduced 'our Kath' to a host of listeners who otherwise knew little of her background and career.

Kathleen Ferrier Night

On 8 October 2003 BBC Radio 3 devoted an evening – three and a half hours – to a programme 'celebrating Ferrier's life, artistry, personality and legacy'.

A wide-ranging discussion was hosted live in the studio by the pianist Ian Burnside, who introduced guests Alice Coote (1992 Decca-Kathleen Ferrier prize winner at the annual Singing Awards); Peggy Reynolds (broadcaster, writer and academic); Christopher Fifield (conductor and editor of *Letters and diaries of Kathleen Ferrier*); and Brian Kay (singer, conductor and radio presenter). Contributions from Lady Barbirolli, Paul Campion, Christopher Cook, Sir John Drummond, Ian Jack, Michael Kennedy, Adèle Leigh and Kenneth Wilkinson enlarged upon aspects of Kathleen's life and career, in particular her artistic relationship with Benjamin Britten; and a number of spoken 'postcards' were included – short pre-recorded talks by Sylvia Alexander, joint Chair of the Kathleen Ferrier Society – from various locations familiar to Kathleen during her Lancashire years. Penelope Wilton was 'the voice of Kathleen Ferrier' in a series of readings of her letters, introduced by Humphrey Carpenter. Archive interviews with Benjamin Britten, Joan Cross, Winifred Ferrier, Bernie Hammond, Roy Henderson, Peter Pears and Bruno Walter were also included.

The programme was also remarkable for its inclusion of a full performance of the recently discovered recording of Berkeley's *Four poems of St Teresa of Avila*, conducted by Hugo Rignold for a BBC broadcast on 7 April 1952; of Brahms' *Alto Rhapsody*, conducted by Erik Tuxen in Oslo on 14 October 1949, and of *Der Abschied* from the Barbirolli/Hallé *Das Lied von der Erde*, originally broadcast by the BBC on 22 April 1952 (these latter two items having recently been released on an APR label CD). Many other recordings, both familiar and less well known, were also played, the programme closing, quite rightly, with *Blow the wind southerly*. Few musicians are granted an evening to themselves on Radio 3 and this presentation, produced by Deborah Preston, Johannah Smith and Lyndon Jones, proved to be a wonderfully inspiring and worthy tribute.

The recordings played, either complete or in part, were:

An die Musik/Schubert

Feinsliebchen (Sweetheart)/Brahms

Now sleeps the crimson petal/Quilter

Oh thou that tellest/Handel

What the Edinburgh Festival has meant to me

I know where I'm going/Hughes

Frauenliebe und Leben/Schumann

Agnus Dei (Mass in B Minor)/Bach

On the Field of Kulikovo/Shaporin

Four poems of St Teresa of Avila/Berkeley

Lachen und Weinen/Schubert

Interview with Eric McLean

Give him this orchid (Lucretia)/Britten

Spring (Spring Symphony)/Britten

O waly, waly/Trad arr. Britten

Alto Rhapsody/Brahms

Will o' the wisp (KF at a Party)

Um Mitternacht/Mahler

Poème de l'amour et de la mer /Chausson

What is life?/Gluck

Erbarm'es Gott ... Können Tränen (Matthäus-Passion)/Bach)

Der Abschied/Mahler

Blow the wind southerly/Trad.

Kathleen Ferrier – An Ordinary Diva

An initiative by the small independent and innovative Forget About It Film and TV company, based in Cardiff, resulted in a refreshing and colourful commemorative film entitled *Kathleen Ferrier – An Ordinary Diva*, developed with the proceeds of the National Lottery through the Arts Council of Wales. It was a co-production with the Dutch broadcasting company AVRO, which screened the programme in the Netherlands. This film was shown six times on BBC4 TV and once on BBC2 between October 2003 and August 2004. In June 2004 Decca released the 58-minute programme as a DVD, together with several extra features. These 'extras' comprise original

hand-written Decca recording cards from Ferrier sessions, a Decca discography, reproductions of 14 LP covers and 24 photographs of Kathleen at different points in her life. Also included is a separate bonus CD containing 19 'of Kathleen Ferrier's best-known recordings', in their 2003 96kHz/24-bit resolution re-mastering.

Forget About It were keen to preserve the recollections of musicians who worked with, knew or saw Kathleen in performance, as well as to use valuable archive footage drawn from the 1968 film *Blow the wind southerly*. The two films of Kathleen herself are included (see Chapter Twenty-One), so she is seen for the first time in colour – the New York party scenes offer the only genuine colour pictures of her to survive.

Kathleen is played by Vivien Parry, mainly in silhouette, shadow or soft focus, in order to give an impression of the great diva rather than a direct impersonation. The strategy works well and, in conjunction with carefully selected musical extracts and many photographs, conveys a real sense of the singer's personality. Photo-montage is used extensively, featuring memorabilia in the Ferrier Collection at Blackburn Museum and Art Gallery; and special footage was filmed at Blackburn, Glyndebourne, in Amsterdam, at the Royal Opera House, Covent Garden and elsewhere in London. Modern technology allows for more visual effects than were available to John Drummond in 1968, and it would be invidious to compare the two features, but both convey a very present sense of Kathleen as a woman and a singer.

Extracts from several of Kathleen's letters are read by the characterful and appropriately spirited Patricia Routledge, with Robert Lindsay as narrator.

The script of *An Ordinary Diva* was written by Sarah Broughton, the director was Suzanne Phillips, the producer Valerie Croft and the executive producer David M Jackson.

Those taking part are: Helen Anderson, Dame Janet Baker, Lady Barbirolli, Alan Blyth, Sir George Christie, Dr Veronica Dunne, Christopher Fifield, Mary Haydock, Ian Jack, Adèle Leigh, Donald Mitchell, Professor Robert Souhami, John Steane and Marion Thorpe.

Contributions taken from *Blow the wind southerly* are by Sir John Barbirolli, Benjamin Britten, Annie Chadwick, Winifred Ferrier, Bernie Hammond, Dr J E Hutchinson and Ena Mitchell.

Kathleen Ferrier – An Ordinary Diva was released on Decca DVD set 074 3067, Region code NTSC 123456, together with additional audio Decca CD 475 6138.

Part II
THE DISCOGRAPHY
by Paul Campion and John Pickstone

Disc and Tape List
Introduction

IN THIS LIST OF KATHLEEN FERRIER'S ISSUED RECORDINGS we have tried to include all major British and USA releases originally made for EMI and Decca. Additionally, a large number of issues from other manufacturers are shown, some of which are taken from live broadcast performances in various countries; increasingly since 1992, companies (principally in Britain and Europe) have copied existing Ferrier material (mostly from Decca originals) and simply re-issued it in a variety of different compilations, and with varying degrees of sound fidelity. Booklet notes from these sources often leave much to be desired in their factual accuracy and in their translations into English. On the other hand, several specialists have produced superb re-masterings of Kathleen's recordings, which can now be heard with a clarity never before achieved. Among such companies are APR, Andante, Dutton, Tahra and Wisp; some of Decca's new releases also show a marked improvement upon earlier issues and EMI maintains its traditionally excellent standards.

Such is the quantity of Ferrier releases now in circulation, it would be well nigh impossible to prepare an entirely comprehensive listing, and we make no claim for completeness this time round. In the discography which follows, European releases are included (we hope not too confusingly) under the general heading of British issues. Examples are Archipel, Danacord, Foyer and Verona; where possible, recordings from companies based in the USA are kept separate, such as the Bruno Walter Society, Educational Media and Music & Arts.

British issues are usually followed by a date in brackets, which is the month or year of release. If a release date has not been traced, the date preceded by 'R' is the month of review in *The Gramophone*. When a date has had to be estimated (e.g. recordings from foreign companies) it may not always be accurate, but will indicate an approximate year; in other instances no guess at an issue date has been attempted.

Under the title of each item the British issues are shown first, in the following order: 78s (10" and 12"), 45s, 33s (10" and 12"), CDs, Cassette Tapes and Stereo 8 Cartridges, marked with the symbols shown below. Below the rule ——————— the USA issues are similarly listed.

Kathleen's early Columbia records were never issued as 78s in the USA, but they have appeared there on LPs and CDs; some of her early Decca 78s were issued in the USA by American Decca on the same number as in the UK, so these numbers have not been duplicated in the American lists.

When her records (including several 78s) were issued on the London and other affiliated labels from the late 1940s, they were given entirely different numbers from their British counterparts, and these are listed below. In the age of CD, most US releases on the London label share the same number as their UK Decca counterpart, but with a different suffix – for example LH or LM, the equivalent of DH or DM.

Eight of Kathleen's recordings were issued both in the original monaural version and in a stereo re-creation which was added to the tapes in 1960. The two versions (*KF 229 – KF 236* for the original mono, and *KF 237 – KF 244* for the stereo remake) are kept distinctly separate from one another, so that the reader may see which issues are in which version. Not all releases since 1960 have been in the stereo re-creation.

Both in Britain and the USA a number of recordings have been subjected to an 'electronic stereo enhancement' process, mainly during the 1960s and 1970s. This should not be confused with the genuine stereo accompaniments referred to above; issues subjected to the electronic process have not been shown separately.

The recordings that Kathleen made for EMI and Decca between 1944 and 1953 have been released in many countries of the world, often with catalogue numbers different from those given here. Only those numbers issued in the United Kingdom and the USA are shown below.

In preparing this updated discography, we have become increasingly aware that some desirable recordings are no longer obtainable. This is frustrating for potential purchasers, but to our regret we have no special information about current availability or sources of supply for those elusive discs.

We are greatly indebted to all those who have helped in the preparation of this discography, particularly Peter Land and Andrew Dalton.

Key to symbols

In the disc and tape list the following symbols are used:

□ 78rpm 10"   ■ 78rpm 12"

◇ 45rpm 7"

O 33rpm 10"   ● 33rpm 12"

★ Compact Disc   oo Tape Cassette   8 Stereo 8 Cartridge

Disc and Tape List
Issue Numbers and Dates

78rpm Records – UK

Columbia
☐ DB 2152 (11.44) ■ DX 1194 (6.45)
☐ DB 2194 (11.45) ■ LX 8939-41 (11.52)
☐ DB 2201 (1.46)

Decca
☐ M 622 (10.48)   ■ K 1465 (Untraced)
☐ M 652 (6.50)   ■ K 1466 (7.46)
☐ M 657 (9.50)   ■ K 1517-21 (R 7.47)
☐ M 679 (2.52)   ■ AK 1517-21 (R 7.47)
☐ M 680 (9.52)   ■ K 1556 (10.46)
☐ M 681 (10.52)   ■ K 1632 (8.47)
                  ■ K 1656-62 (R 12.47)
☐ F 9300 (12.49) ■ AK 1656-62 (R 12.47)
                  ■ K 1673-9 (R 1.48)
                  ■ AK 1673-9 (R 1.48)
                  ■ K 1847-8 (6.48)
                  ■ AK 1847-8 (6.48)
                  ■ AK 2001-21 (11.48)
                  ■ K 2135 (5.49)
                  ■ K 2289 (12.49)

                  ■ AX 347-8 (9.50)
                  ■ AX 399-401 (3.51)
                  ■ AX 563-4 (10.51)

78rpm Records – USA

London
☐ R 10102   ■ T 5052
☐ R 10103   ■ T 5349
☐ R 10104   ■ T 5434
            ■ T 5435
            ■ T 5647

45rpm Records – UK

Columbia
◇ SED 5526 (10.55)
◇ SED 5530 (3.56)   ◇ SCD 2143 (11.60)

Decca
◇ 45-71034 (12.54) ◇ CEP 518 (12.57)
◇ 45-71035 (12.54) ◇ CEP 550 (7.58)
◇ 45-71036 (12.54) ◇ CEP 569 (11.58)
◇ 45-71037 (12.54) ◇ CEP 587 (3.59)
◇ 45-71038 (12.54) ◇ CEP 663 (7.60)
◇ 45-71039 (12.54) ◇ CEP 719 (3.62)
◇ 45-71072 (4.55)   ◇ CEP 720 (3.62)
◇ 45-71108 (12.55) ◇ CEP 721 (3.62)
◇ 45-71112 (5.56)   ◇ CEP 722 (3.62)
◇ 45-71130 (6.56)   ◇ CEP 723 (3.62)
◇ 45-71135 (4.56)   ◇ CEP 724 (3.62)
◇ 45-71138 (6.56)   ◇ CEP 725 (3.62)
◇ 45-71139 (6.56)   ◇ CEP 726 (3.62)
                    ◇ CEP 5508 (4.63)

45rpm Re-created Stereo – Decca
◇ SEC 5099 (10.61)

45rpm Records – USA

London
◇ 45-40166
◇ D 18060

33rpm Records – UK

Columbia
○ 33C 1009 (11.52)

Decca
○ LX 3006 (6.50)
○ LX 3007 (6.50)
○ LX 3040 (5.51)
○ LX 3098 (11.52)
○ LX 3133 (6.54)

33rpm UK – Decca *(continued)*

○ LW 5072 (12.53)   ● LXT 2556 (1.51)
○ LW 5076 (1.54)   ● LXT 2721 (9.52)
○ LW 5083 (1.54)   ● LXT 2722 (9.52)
○ LW 5089 (2.54)   ● LXT 2757 (1.53)
○ LW 5094 (3.54)   ● LXT 2850 (11.53)
○ LW 5098 (3.54)   ● LXT 2893 (2.54)
○ LW 5123 (9.54)   ● LXT 5324 (5.57)
○ LW 5225 (3.56)   ● LXT 5382 (11.57)
○ LW 5353 (10.59) ● LXT 5576 (10.60)

○ BR 3052 (6.60)   ● LXT 6278 (4.67)
               ● LXT 6907 (10.78)
               ● LXT 6934 (9.79)

● ACL 52 (9.59)   ● 414 095-1DH (3.85)
● ACL 109-11 (11.60) ● 414 194-1DM (5.86)
(Three-record set – ● 414 611-1DG (2.86)
St Matthew Passion) ● 414 623-1DG (6.86)
● ACL 293 (11.66)
● ACL 305 (9.68)   ● 417 182-1DM (5.86)
● ACL 306 (9.68)   ● 417 466-1DM (1.87)
● ACL 307 (9.68)   ● 417 634-1DM (11.87)
● ACL 308 (10.68)
● ACL 309 (10.68)
● ACL 310 (10.68)
● ACL 318 (6.69)

● ECS 562 (10.70) ● PA 172 (10.71)
● ECS 2178 (11.77)

● SPA 205 (3.72)
● SPA 316 (12.73)
● SPA 355 (7.74)
● SPA 433 (9.75)
● SPA 524 (6.78)

● 6 BB 197-8 (11.75) (Two-record set – Edinburgh Festival recital and last BBC broadcast recital)
● D 42 D 3 (4.77) (Three-record set – *St Matthew Passion*)
● D 264 D 2 (9.82) (Two-record set – Mahler's *Second Symphony*)
● DPA 623-4 (12.78) (Two-record set – *Favourite composers – Schumann*)
● DPA 627-8 (12.79) (Two-record set – *The music of England*)

● AKF 1-7 (10.73) (Seven-record set) N.B. AKF 4 is in Re-created Stereo

33rpm – Decca Re-created Stereo

● SXL 2234 (9.60)
● DPA 551-2 (9.76) (Two-record set – *Favourite composers – Handel*)
● SDD 286 (10.71)
● SDD M 432-4 (9.74) (Three-record set – *Festival of Sacred Music*)
● AKF 4 (10.73)

● SPA 297 (12.73)
● SPA 322 (9.74)
● SPA 448 (8.76)
● SPA 531 (10.78)
● SPA 566 (9.80)
● SPA 588 (4.81)

HMV

● HLM 7002 (3.72)
● HLM 7145 (12.78) (*Great British Mezzo-Sopranos and Contraltos*)
● HQM 1072 (2.67)
● RLS 725 (4.78) (Two-record set – *Orfeo ed Euridice*)
● EX 7697431 (4.89) (Eight-record set – *The Record of Singing Volume 4*)

Rococo

● 5265

Rodolphe

● RP 12407

BBC Artium

● REGL 368 (R 12.79) (*Kathleen Ferrier – The Singer and the Person*)

Danacord

● DACO 114 (1985)

Foyer

● FO 1046 (1986) (Four-record set – *Matthäus-Passion*)

33rpm Records – USA

London

O LD 9066	● LLP 271
O LD 9088	● LLP 625-6
O LD 9096	● LLP 688
O LD 9097	● LLP 845
O LD 9098	● LLP 903
O LD 9099	● LLP 924
O LD 9137	● LLP 1529
O LD 9229	● LLP 1670
	● 5020
O LPS 48	● 5069-70
O LPS 104	● 5083
O LPS 160	● 5092
O LPS 161	● 5098
O LPS 538	● 5103
O LPS 1032	● 5258
	● 5291
	● 5411
● 414 095-1LH	
● 414 194-1LJ	
● 414 611-1LJ	● STS 15200
● 414 623-1LJ	● STS 15201
● 417 466-1LJ	● STS 15202

● 2-LONDON A-4212 (Two-record set – *Das Lied von der Erde* and *Three Rückert Lieder*)

American Columbia
O Masterworks ML 2187
● Masterworks ML 4980

Arabesque
● Arabesque 8070

Bruno Walter Society (Educ Media)
● IGI 369

● IGI 374 (Two-record set – Mahler's *Second Symphony* and two songs from *Das Lied von der Erde*)

● BWS 707

● BWS 742	● DIS 3700

Capitol Seraphim
● Seraphim M 60044
● Seraphim M 60203

● IH-6150 (Eight-record set – *The Record of Singing Volume 4*)

CBS Odyssey
● 2-Odyssey 32 26 0016 (Two-record set – *Kindertotenlieder* and Mahler's *Fifth Symphony*)

Richmond

● R 23182	● R 23186
● R 23183	● R 23187
● R 23184	● R 23206
● R 23185	

● 3-RICHMOND A 43001 (Three-record set – *St Matthew Passion*)

Compact Discs – UK

EMI
★ CDH 7 61003-2 (1.88)

★ CZS 5 69743-2 (3.97) (Four-CD set – *Les Introuvables de Walter Legge*)

★ CZS 5 75133-2 (3.02) (Two-CD set – *Great Conductors – Bruno Walter*)

★ CDM 5 66911-2 (10.98)

★ CMS 5 66182-2 (2.97) (Eleven-CD set – *EMI Centenary Box*)

★ CMS 7 63790-2 (11.90) (Five-CD set – *Elisabeth Schwarzkopf*)

★ CDM 7 63655-2 (12.90) *Unpublished recordings of Elisabeth Schwarzkopf*

★ CHS 7 69741-2 (12.91) (Seven-CD set – *The Record of Singing Volume 4*)

★ CHS 5 67207-2 (1.00) (Two-CD set – EMI's *B Minor Mass* plus five rehearsal items)

★ 7243 5 86194 2 3 (11.04) (Two-CD set – *Orfeo ed Euridice*)

Decca
★ 414 194-2DH (10.84)
★ 414 611-2DH (4.88)
★ 414 623-2DH (12.85)
★ 417 192-2DH (4.88)
★ 421 299-2DH (4.88)

★ 425 970-2DM (11.90)
★ 425 995-2DM (3.92)

CDs UK – Decca (contd.)

★ 430 096-2DWO (9.90) (*The World of Kathleen Ferrier*)

★ 430 499-2DWO (R10.91) (*The World of Bach*)

★ 433 332-2DM (R2.92) (Twelve-CD set – *Vienna Philharmonic 150th Anniversary*)

★ 433 468-2DM (4.92)

★ 433 469-2DM (4.92)

★ 433 470-2DM (4.92)

★ 433 471-2DM (4.92)

★ 433 472-2DM (4.92)

★ 433 473-2DM (4.92)

★ 433 474-2DM (4.92)

★ 433 475-2DM (4.92)

★ 433 476-2DM (4.92)

★ 433 477-2DM (4.92)

★ 433 802 – 2DM10 (4.92) (Ten-CD set *The Kathleen Ferrier Edition*)

★ 436 404-2DWO (3.93) (*The World of Sacred Music*)

★ 436 928-2DWO (*The World of British Music*)

★ 440 063-2DM (8.94)

★ 443 393-2DWO (12.94) (*The World of Henry Purcell*)

★ 444 543-2DF2 (7.96) (*Essential Handel*)

★ 448 055-2DWO (12.95) (*The World of Kathleen Ferrier vol 2*)

★ 458 270-2DH (1997)

★ 466 576-2DM (9.00)

★ 467 782-2DWO (2.01) (*The World of English Folksongs*)

★ 470 189-2 (2002) (*British Music Collection – Bridge*)

★ 470 195-2 (2002) (*British Music Collection – Ireland, Rubbra and Quilter*)

★ 470 384-2 (2002) (*British Music Collection –Stanford*)

★ 475 078-2DX2 (R 8.03) (Two-CD set *Kathleen Ferrier – A Tribute*)

★ 475 6060 DC10 (Ten-CD set *The Kathleen Ferrier Edition*) (6.04)

★ 475 6138 (6.04) Bonus CD with the DVD *An Ordinary Diva*

★ 475 6411-9DM (12.04) (Re-created stereo *Bach and Handel arias*)

Andante

★ 4973 (2002) (Four-CD set – including *Das Lied von der Erde*)

★ A1170 (2003) (Three-CD set – *Matthäus-Passion*)

Appian Publications and Recordings

★ APR 5544 (1997)

★ APR 5579 (2003)

Archipel

★ ARPCD0033 (2001)

★ ARPCD00243 (2001) (Three-CD set – *Matthäus-Passion*)

★ ARPCD00312 (2001) (Two-CD set – *Mass in B Minor*)

Audiophile

★ APL 101.567 (2003)

Aura

★ AUR2482 (2003)

BBC Legends

★ BBCL 4007-8 (1998) (Two-CD set – *Mass in B Minor*)

★ BBCL 4100-2 (2002)

Belart

★ 450 020-2 (1995)

Cantus Classics

★ 5.00276 (2002) (Two-CD set – *Orfeo ed Euridice* with a French version of the opera on the second CD)

Classic Options

★ CO 3540 (1991)

★ CO 3541 (1991)

Danacord

★ DACO CD 301 (1986)

Documents (*Membran*)

★ 221538-303 (2003) (Two-CD set – *Orfeo ed Euridice* plus other Ferrier titles)

★ 221362-205 (1.05)
★ 221917 (1.05)

Dutton
★ CDLX 7020 (1997)
★ CDLX 7024 (1997)
★ CDLX 7025 (1997)

★ CDEA 5015 (1998)
★ 2CDAX 2005 (1999)
★ CDAX 8019 (1999)
★ CDK 1210 (2000)

Foyer
★ 3CF 2013 (1988) (Three-CD set –
Matthäus-Passion)
★ 2CF 2022 (1988) (Two-CD set –
Mass in B Minor)

Gala
★ GL 100.612 (1999) (Three-CD set –
Matthäus-Passion)
★ GL100.560 (2000) (Two-CD set –
The Rape of Lucretia)
★ GL 307 (1990)
★ GL 318 (1993) Songs my Father taught me,
also including interviews

Going for a Song
★ GFS635 (2004)

Guild Historical
★ GHCD 2210 (2002)
★ GHCD 2260/2 (2003)

Laserlight Classics
★ 14 262 (1995)

Living Era
★ CD AJA 5536 (2004)

Memoir Classics
★ CDMOIR 440 (1997)

Naxos
★ 8.110029 (2.99)
★ 8.110871 (4.03)
★ 8.110876 (8.03)
★ 8.111009 (10.04)
★ 8.111081 (3.05)

Nimbus
★ NI 7864 (1994) More Legendary Voices

Regis
★ RRC 1057 (2001)
★ RRC 1146 (2003)
★ RRC 1164 (2003)
★ RRC 1153 (2004)

Pearl
★ GEMS 0231 (08.05) (Two-CD set –
The Rape of Lucretia)

Prism Leisure
★ PLATCD 640 (2000)

Tahra
★ TAH 462 (2002) Hommage à Kathleen
Ferrier
★ TAH 482 (2003) In Memoriam

Urania
★ URN22.194 (2001) (Extracts from
Matthäus-Passion and Mass in B Minor)
★ URN22185 (2001) (Three-CD set
Matthäus-Passion)

Verona
★ 27016/7 (1989) (Two-CD set –
Orfeo ed Euridice)
★ 30004/5 (2001) (Two-CD set –
Orfeo ed Euridice)
★ 30001/3 (2001) (Three-CD set –
Matthäus-Passion)
★ 27062/3 (1990) (Two-CD set – Mahler's
Second Symphony and Lieder eines
fahrenden Gesellen with Fischer-
Dieskau)
★ 27070/2 (1989) (Three-CD set –
Matthäus-Passion)
★ 27073/4 (1989) (Two-CD set –
Mass in B Minor)
★ 27076 (1990)
★ 30015/16 (2001) (Two-CD set –
Mahler's Second Symphony plus other
Ferrier titles
★ 30006/7 (2001) (Two-CD set – Mass in B
Minor)

CDs – UK *(continued)*

Vocal Archives
★ VA 1169 (1998)

Wisp
★ WISPCD 25963 (1996)
★ WISPCD 25965 (1996)
★ WISPCD 25966/7 (1996)
★ WISPCD 25971 (1999)

Compact Discs – USA

London
★ 414 194-2LH
★ 414 623-2LH
★ 425 970-2LM
★ 425 995-2LM
★ 430 061-2LM (11.90)
★ 430 096-2LWO

★ 433 468-2LM	★ 433 473-2LM
★ 433 469-2LM	★ 433 474-2LM
★ 433 470-2LM	★ 433 475-2LM
★ 433 471-2LM	★ 433 476-2LM
★ 433 472-2LM	★ 433 477-2LM

★ 448 150-2LM (*Great Voices of the Fifties Vol 1*)

Angel
★ CDH-61003
★ CDM-63655

Music & Arts
★ CD 733
★ CD 901 (03.96)

New York Philharmonic
★ NYP9801/12 (1999) (Twelve-CD set *Mahler broadcasts 1948-1982*)

PGD London Classics

★ 33468	★ 33473
★ 33469	★ 33474
★ 33470	★ 33475
★ 33471	★ 33476
★ 33472	★ 33477

Tape Cassettes – UK

BBC Artium
oo ZCF 368 (R 12.79)

Decca
oo KACC 309 (11.73)

oo KCSP 172 (6.72)
oo KCSP 205 (5.72)
oo KCSP 316 (1.74)
oo KCSP 355 (8.74)
oo KCSP 433 (9.75)
oo KCSP 524 (6 78)

oo KDPC 623-4 (12.78) (Two tapes – *Favourite composers – Schumann*)
oo KDPC 627-8 (12.79) (Two tapes – *Music of England*)
oo K 160 K54 (9.79) (Four tapes – Nos 160 K l-4) NB Cassette 160 K2 is in Re-created Stereo
oo KECC 2178 (11.77)
oo K MON2 7050 (2.78)
oo KLXTC 6934 (9.79)
oo K 264 K22 (9.82) (Two tapes – Mahler's *Second Symphony*)

oo 414 095-4DH (3.85)
oo 414 194-4DM (5.86)
oo 414 611-4DG (2.86)
oo 414 623-4DG (6.86)
oo 417 182-4DM (5.86)
oo 417 466-4DM (1.87)
oo 417 634-4DM (11.87)

oo 430 061-4LM (11.90)
oo 430 096-4DWO (9.90) (*The World of Kathleen Ferrier*)
oo 430 499-4DWO (R10.91) (*The World of Bach*)
oo 433 468-4DM (4.92)
oo 433 469-4DM (4.92)
oo 433 470-4DM (4.92)
oo 433 471-4DM (4.92)
oo 433 472-4DM (4.92)
oo 433 473-4DM (4.92)
oo 433 474-4DM (4.92)
oo 433 475-4DM (4.92)

oo 433 476-4DM (4.92)

oo 433 477-4DM (4.92)

oo 436 404-4DWO (1993)
(*The World of Sacred Music*)

oo 436 928-4DWO
(*The World of British Music*)

oo 444 543-4DF2 (7.96) (*Essential Handel*)

oo 448 055-2DWO (12.95)
(*The World of Kathleen Ferrier Vol 2*)

oo 452 450-4DF2 (*The Joy of Christmas*)

oo 458 270-4DH (1997)

EM1
oo EG 7 63655-4 (12.90)

Gala
oo GL 6318 (1993) *Songs my Father taught
me* (also including interviews)

Rodolphe
oo RPK 22407

Re-created Stereo Tape Cassettes – Decca
oo KCSP 297 (11.73)
oo KCSP 322 (8.74)
oo KCSP 448 (8.76)
oo KCSP 531 (10.78)
oo KCSP 566 (9.80)
oo KCSP 588 (4.81)

oo KDPC 551-2 (9.76) (Two tapes –
Favourite composers – Handel)

oo KSDC 286 (11.73)

oo 160 K2 (9.79)

oo 411 887-4DN (9.84)
oo 414 047-4DN (1.85)
oo 414 048-4DN (1.85)
oo 421 175-4DC (2.88)

Tape Cassettes – USA

London
oo 414 095-4LH
oo 414 194-4LJ
oo 414 611-4LJ
oo 414 623-4LJ
oo 417 466-4LJ
oo 433 469-4LM

Arabesque
oo Arabesque 9070

Stereo 8 Cartridges

Decca
8 ECSP 172 (19.73)
8 ECSP 205 (11.72)
8 ECSP 316 (1.74)
8 ECSP 355 (8.74)

Re-created Stereo – Stereo 8 – Decca
8 ECSP 322 (8.74)

Disc and Tape List
Title-by-title Listing

KF 1 *What is life?*
- ● HLM 7145
- ★ APR 5544
- ★ CZS 5 69743-2
- ★ CDLX 7024

KF 2 *Constancy*
- ● HLM 7145
- ★ CZS 5 69743-2
- ★ VA 1169
- ★ APR 5544

KF 3 *Sweetheart*
- ● HLM 7145
- ★ CZS 5 69743-2
- ★ VA 1169
- ★ APR 5544

KF 4 *My work is done ... It is because ...*
- ● HLM 7145
- ★ CZS 5 69743-2
- ★ CDAX 8019
- ★ VA 1169
- ★ APR 5544

KF 6 *I will lay me down in peace*
- □ DB 2152
- ◇ SED 5530
- ● HLM 7002
- ● M 60203
- ★ CZS 5 69743-2
- ★ CDM 5 66911-2
- ★ CO 3541
- ★ VA 1169
- ★ APR 5544
- ★ CDMOIR 440
- ★ CDH 7 61003-2
- ★ CDH-61003

KF 7 *O praise the Lord*
- □ DB 2152
- ◇ SED 5530
- ● HLM 7002
- ● M 60203
- ★ CZS 5 69743-2
- ★ CDM 5 66911-2
- ★ CO 3541
- ★ VA 1169
- ★ APR 5544
- ★ CDMOIR 440
- ★ CDH 7 61003-2
- ★ CDH-61003

KF 11 *Spring is coming*
- ■ DX 1194
- ◇ SED 5526
- ◇ SCD 2143
- ● HLM 7002
- ● M 60203
- ★ CDM 5 66911-2
- ★ CO 3541
- ★ VA 1169
- ★ CD AJA 5536
- ★ CDMOIR 440
- ★ APR 5544
- ★ CDH 7 61003-2
- ★ PLATCD 640
- ★ CDH-61003

KF 12 *Come to me, soothing sleep*
- ★ CDM 5 66911-2
- ★ CO 3541

KF 12   Come to me, soothing sleep (continued)

                          ★ VA 1169
                          ★ CD AJA 5536
                          ★ CDMOIR 440
                          ★ APR 5544

◇ SED 5526   ★ CDH 7 61003-2
■ DX 1194   ◇ SCD 2143   ● HLM 7002   ★ PLATCD 640

                      ● M 60203   ★ CDH-61003

KF 16   Sound the trumpet

                          ★ CDM 5 66911-2
                          ★ CO 3541
                          ★ VA 1169
                          ★ CD AJA 5536
                          ★ APR 5544
                          ★ CDMOIR 440

                          ★ CDH 7 61003-2
□ DB 2201   ◇ SED 5530   ● HLM 7002   ★ PLATCD 640

                      ● M 60203   ★ CDH-61003

KF 17   Let us wander

                          ★ CDM 5 66911-2
                          ★ CO 3541
                          ★ VA 1169
                          ★ APR 5544
                          ★ CDMOIR 440

□ DB 2201   ◇ SED 5530   ● HLM 7002   ★ CDH 7 61003-2

                      ● M 60203   ★ CDH-61003

KF 18   Shepherd, leave decoying

                          ★ CDM 5 66911-2
                          ★ CDMOIR 440
                          ★ APR 5544

                          ★ CDH 7 61003-2
□ DB 2201   ◇ SED 5530   ● HLM 7002   ★ PLATCD 640

                      ● M 60203   ★ CDH-61003

KF 19   I would that my love

                          ★ CDM 5 66911-2
                          ★ CO 3541
                          ★ CD AJA 5536
                          ★ APR 5544
                          ★ CDMOIR 440
                          ★ CDH 7 61003-2

□ DB 2194   ◇ SED 5526   ● HLM 7002   ★ PLATCD 640

                      ● M 60203   ★ CDH-61003

KF 20   Greeting

                          ★ CDM 5 66911-2
                          ★ APR 5544

                      ● HLM 7002   ★ CDMOIR 440
□ DB 2194   ◇ SED 5526   ● HQM 1072   ★ PLATCD 640

                      ● M 60044
                      ● M 60203

KF 26   Have mercy, Lord, on me

                          ★ 475 6138
                          ★ GFS635
                          ★ RRC1057
                          ★ CDMOIR 440

KF 26   Have mercy, Lord, on me (continued)

		★ 430 096-2DWO	oo KLXTC 6934
		★ 433 470-2DM	oo 417 466-4DM
		★ 458 270-2DH	oo 430 096-4DWO
	● LXT 6934	★ 475 078-2DX2	oo 433 470-4DM
■ K 1465 ◇ 45-71037	● 417 466-1DM	★ 475 6060 DC10	oo 458 270-4DH
	● 417 466-1LJ	★ 433 470-2LM	oo 417 466-4LJ
		★ 430 096-2LWO	
		★ 33470	

KF 27   Art thou troubled?

		★ 475 6138	
		★ CDLX 7020	
		★ GFS635	
		★ CD AJA 5536	
		★ 475 6060DC10	
		★ CDMOIR 440	
		★ 430 096-2DWO	oo KCSP 172
	○ LW 5072	★ 433 470-2DM	oo 430 096-4DWO
	● AKF 3	★ 458 270-2DH	oo 160 K4
	● ACL 308	★ 475 078-2DX2	oo 433 470-4DM
■ K 1466 ◇ 45-71034	● PA 172	★ 221538-303	oo 458 270-4DH
■ T 5434		★ PLATCD 640	8 ECSP 172
	○ LD 9066	★ 433 470-2LM	
	● LLP 1529	★ 430 096-2LWO	
	● 5258	★ 33470	
	● R 23185		

KF 28   What is life?

		★ 475 6138	
		★ CDLX 7020	
		★ GFS635	
		★ CD AJA 5536	
		★ 430 096-2DWO	oo KCSP 172
		★ 433 470-2DM	oo KCSP 355
		★ 458 270-2DH	oo 430 096-4DWO
	○ LW 5072	★ 475 078-2DX2	oo 160 K4
	● AKF 3	★ PLATCD 640	oo 433 470-4DM
	● ACL 308	★ 475 6060 DC10	oo 458 270-4DH
◇ 45-71034	● PA 172	★ CDMOIR 440	8 ECSP 172
■ K 1466 ◇ CEP 724	● SPA 355	★ RRC1057	8 ECSP 355
■ T 5434			
	○ LD 9066	★ 433 470-2LM	
	● LLP 1529	★ 430 096-2LWO	
	● 5258	★ 33470	
	● R 23185		

KF 29   Stabat Mater

■ K 1517-21
■ AK 1517-21

		★ 475 6060 DC10	
	● LXT 6907	★ 433 470-2DM	oo 417 466-4DM
	● 417 466-1DM	★ 2CDAX 2005	oo 433 470-4DM
	● 417 466-1LJ	★ 433 470-2LM	oo 417 466-4LJ
		★ 33470	

KF 29a   Quae Moerebat

★ 221538-303

KF 29b   Eia, Mater

★ 221538-303

KF 29c   Sancta Mater

★ 221538-303
★ CDMOIR 440

KF 29d *Fac ut portem*

★ 221538-303
★ PLATCD 640
★ CDMOIR 440
★ RRC1057

KF 31 *O rest in the Lord*

★ CDLX 7025
★ GFS635
★ CD AJA 5536
★ RRC1057
★ CDMOIR 440

■ K 1556 ◊ 45-71039 O LW 5072 ★ 430 096-2DWO oo KCSP 316
◊ CEP 724 ● AKF 3 ★ 433 470-2DM oo KCSP 433
● ACL 308 ★ 458 270-2DH oo 430 096-4DWO
● SPA 316 ★ 475 078-2DX2 oo 160 K4
● SPA 433 ★ 221538-303 oo 433 470-4DM
★ PLATCD 640 oo 458 270-4DH
★ 475 6060 DC10 **8** ECSP 316

◊ D 18060 O LD 9066 ★ 433 470-2LM
● LLP 1529 ★ 430 096-2LWO
● 5258 ★ 33470
● R 23185

KF 32 *Woe unto them*

★ CDLX 7025
★ RRC1057
★ CDMOIR 440
★ 475 6060 DC10
★ 475 078-2DX2
★ 221538-303
★ PLATCD 640

□ K 1556 ◊ 45-71112 ● AKF 3 ★ 430 096-2DWO oo 430 096-4DWO
◊ CEP 724 ● ACL 308 ★ 433 470-2DM oo 433 470-4DM

● R 23185 ★ 433 470-2LM
★ 430 096-2LWO
★ 33470

KF 33 *The Rape of Lucretia*

★ GL100.560
★ WISPCD25966/7

KF 33a *Rome is now ruled*
KF 33b *My horse! My horse!*
KF 33c *She sleeps as a rose*
KF 33d *Flowers bring*
KF 33e *Lucretia, Lucretia*

(Five extracts) ● IGI 369 ★ CD 901

KF 34 *The Rape of Lucretia* ★ GEMS 0231

KF 34a *Hush, here she comes ... Flowers bring* ★ CDMOIR 440

KF 34b *Lucretia, Lucretia* ★ GL 318 oo GL 6318
● REGL 368 ★ CDMOIR 440 oo ZCF 368

● Arabesque 8070 oo Arabesque 9070

KF 36 *Gretchen am Spinnrade* ★ RRC1057
★ PLATCD 640

KF 36   Gretchen am Spinnrade (continued)

■ K 1632	◇ CEP 663	○ LW 5098	★ 475 6060 DC10	
		● AKF 6	★ 430 096-2DWO	oo 430 096-4DWO
		● ACL 307	★ 433 471-2DM	oo 160 K4
			★ 475 078-2DX2	oo 433 471-4DM
■ T 5435		○ LD 9099	★ 433 471-2LM	
		● LLP 1529	★ 430 096-2LWO	
		● 5258	★ 33471	
		● R 23184		

KF 37   Die junge Nonne

			★ RRC1057	
			★ PLATCD 640	
			★ 475 6060 DC10	
□ K 1632	◇ CEP 663	○ LW 5098	★ 430 096-2DWO	oo 430 096-4DWO
		● AKF 6	★ 433 471-2DM	oo 433 471-4DM
		● ACL 307	★ 475 078-2DX2	
□ T 5435		○ LD 9099	★ 433 471-2LM	
		● LLP 1529	★ 430 096-2LWO	
		● 5258	★ 33471	
		● R 23184		

KF 38   Orfeo ed Euridice – Concise

			★ 5.00276	
□ K 1656-62		● LXT 2893	★ 433 468-2DM	oo 417 182-4DM
□ AK 1656-62		● ACL 293	★ CDEA 5015	oo 433 468-4DM
		● 417 182-1DM	★ 221538-303	
			★ 475 6060 DC10	
		● LLP 924	★ 433 468-2LM	
		● 5103	★ 33468	

KF 38a   Euridice ... Piango il mio ben   ★ VA 1169

KF 38b   Deh placatevi!   ★ VA 1169

KF 38c   Mille pene   ★ VA 1169

KF 38d   Che puro ciel

	★ 475 6138	
	★ 448 055-2DWO	
	★ VA 1169	
	★ RRC1164	oo 448 055-2DWO
○ LW5225	★ PLATCD 640	oo KCSP 172
● PA 172	★ 475 078-2DX2	oo ECSP 172
○ LD 9229		

KF 38e   Che farò?

★ RRC1164	
★ 458 270-2DH	oo 458 270-4DH

KF 40   St Matthew Passion – abridged
■ K 1673-9 (For excerpts, see under *KF 41*)
■ AK 1673-9

KF 41   St Matthew Passion – (almost) complete

■ AK 2001-21	● ACL 109-11	
	● D 42 D3	★ 2CDAX 2005
	● A 43001	

KF 41a   Come, ye daughters
- AK 2001-2-3

★ 433 469-2DM
★ 475 6060 DC10   oo 433 469-4DM

★ 433 469-2LM   oo 433 469-4LM
★ 33469

KF 41b   My Master and my Lord . . . Grief for sin
- AK 2004-5   ● ACL 308
- K 1673 (Aria only)
- AK 1673 (Aria only)

★ RRC1057
★ 433 469-2DM   oo 433 469-4DM
★ 221538-303
★ PLATCD 640
★ 475 6060 DC10

      ● R 23185

★ 433 469-2LM   oo 433 469-4LM
★ 33469

KF 41c   Behold, my Saviour ... Have lightnings
- AK 2008-9

★ 433 469-2DM
★ 475 6060 DC10   oo 433 469-4DM

★ 433 469-2LM   oo 433 469-4LM
★ 33469

KF 41d   Ah! Now is my Saviour gone
- AK 2012-3   ● AKF 3
      ● ACL 308

★ 433 469-2DM   oo 433 469-4DM
★ 475 6060 DC10

      ● R 23185

★ 433 469-2LM   oo 433 469-4LM
★ 33469

KF 41e   Have mercy, Lord, on me   ★ CD AJA 5536
- AK 2012-1   ● AKF 3
- K 1676   ● ACL 308
- AK 1676   ● PA 172

★ 433 469-2DM   oo KCSP 172
★ 221538-303   oo 433 469-4DM
★ PLATCD 640   8ECSP 172
★ 475 6060 DC10

      ● R 23185

★ 433 469-2LM   oo 433 469-4LM
★ 33469

KF 41f   Lamb of God
- K 1676
- AK 1679
- AK 2011

★ 433 469-2DM   oo 433 469-4DM
★ 475 6060 DC10

★ 433 469-2LM   oo 433 469-4LM
★ 33469

KF 41g   O gracious God! ... If my tears be unavailing
- AK 2017-8   ● AKF 3
      ● ACL 308

★ 433 469-2DM   oo 433 469-4DM
★ 2CDAX 2005 (unpub. take)
★ 221538-303
★ 475 6060 DC10

      ● R 23185

★ 433 469-2LM   oo 433 469-4LM
★ 33469

KF 41h   O sacred Head
- AK 2019

★ 433 469-2DM
★ 475 6060 DC10   oo 433 469-4DM

KF 41h   *O sacred Head (continued)*   ★ 433 469-2LM   oo 433 469-4LM
                              ★ 33469

KF 41i   *Ah, Golgotha! ... See the Saviour's outstretched hands*
■ AK 2020-1   ● AKF 3   ★ 433 469-2DM   oo 433 469-4DM
■ K 1678 (Aria only)   ● ACL 308   ★ 475 6060 DC10
■ AK 1676 (Aria only)

                      ● R 23185   ★ 433 469-2LM   oo 433 469-4LM
                                         ★ 33469

KF 41j   *Be near me, Lord*
■ K 1678   ★ 433 469-2DM   oo 433 469-4DM
■ AK 1675   ★ 475 6060 DC10
■ AK 2020

                                     ★ 433 469-2LM   oo 433 469-4LM
                                     ★ 33469

KF 41k   *And now the Lord*
■ AK 2017   ★ 433 469-2DM   oo 433 469-4DM
                                     ★ 475 6060 DC10

                                     ★ 433 469-2LM   oo 433 469-4LM
                                     ★ 33469

KF 41l   *In tears of grief*
■ K 1679   ★ 433 469-2DM   oo 433 469-4DM
■ AK 1674-3   ★ 475 6060 DC10
■ AK 2016-5

                                     ★ 433 469-2LM   oo 433 469-4LM
                                     ★ 33469

KF 51   *Beethoven's Symphony No. 9*

                       ● BWS 742   ★ CD 733

KF 55   *Alto Rhapsody*   ★ CDK 1210
                                       ★ 30015/16
                                       ★ GL 307
                                       ★ RRC 1146
                                       ★ VA 1169
                                       ★ 475 6060 DC10
■ K 1847-8   ◊ CEP 569   ● LXT 2850   ★ 421 299-2DH   oo 433 477-4DM
■ AK 1847-8   ● AKF 5   ★ 433 477-2DM
                                 ● ACL 306   ★ 8.111009

                                 ● LLP 903   ★ 433 477-2LM
                                 ● 5098   ★ 33477
                                 ● R 23183
                                 ● STS 15201

KF 56   *Das Lied von der Erde*   ★ 221362-205
                                       ★ 8.110029

                                       ★ NYP9801/12

KF 56a   *Von der Schönheit*   ★ WISPCD25965

                       ● IGI 374

KF 56b   Der Abschied

★ WISPCD25966/7

● IGI 374

KF 58   Four poems of St Teresa of Avila

● REGL 368

★ WISPCD 25971
★ GL 318

oo GL 6318
oo ZCF 368

● Arabesque 8070

oo Arabesque 9070

KF 66   Silent night, holy night

☐ M 622   ◇ 45-71036
            ◇ CEP 518

● LXT 6934
● PA 172

8 ECSP 172
★ 433 471-2DM   oo KLXTC 6934
★ 475 6060 DC10   oo KCSP 172
★ RRC1057   oo 433 471-4DM

■ T 5052   ◇ 45-40166

★ 433 471-2LM
★ 33471

KF 67   O come all ye faithful

☐ M 622   ◇ 45-71036
            ◇ CEP 518

● LXT 6934

★ 433 471-2DM   oo KLXTC 6934
★ 475 6060 DC10   oo 433 471-4DM

■ T 5052   ◇ 45-40166

★ 433 471-2LM
★ 33471

KF 68   Love is a bable

● REGL 368

oo ZCF 368

● Arabesque 8070

oo Arabesque 9070

KF 69   Frondi tenere ... Ombra mai fu

★ GFS635
★ RRC1057
★ 475 078-2DX2
★ 221538-303
★ PLATCD 640
★ 475 6060 DC10

■ K 2135   ◇ 45-71039
            ◇ CEP 724

O LW 5072
● AKF 3
● ACL 308

★ 430 096-2DWO   oo 430 096-4DWO
★ 433 470-2DM   oo 433 470-4DM
★ 458 270-2DH   oo 458 270-4DH

■ T 5349   ◇ D 18060

O LD 9066
O LPS 104
● LLP 1529
● 5258
● R 23185

★ 433 470-2LM
★ 430 096-2LWO
★ 33470

KF 71   Four Serious Songs

● LXT 6934
● 414 095-1DH

★ 433 472-2DM   oo KLXTC 6934
★ GHCD 2260/2   oo 414 095-4DH
★ 475 6060 DC10   oo 433 472-4DM

● 414 095-1LH

★ 433 472-2LM   oo 414 095-4LH
★ 33472

KF 72   Blow the wind southerly

★ 8.111081
★ 475 6138
★ 436 928-2DWO
★ 450 020-2
★ 467 782-2DWO
★ NI 7864   oo 436 928-4DWO

☐ F 9300   ◇ 45-71135
            ◇ CEP 725

O LX 3040
O LW 5225
O BR 3052

★ 417 192-2DH   oo KACC 309
★ 430 096-2DWO   oo KCSP 172
★ 433 475-2DM   oo KCSP 205

215

KF 72   Blow the wind southerly (continued)

- AKF 1
- ACL 309
- PA 172
- SPA 205
- DPA 627
- ECS 2178

★ 458 270-2DH
★ 475 078-2DX2
★ PLATCD 640
★ 475 6060 DC10
★ RRC1057
★ RRC1164
★ CD AJA 5536
★ GFS635

oo KECC 2178
oo KDPC 627
oo 430 096-4DWO
oo 160 K4
oo 433 475-4DM
oo 458 270-4DH
8 ECSP 172
8 ECSP 205

☐ R 10102

○ LD 9229
○ LPS 48
- 5411
- R 23186

★ 433 475-2LM
★ 430 096-2LWO
★ 33475

KF 73   Ma bonny lad

★ 8.111081
★ 475 6138
★ 467 782-2DWO
★ RRC1057

☐ F 9300

◇ 45-71135
◇ CEP 725

○ LX 3040
○ BR 3052
- AKF 1
- ACL 309
- PA 172

★ 417 192-2DH
★ 430 096-2DWO
★ 433 475-2DM
★ 458 270-2DH
★ 475 078-2DX2
★ PLATCD 640
★ 475 6060 DC10

oo KACC 309
oo KCSP 172
oo 430 096-4DWO
oo 160 K4
oo 433 475-4DM
oo 458 270-4DH
8 ECSP 172

☐ R 10102

○ LPS 48
- 5411
- R 23186

★ 433 475-2LM
★ 430 096-2LWO
★ 33475

KF 74   The keel row

★ 8.111081
★ 475 6138
★ 436 928-2DWO
★ 450 020-2
★ 467 782-2DWO
★ GFS635
★ CD AJA 5536

☐ F 9300

◇ 45-71135

○ LX 3040
- AKF 1
- ACL 309
- PA 172
- DPA 627

★ 417 192-2DH
★ 430 096-2DWO
★ 433 475-2DM
★ 475 078-2DX2
★ PLATCD 640
★ 475 6060 DC10
★ RRC1057

oo 436 928-4DWO
oo KACC 309
oo KCSP 172
oo KDPC 627
oo 430 096-4DWO
oo 160 K4
oo 433 475-4DM
8 ECSP172

☐ R 10102

○ LPS 48
- 5411
- R 23186

★ 433 475-2LM
★ 430 096-2LWO
★ 33475

KF 75   Have you seen but a whyte lillie grow?

◇ CEP 725

○ LX 3040
○ BR 3052
- AKF 1
- ACL 309

★ 417 192-2DH
★ 433 475-2DM
★ 475 6060 DC10
★ 8.111081

oo KACC 309
oo 433 475-4DM

☐ R 10103

○ LPS 48
- 5411
- R 23186

★ 433 475-2LM
★ 33475

KF 76 *Willow, willow*

	◇ CEP 725	○ LX 3040	★ 417 192-2DH	○○ KACC 309
		○ BR 3052	★ 433 475-2DM	○○ 160 K4
		● AKF 1	★ 475 6060 DC10	○○ 433 475-4DM
		● ACL 309	★ 8.111081	

☐ R 10103		○ LPS 48	★ 433 475-2LM	
		● 5411	★ 33475	
		● R 23186		

KF 77 *The Lover's Curse*

	◇ CEP 725	○ LX 3040	★ 417 192-2DH	○○ KACC 309
		○ BR 3052	★ 433 475-2DM	○○ 160 K4
		● AKF 1	★ 475 6060 DC10	○○ 433 475-4DM
		● ACL 309	★ 8.111081	

☐ R 10104		○ LPS 48	★ 433 475-2LM	
		● 5411	★ 33475	
		● R 23186		

KF 78 *Down by the salley gardens*

			★ 8.111081	
			★ 475 6138	
			★ 450 020-2	
			★ 448 055-2DWO	
			★ 470 195-2	
			★ CD AJA 5536	
			★ 475 6060 DC10	
	◇ 45-71135	○ LX3040	★ RRC1057	○○ 448 055-2DWO
	◇ CEP 518	○ BR3052	★ 417192-2DH	○○ KACC 309
	◇ CEP 725	● AKF 1	★ 433 475-2DM	○○ 433 475-4DM
		● ACL 309	★ 458 270-2DH	○○ 458 270-4DH
			★ 475 078-2DX2	

☐ R 10104		○ LPS 48	★ 433 475-2LM	
		● 5411	★ 33475	
		● R 23186		

KF 80 *An die Musik*

			★ 475 6138	
			★ GFS635	
			★ CD AJA 5536	
☐ M 652	◇ CEP 663	○ LW 5098	★ 430 096-2DWO	○○ KCSP 172
	◇ CEP 719	● AKF 6	★ 433 471-2DM	○○ 430 096-4DWO
		● ACL 307	★ 458 270-2DH	○○ 160 K4
		● PA 172	★ 475 078-2DX2	○○ 433 471-4DM
		● SPA 524	★ 475 6060 DC10	○○ 458 270-4DH
			★ RRC1057	8 ECSP 172

		○ LD 9099	★ 433 471-2LM	
		● LLP 1529	★ 430 096-2LWO	
		● 5258	★ 33471	
		● R 23184		

KF 81 *Gestillte Sehnsucht*

			★ CD AJA 5536	
			★ 475 6060 DC10	
■ K 2289	◇ CEP 720	● LXT 2850	★ 421 299-2DH	○○ 433 477-IDM
		● AKF 5	★ 433 477-2DM	
		● ACL 306	★ 8.111009	

■ T 5647		● LLP 903	★ 433 477-2LM	
		● 5098	★ 33476	
		● R 23183		

217

KF 82   Geistliches Wiegenlied

                                              ★ 448 055-2DWO
    ★ CD AJA 5536
    ★ 475 6060 DC10

■ K 2289   ◇ CEP 720   ● LXT 2850   ★ 421 299-2DH   oo 433 477-4DM
                           ● AKF 5   ★ 433 477-2DM   oo 448 055-2DWO
                           ● ACL 306   ★ 475 078-2DX2
    ★ 8.111009

■ T 5647   ● LLP 903   ★ 433 477-2LM
                           ● 5098   ★ 33476
                           ● R 23183

KF 83   Kathleen Ferrier at a Party

    ★ 30015/16
    ★ GL 318
    ★ WISPCD25965   oo GL 6318

KF 83a   The Floral Dance   ● REGL 368   oo ZCF 368

                               ● Arabesque 8070   oo Arabesque 9070

KF 86   Spring Symphony

    ★ APL 101.567
    ★ 440 063-2DM

KF 87   Die junge Nonne
KF 88   Der Vollmond strahlt

    ★ 458 270-2DH   oo 458 270-4DH
    ★ 475 078-2DX2   oo 448 055-2DWO
    ★ RRC1164
    ★ 448 055-2DWO

KF 89   Du liebst mich nicht
KF 90   Der Tod und das Mädchen
KF 91   Suleika 1
KF 92   Du bist die Ruh'

    ★ 475 6138
    ★ 475 078-2DX2
    ★ RRC1164
    ★ 448 055-2DWO   oo 448 055-2DWO

KF 93   Frauenliebe und Leben
KF 94   Immer leiser wird mein Schlummer
KF 95   Der Tod, das ist die kühle Nacht
KF 96   Botschaft
KF 97   Von ewiger Liebe
All eleven items, KF 87-97

    ★ 448 055-2DWO   oo 448 055-2DWO

                ● 6BB 197-8   ★ 414 611-2DH   oo 414 611-4DG
                ● 414 611-1DG   ★ 433 476-2DM   oo 160 K3
    ★ 475 6060 DC10   oo 433 476-4DM

                ● 414 611-1LJ   ★ 433 476-2LM   oo 414 611-4LJ
                ● BWS 707   ★ 33476

KF 93   Frauenliebe und Leben only

                ● DIS 3700

KF 98   What the Edinburgh Festival has meant to me

    ★ 475 6138
    ★ 475 6060 DC10
                ● 6BB 197   ★ 414 611-2DH   oo 414 611-4DG
                ● 414 611-1DG   ★ 433 476-2DM   oo 433 476-4DM

KF 98   *What the Edinburgh Festival has meant to me (continued)*

        ● 414 611-1LJ   ★ 433 476-2LM   oo 414 611-4LJ
                                  ★ 33476

KF 98a   **Extract from talk**

        ● REGL 368   ★ WISPCD25963   oo ZCF 368

        ● Arabesque 8070   oo Arabesque 9070

KF 99   **Kindertotenlieder**

                                 ★ CDM 5 66911-2
                                 ★ 30015/16
                                 ★ GL 307
                                 ★ RRC 1153
■ LX 8939-41   ○ 33C 1009   ★ CDH 7 61003-2
                  ● HLM 7002   ★ 8.110876

                  ○ ML 2187   ★ CDH-61003
                  ● ML 4980
                  ● M 60203
                  ● 32 26 0016

KF 99a   *Nun will die Sonn'*

                                 ★ CZS 5 75133-2

KF 99b   *Oft denk' ich*

                                 ★ CMS 5 66182-2

KF 100-102   *Alto Rhapsody*
                  Von ewiger Liebe
                  Wir wandelten   *(three items)*
                  ● DACO 114   ★ DACO CD 301

KF 103   *Alto Rhapsody*

                                 ★ APR 5579

KF 104   *Hark! The echoing air*

                                 ★ 448 055-2DWO
                                 ★ 475 6060 DC10
                  ● LXT 5324   ★ 433 473-2DM   oo 433 473-4DM
                  ● AKF 2   ★ GHCD 2260/2   oo 448 055-2DWO
                  ● ACL 310   ★ 475 078-2DX2

                  ● LLP 1670   ★ 433 473-2LM
                  ● 5291   ★ 33473
                  ● R 23187

KF 105   *Like as the love-lorn turtle*

                                 ★ 448 055-2DWO
                                 ★ 475 6060 DC10
       ◇ CEP 587   ● LXT 5324   ★ 433 473-2DM   oo 433 473-4DM
                  ● AKF 2   ★ GHCD 2260/2   oo 448 055-2DWO
                  ● ACL 310   ★ 475 078-2DX2

                  ● LLP 1670   ★ 433 473-2LM
                  ● 5291   ★ 33473
                  ● R 23187

KF 106   *How changed the vision*

                  ● LXT 5324   ★ 433 473-2DM   oo 433 473-4DM
                  ● AKF 2   ★ GHCD 2260/2
                  ● ACL 310   ★ 475 6060 DC10

                  ● LLP 1670   ★ 433 473-2LM
                  ● 5291   ★ 33473
                  ● R 23187

KF 107 *Mad Bess of Bedlam*

            ◊ CEP 5508

		★ 443 393-2DWO	
		★ 475 6060 DC10	
◊ CEP 5508	● AKF 3	★ 433 473-2DM	oo 433 473-4DM
	● ACL 310	★ GHCD 2260/2	oo 443 393-4DWO
	● R 23187	★ 433 473-2LM	
		★ 33473	

KF 108 *Verborgenheit*

● LXT 5324	★ 433 473-2DM	oo 433 473-4DM
● AKF 2	★ GHCD 2260/2	
● ACL 307	★ 475 6060 DC10	
● LLP 1670	★ 433 473-2LM	
● 5291	★ 33473	
● R 23184		

KF 109 *Der Gärtner*

● LXT 5324	★ 433 473-2DM	oo 433 473-4DM
● AKF 2	★ GHCD 2260/2	
● ACL 307	★ 475 6060 DC10	
● LLP 1670	★ 433 473-2LM	
● 5291	★ 33473	
● R 23184		

KF 110 *Auf ein altes Bild*

            ◊ CEP 587

● LXT 5324	★ 433 473-2DM	oo 433 473-4DM
● AKF 2	★ GHCD 2260/2	
● ACL 307	★ 475 6060 DC10	
● LLP 1670	★ 433 473-2LM	
● 5291	★ 33473	
● R 23184		

KF 111 *Auf einer Wanderung*

● LXT 5324	★ 433 473-2DM	oo 433 473-4DM
● AKF 2	★ GHCD 2260/2	
● ACL 307	★ 475 6060 DC10	
● LLP 1670	★ 433 473-2LM	
● 5291	★ 33473	
● R 23184		

KF 112 *Altar*   ◊ CEP 587

● LXT 5324	★ 433 473-2DM	oo KCSP 172
● AKF 2	★ GHCD 2260/2	oo 433 473-4DM
● PA 172	★ 475 6060 DC10	8 ECSP 172
● LLP 1670	★ 433 473-2LM	
● 5291	★ 33473	

KF 113 *Cantata No. 11 (78rpm version)*
■ AX 399-401

KF 114 *Cantata No. 11 (33rpm version)*

O LX3006	oo 417 466-4DM
● ACL 52	
● ECS 562	
● 417 466-1DM	
O LPS 160	oo 417 466-4LJ
● LLP 845	

KF 114   Cantata No. 11 (33rpm version) (continued)
- ● 5092
- ● R 23206
- ● 417 466-1LJ

*KF 114a   **Ah, tarry yet, my dearest Saviour***
- ● LXT 6934
  - ★ RRC1057
  - ★ 433 470-2DM
  - ★ 221538-303
  - ★ 475 6060 DC10
  - oo KLXTC 6934
  - oo 433 470-4DM

  - ★ 433 470-2LM
  - ★ 33470

*KF 115   **Cantata No. 67 (78rpm version)***
- ■ AX 347-8

*KF 116   **Cantata No. 67 (33rpm version)***
- O LX 3007
- ● ACL 52
- ● ECS 562

- O LPS 161
- ● 5092
- ● R 23206

*KF 122   **Vergiss mein nicht***
- ● 414 095-1DH
  - ★ 433 473-2DM
  - ★ 475 6060 DC10
  - oo 414 095-4DH
  - oo 433 473-4DM

- ● 414 095-1LH
  - ★ 433 473-2LM
  - ★ 33473
  - oo 414 095-4LH

*KF 123   **Ach, dass nicht die letzte Stunde***
- ● 414 095-1DH
  - ★ 433 473-2DM
  - ★ 475 6060 DC10
  - oo 414 095-4DH
  - oo 433 473-4DM

- ● 414 095-1LH
  - ★ 433 473-2LM
  - ★ 33473
  - oo 414 095-4LH

*KF 125   **Sapphische Ode***
  - ★ RRC1164
  - ★ 475 6060 DC10
- ◇ 45-71130
- ◇ CEP 719
  - ● LXT 2850
  - ● AKF 5
  - ● ACL 306
  - ● PA 172
  - ★ 430 096-2DWO
  - ★ 433 471-2DM
  - ★ 458 270-2DH
  - ★ 475 078-2DX2
  - ★ 8.111009
  - oo KCSP 172
  - oo 430 096-4DWO
  - oo 433 471-4DM
  - oo 458 270-4DH
  - 8 ECSP 172

  - ● LLP 903
  - ● 5098
  - ● R 23183
  - ★ 433 471-2LM
  - ★ 430 096-2LWO
  - ★ 33471

*KF 126   **Botschaft***
  - ★ 475 6138
  - ★ RRC1164
  - ★ 475 6060 DC10
- ◇ 45-71130
- ◇ CEP 719
  - ● LXT 2850
  - ● AKF 5
  - ● ACL 306
  - ★ 430 096-2DWO
  - ★ 433 471-2DM
  - ★ 475 078-2DX2
  - ★ 8.111009
  - oo 430 096-4DWO
  - oo 433 471-4DM

  - ● LLP 903
  - ● 5098
  - ● R 23183
  - ★ 433 471-2LM
  - ★ 430 096-2LWO
  - ★ 33471

KF 127   Der Musensohn

			★ 475 6138	
			★ GFS635	
			★ CD AJA 5536	**8** ECSP 172
□ M 652	◊ CEP 719	O LW 5098	★ 430 096-2DWO	oo KCSP 172
	◊ CEP 663	● AKF 6	★ 433 471-2DM	oo KCSP 524
		● ACL 307	★ 475 078-2DX2	oo 430 096-4DWO
		● PA 172	★ 475 6060 DC10	oo 160 K4
		● SPA 524	★ RRC1057	oo 433 471-4DM
		O LD 9099	★ 433 471-2LM	
		● LLP 1529	★ 430 096-2LWO	
		● 5258	★ 33471	
		● R 23184		

KF 131   Bist du bei mir

★ 475 6060 DC10	
★ 458 270-2DH	oo 458 270-4DH
★ 433 473-2DM	oo 433 473-4DM
★ 433 473-2LM	
★ 33473	

KF 134   Interview complete

★ WISPCD25965

KF 134a   Interview excerpt

● REGL 368	★ GL 318	oo GL 6318
	★ RRC1057	oo ZCF 368
● Arabesque 8070		oo Arabesque 9070

KF 136   Matthäus-Passion (complete)

★ URN22185
★ GL 100.612
● FO 1046   ★ Foyer 3CF 2013
★ Verona CD 27070/2
★ Andante A1170
★ Verona 30001/3

KF 136a   Du lieber Heiland du ... Buss' und Reu'

★ URN22.194
★ TAH 462
★ CO 3540
★ Verona CD 27076
★ WISPCD 25971

KF 136b   So ist mein Jesus nun gefangen

★ URN22.194
★ Verona CD 27076

KF 136c   Ach, nun ist mein Jesus hin

★ CO 3540
★ URN22.194
★ Verona CD 27076
★ WISPCD 25971

KF 136d   Erbarme dich, mein Gott   ★ TAH 462

★ CO 3540
★ URN22.194
★ Verona CD 27076
★ WISPCD 25971

KF 136e   Erbarm' es Gott ... Können Tränen

★ TAH 462
★ URN22.194
★ Verona CD 27076
★ WISPCD 25971

KF 136f *Ach Golgatha ... Sehet, Jesus*	★ TAH 462 ★ URN22.194 ★ Verona CD 27076 ★ WISPCD 25971	
KF 136g *Nun ist der Herr*	★ WISPCD 25971	
KF 137 *Christe eleison*	★ CHS 5 67207-2 ★ CDM 7 63655-2 ★ CMS 7 63790-2	oo EG 763655-4
	★ CDM-63655	
KF 138 *Laudamus Te*	★ CHS 5 67207-2 ★ CDM 7 63655-2 ★ CMS 7 63790-2	oo EG 763655-4
	★ CDM-63655	
KF 139 *Qui sedes*	★ CHS 5 67207-2	
KF 140 *Agnus Dei*	★ CHS 5 67207-2 ★ CHS 7 69741-2	
KF 141 *Et in unum Dominum*	★ CHS 5 67207-2 ★ CDM 7 63655-2 ★ CMS 7 63790-2	oo EG 763655-4
KF 142 *Mass in B Minor*	★ CDM-63655 ★ Foyer 2CF 2022 ★ Verona CD 27073-4 ★ GHCD 2260/2 ★ ARPCD00312 ★ Verona 30006/7	
KF 142a *Christe eleison*	★ URN22.194 ★ Verona CD 27076	
KF 142b *Qui sedes*	★ URN22.194 ★ Verona CD 27076	
KF 142c *Et in unum Dominum*	★ URN22.194 ★ Verona CD 27076	
KF 142d *Agnus Dei*	★ URN22.194 ★ Verona CD 27076 ★ CO 3540	

KF 146 *Frauenliebe und Leben*	O LW 5089 ● LXT 2556 ● AKF 6 ● ACL 307 ● DPA 624	★ 433 471-2DM ★ 8.111009 ★ 475 6060 DC10	oo KDPC 624 oo 433 471-4DM
	O LD 9098 ● LLP 271 ● 5020 ● R 23184	★ 433 471-2LM ★ 33471	

KF 146a Er, der herrlichste von allen

★ 448 055-2DWO
★ 458 270-2DH   oo 458 270-4DH
★ 475 078-2DX2   oo 448 055-2DWO

KF 146b Ich kann's nicht fassen

★ 475 078-2DX2

KF 147 Widmung

◊ 45-71130   O LW 5098   ★ 433 471-2DM   oo 433 471-4DM
◊ CEP 719   ● AKF 6   ★ 475 6060 DC10
               ● ACL 307   ★ RRC1057

               O LD 9099   ★ 433 471-2LM
               ● LLP 1529   ★ 33471
               ● 5258
               ● R 23184

KF 148 Volksliedchen

◊ 45-71130   O LW5098   ★ 433 471-2DM   oo 433 471-4DM
◊ CEP 719   ● AKF 6   ★ 475 6060 DC10
               ● ACL 307   ★ RRC1057

               O LD 9099   ★ 433 471-2LM
               ● LLP 1529   ★ 33471
               ● 5258
               ● R 23184

KF 149 Vier ernste Gesänge
■ AX 563-4
                              ★ RRC 1153
               O LW 5094   ★ 421 299-2DH   oo 433 477-4DM
               ● LXT 2556   ★ 433 477-2DM
               ● AKF 5   ★ 8.111009
               ● ACL 306   ★ 475 6060 DC10

               O LD 9097   ★ 433 477-2LM
               ● LLP 271   ★ 33476
               ● 5020
               ● R 23183

KF 150 The fidgety bairn

                              ★ 8.111081
                              ★ 467 782-2DWO
                              ★ 475 6060 DC10
□ M 657   ◊ CEP 5508   ● AKF 1   ★ 417 192-2DH   oo KACC 309
                              ● ACL 309   ★ 433 475-2DM   oo 433 475-4DM

                              ● R 23186   ★ 433 475-2LM
                                              ★ 33475

KF 151 Ca' the yowes

                              ★ 8.111081
                              ★ RRC1057
□ M 657   ◊ 45-71072   ● AKF 1   ★ 417 192-2DH   oo KACC 309
               ◊ CEP 5508   ● ACL 309   ★ 433 475-2DM   oo 160 K4
                              ● EX 7697431   ★ 475 6060 DC10   oo 433 475-4DM

                              ● R 23186   ★ 433 475-2LM
                              ● IH-6150   ★ 33475

KF 156 Where'er you walk

                              ★ CO 3541   oo GL 6318
                              ★ GL 318
                              ★ 30015/16

KF 157 *Like as the love-lorn turtle*		★ CO 3541	
KF 158 *Hark! The echoing air*		★ CO 3541	
KF 159 *Lasciatemi morire*		★ GL 318 ★ 30015/16	oo GL 6318
KF 160 *Pur dicesti*		★ CO 3541 ★ GL 318 ★ 30015/16	oo GL 6318
KF 161 *Ah diletta, Euridice ... Che farò?*		★ CO 3541 ★ GL 318	oo GL 6318
KF 162 *Lachen und Weinen*		★ CO 3541 ★ GL 318	oo GL 6318
KF 163 *Sonntag*		★ CO 3541 ★ GL 318 ★ 30015/16	oo GL 6318
KF 164 *Love is a bable*		★ CO 3541	
KF 165 *The fairy lough*			
KF 166 *Ca' the yowes*			
All eleven items KF 156-166	● Rococo 5265 ● RP 12407	★ WISPCD25965 ★ 14 262 ★ TAH 462	oo RPK 22407
KF 167 *The Spanish Lady*	● Rococo 5265 ● RP 12407 ● REGL 368	★ WISPCD 25965 ★ GL 318 ★ CO 3541 ★ 14 262 ★ TAH 462	oo RPK 22407 oo ZCF 368 oo GL 6318
	● Arabesque 8070		Arabesque 9070
KF 168 *Poème de l'amour et de la mer*	● 414 095-1DH	★ 433 472-2DM ★ 475 6060 DC10	oo 414 095-4DH oo 433 472-4DM
	● 414 095-1LH	★ 433 472-2LM ★ 33472	oo 414 095-4LH
KF 171 *Orfeo ed Euridice*	● RLS 725	★ Verona 30004/5 ★ Verona CD 27016-7 ★ 7243 5 86194 2 3	

KF 171a *Chiamo il mio ben*

KF 171b *Chi mai dell' Erebo*

KF 171c *Deh! Placatevi con me*

KF 171d *Che puro ciel!*

KF 171e *Che ho fatto ... Che farò?* Four excerpts, a, b, d, e Four excerpts, a, c, d, e		★ CO 3540 ★ CDH 7 61003-2 ★ CDM 5 66911-2
		★ CDH-61003

KF 171f *Ah più non m'ode ... Che farò?*
- REGL 368   oo ZCF 368
- Arabesque 8070   oo Arabesque 9070

KF 172 *Kindertotenlieder*
- 417 634-1DM   ★ 425 995-2DM   oo 417 634-4DM
-       ★ 425 995-2LM

KF 173 *Mahler's Symphony No. 2*
- ★ AUR2482
- ★ ARPCD0033
- ★ 30015/16
- ★ 221917
- ★ 425 970-2DM
- ★ GHCD 2210
- D 264 D2   ★ Verona CD 27062   oo K 264 K2
- IGI 374   ★ 425 970-2LM

KF 173a *Urlicht*
- ★ Verona CD 27076
- ★ CO 3540

KF 174 *Mass in B Minor*   ★ BBCL 4007-8

KF 174a *Christe eleison*   ★ WISPCD 25971

KF 174b *Laudamus Te*   ★ WISPCD 25971

KF 174c *Qui sedes*   ★ WISPCD 25971

KF 174d *Et in unum Dominum*   ★ WISPCD 25971

KF 174e *Agnus Dei*   ★ WISPCD 25971

KF 182 *Land of Hope and Glory*   ★ BBCL 4100-2

KF 183 *O waly, waly*
- ★ 8.111081
- ★ 467 782-2DWO
- ★ GFS635
- ◇ 45-71072   O LX 3098   ★ 417 192-2DH   oo KACC 309
- ◇ CEP 726   ● BR 3052   ★ 433 475-2DM   oo 433 475-4DM
-    ● AKF 1   ★ 475 6060 DC10
-    ● ACL 309   ★ CD AJA 5536
-    O LPS 538   ★ 433 475-2LM
-    ● 5411   ★ 33475
-    ● R 23186

KF 184 *I have a bonnet*
- ★ 8.111081
- ★ 448 055-2DWO
- ★ 467 782-2DWO
- ★ GFS635
- ★ CD AJA 5536
- ★ 475 6060 DC10   oo 448 055-2DWO
- ◇ 45-71108   O LX 3098   ★ 417 192-2DH   oo KACC 309
-    ● AKF 1   ★ 433 475-2DM   oo 433 475-4DM
-    ● ACL 309   ★ 475 078-2DX2
-    O LPS 538   ★ 433 475-2LM
-    ● 5411   ★ 33475
-    ● R 23186

KF 185   My boy Willie

◇ 45-71108	○ LX 3098
	● AKF 1
	● ACL 309
	○ LPS 538
	● 5411
	● R 23186

★ 467 782-2DWO
★ 475 6060 DC10
★ 417 192-2DH   oo KACC 309
★ 433 475-2DM   oo 433 475-4DM
★ 8.111081

★ 433 475-2LM
★ 33475

KF 186   I will walk with my love

□ M 681

◇ 45-71108	○ LX 3098
◇ CEP 725	○ BR 3052
	● AKF 1
	● ACL 309
	○ LPS 538
	● 5411
	● R 23186

★ 417 192-2DH   oo KACC 309
★ 433 475-2DM   oo 433 475-4DM
★ 475 6060 DC10
★ 8.111081

★ 433 475-2LM
★ 33475

KF 187   The Stuttering Lovers

★ 8.111081
★ 448 055-2DWO
★ 467 782-2DWO
★ RRC1164
★ 475 6060 DC10   oo 448 055-2DWO

□ M 681   ◇ 45-71108

○ LX 3098
● AKF 1
● ACL 309
○ LPS 538
● 5411
● R 23186

★ 417 192-2DH   oo KACC 309
★ 433 475-2DM   oo 433 475-4DM
★ 475 078-2DX2

★ 433 475-2LM
★ 33475

KF 188   Now sleeps the crimson petal

★ 8.111081
★ 470 195-2
★ RRC1164

□ M 680

◇ 45-71139	○ LX 3098
◇ CEP 726	○ BR 3052
	● AKF 1
	● ACL 309
	○ LPS 538
	● 5411
	● R 23186

★ 417 192-2DH   oo KACC 309
★ 433 475-2DM   oo 433 475-4DM
★ 458 270-2DH   oo 458 270-4DH
★ 475 6060 DC10

★ 433 475-2LM
★ 33475

KF 189   I know where I'm going

★ 8.111081
★ 467 782-2DWO
★ RRC1164

□ M 681   ◇ CEP 726

○ LX3098
○ BR 3052
● AKF 1
● ACL 309
○ LPS 538
● 5411
● R 23186

★ 417 192-2DH   oo KACC 309
★ 433 475-2DM   oo 433 475-4DM
★ 458 270-2DH   oo 458 270-4DH
★ 475 6060 DC10

★ 433 475-2LM
★ 33475

KF 190 *The fair house of joy*

			★ 8.111081	
			★ 470 195-2	
			★ 475 6060 DC10	
	◇ 45-71139	○ LX 3098	★ 417 192-2DH	oo KACC 309
		● AKF 1	★ 433 475-2DM	oo 433 475-4DM
		● ACL 309	★ 458 270-2DH	oo 458 270-4DH
		○ LPS 538	★ 433 475-2LM	
		● 5411	★ 33475	
		● R 23186		

KF 191 *To Daisies*

			★ 8.111081	
			★ 470 195-2	
			★ 475 6060 DC10	
			★ 458 270-2DH	oo 458 270-4DH
□ M 680	◇ 45-71139	● AKF 1	★ 417 192-2DH	oo KACC 309
		● ACL 309	★ 433 475-2DM	oo 433 475-4DM
		● R 23186	★ 433 475-2LM	
			★ 33475	

KF 192 *Over the mountains*

			★ 8.111081	
			★ 470 195-2	
	◇ 45-71139	○ LX 3098	★ 417 192-2DH	oo KACC 309
	● AKF 1	★ 433 475-2DM	oo 433 475-4DM	
		● ACL 309	★ 475 6060 DC10	
		○ LPS 538	★ 433 475-2LM	
		● 5411	★ 33475	
		● R 23186		

KF 193 *Ye banks and braes*

			★ 8.111081	
			★ 448 055-2DWO	
			★ 470 195-2	
			★ GFS635	
			★ RRC1164	
			★ 475 6060 DC10	oo 448 055-2DWO
□.M.679	◇ 45-71035	○ LX 3098	★ 417 192-2DH	oo KACC 309
	◇ CEP 518	○ BR 3052	★ 433 475-2DM	oo 160 K4
	◇ CEP 726	● AKF 1	★ 458 270-2DH	oo 433 475-4DM
		● ACL 309	★ 475 078-2DX2	oo 458 270-4DH
		○ LPS 538	★ 433 475-2LM	
		● 5411	★ 33475	
		● R 23186		

KF 194 *Drink to me only*

			★ 8.111081	
			★ 450 020-2	
			★ 448 055-2DWO	
			★ 470 195-2	
			★ 467 782-2DWO	
			★ CD AJA 5536	
			★ RRC1164	
			★ 475 6060 DC10	oo 448 055-2DWO
□ M 679	◇ 45-71035	○ LX 3098	★ 417 192-2DH	oo KACC 309
	◇ CEP 518	○ BR 3052	★ 433 475-2DM	oo 160 K4
	◇ CEP 726	● AKF 1	★ 458 270-2DH	oo 433 475-4DM
		● ACL 309	★ 475 078-2DX2	oo 458 270-4DH

KF 194 Drink to me only *(continued)*	○ LPS 538 ● 5411 ● R 23186	★ 433 475-2LM ★ 33475	
KF 196 Ganymed		★ 475 6060 DC10 ★ 433 471-2DM	oo 433 471-4DM
		★ 433 471-2LM ★ 33471	
KF 197 Du liebst mich nicht		★ 475 6060 DC10 ★ 433 471-2DM	oo 433 471-4DM
		★ 433 471-2LM ★ 33471	
KF 198 Lachen und Weinen		★ 475 6060 DC10 ★ 433 471-2DM	oo 433 471-4DM
		★ 433 471-2LM ★ 33471	
KF 199 Ruhe Süssliebchen in Schatten	● REGL 368	★ 30015/16 ★ GL 318	oo GL 6318 oo ZCF 368
	● Arabesque 8070		oo Arabesque 9070
KF 200 Auf dem See	● REGL 368	★ 30015/16 ★ GL 318	oo GL 6318 oo ZCF 368
	● Arabesque 8070		oo Arabesque 9070
KF 202 Es schauen die Blumen	● REGL 368	★ GL 318	oo GL 6318 oo ZCF 368
	● Arabesque 8070		oo Arabesque 9070
KF 203 Der Jäger	● REGL 368	★ 30015/16 ★ GL 318	oo GL 6318 oo ZCF 368
	● Arabesque 8070		oo Arabesque 9070
KF 205 Das Lied von der Erde		★ APR 5579	
KF 206 Das Lied von der Erde	● LXT 2721-2 ● LXT 5576 ● LXT 6278 ● AKF 7 ● ACL 305 ● 414 194-1DM	★ 414 194-2DH ★ 8.110871 ★ RRC 1146 ★ 466 576-2DM ★ 433 332-2DM	oo KMON 2 7050 oo 414 194-4DM oo 160 K1
	● LLP 625-6 ● 5069-70 ● R 23182 ● STS 15200 ● 2-London A-4212 ● 414 194-1LJ	★ 414 194-2LH	oo 414 194-4LJ

KF 207 *Ich bin der Welt abhanden gekommen*

★ 475 6138
★ 448 055-2DWO
★ 466 576-2DM
★ RRC 1153
★ 8.110871

○ LW 5123 ★ 421 299-2DH oo KMON 2 7050
● LXT 2721 ★ 433 477-2DM oo 160 K1
● AKF 6 ★ 475 078-2DX2 oo 433 477-4DM
● ACL 318 ★ 475 6060 DC10 oo 448 055-2DWO

○ LD 9137 ★ 433 477-2LM
● LLP 625 ★ 448 150-2LM
● 5069 ★ 33476
● STS 15202
● 2-London A-4212

KF 208 *Ich atmet' einen linden Duft*

★ 475 6138
★ 466 576-2DM
★ RRC 1153
★ 8.110871
★ CD AJA 5536

○ LW 5123 ★ 421 299-2DH oo KMON 2 7050
● LXT 2721 ★ 433 477-2DM oo 160 K1
● AKF 6 ★ 475 078-2DX2 oo 433 477-4DM
● ACL 318 ★ 475 6060 DC10

○ LD 9137 ★ 433 477-2LM
● LLP 625 ★ 448 150-2LM
● 5069 ★ 33476
● STS 15202
● 2-London A-4212

KF 209 *Um Mitternacht*

★ 475 6138
★ 466 576-2DM
★ RRC 1153
★ 8.110871
★ CD AJA 5536

○ LW 5123 ★ 421 299-2DH oo KMON 2 7050
○ LW 5225 ★ 430 096-2DWO oo KCSP 172
● LXT 2721 ★ 433 477-2DM oo 430 096-4DWO
● AKF 6 ★ 458 270-2DH oo 160 K1
● ACL 318 ★ 475 078-2DX2 oo 433 477-4DM
● PA 172 ★ 475 6060 DC10 oo 458 270-4DH
★ RRC1164 8 ECSP 172

○ LD 9137 ★ 433 477-2LM
○ LD 9229 ★ 448 150-2LM
● LLP 625 ★ 430 096-2LWO
● 5069 ★ 33476
● STS 15202
● 2-London A-4212

KF 210 *Das Lied von der Erde*

★ WISPCD25963
★ 4974/7
★ TAH 482

KF 211 *The fairy lough*

★ 8.111081
★ 470 384-2
○ LX 3133 ★ 430 061-2LM oo 430 061-4LM

KF 211	*The fairy lough (continued)*	O LW 5353 ● AKF 2 ● ACL 310	★ 433 473-2DM ★ GHCD 2260/2 ★ 475 6060 DC10	oo 160 K4 oo 433 473-4DM
		O LPS 1032 ● R 23187	★ 433 473-2LM ★ 33473	
KF 212	*A soft day*		★ 8.111081 ★ 470 384-2 ★ 475 6060 DC10	
		O LX 3133 O LW 5353 ● AKF 2 ● ACL 310	★ 430 061-2LM ★ 433 473-2DM ★ GHCD 2260/2 ★ 475 078-2DX2	oo 430 061-4LM oo 433 473-4DM
		O LPS 1032 ● R 23187	★ 433 473-2LM ★ 33473	
KF 213	*Love is a bable*	O LX 3133 O LW 5353 ● AKF 2 ● ACL 310	★ 430 061-2LM ★ 433 473-2DM ★ GHCD 2260/2 ★ 8.111081	oo 430 061-4LM oo 433 473-4DM
		O LPS 1032 ● R 23187	★ 433 473-2LM ★ 33473	
KF 214	*Silent Noon*		★ 8.111081 ★ RRC 1164	
		O LX 3133 O LW 5353 ● AKF 2 ● ACL 310	★ 430 061-2LM ★ 433 473-2DM ★ GHCD 2260/2 ★ 475 6060 DC10	oo 430 061-4LM oo 160 K4 oo 433 473-4DM
		O LPS 1032 ● R 23187	★ 433 473-2LM ★ 33473	
KF 215	*Go not, happy day*		★ 8.111081 ★ 470 195-2	
		O LX 3133 O LW 5353 ● AKF 2 ● ACL 310 ● PA 172	★ 430 061-2LM ★ 430 096-2DWO ★ 433 473-2DM ★ 458 270-2DH ★ GHCD 2260/2 ★ 475 078-2DX2 ★ 475 6060 DC10	oo KCSP 172 oo 430 061-4LM oo 430 096-4DWO oo 160 K4 oo 433 473-4DM oo 458 270-4DH **8** ECSP 172
		O LPS 1032 ● R 23187	★ 433 473-2LM ★ 430 096-2LWO ★ 33473	
KF 216	*Sleep*		★ 8.111081	
		O LX 3133 O LW 5353 ● AKF 2 ● ACL 310	★ 430 061-2LM ★ 433 473-2DM ★ GHCD 2260/2 ★ 475 6060 DC10	oo 430 061-4LM oo 433 473-4DM
		O LPS 1032 ● R 23187	★ 433 473-2LM ★ 33473	

KF 217 Pretty ring time

	★ 8.111081	
○ LX 3133	★ 430 061-2LM	○○ 430 061-4LM
○ LW 5353	★ 433 473-2DM	○○ 433 473-4DM
● AKF 2	★ GHCD 2260/2	
● ACL 310	★ 475 6060 DC10	
○ LPS 1032	★ 433 473-2LM	
● R 23187	★ 33473	

KF 218 O waly, waly

	★ 475 6060 DC10	
○ LX 3133	★ 430 061-2LM	○○ 430 061-4LM
○ LW 5353	★ 433 473-2DM	○○ 433 473-4DM
○ LPS 1032	★ 433 473-2LM	
	★ 33473	

KF 219 Come you not from Newcastle?

	★ 8.111081	
	★ 475 6138	
	★ RRC1164	
	★ 475 6060 DC10	**8** ECSP 172
○ LX 3133	★ 430 061-2LM	○○ KCSP 172
○ LW 5353	★ 430 096-2DWO	○○ 430 061-4LM
● AKF 2	★ 433 473-2DM	○○ 430 096-4DWO
● ACL 310	★ GHCD 2260/2	○○ 160 K4
● PA 172	★ 475 078-2DX2	○○ 433 473-4DM
○ LPS 1032	★ 433 473-2LM	
● R 23187	★ 430 096-2LWO	
	★ 33473	

KF 220 Kitty my love

	★ 8.111081	
	★ RRC1164	
	★ 467 782-2DWO	
	★ GFS635	
○ LX 3133	★ 430 061-2LM	○○ KCSP 172
○ LW 5353	★ 430 096-2DWO	○○ 430 061-4LM
● AKF 2	★ 433 473-2DM	○○ 430 096-4DWO
● ACL 310	★ GHCD 2260/2	○○ 160 K4
● PA 172	★ 475 078-2DX2	○○ 433 473-4DM
	★ 475 6060 DC10	**8** ECSP 172
○ LPS 1032	★ 433 473-2LM	
● R 23187	★ 430 096-2LWO	
	★ 33473	

KF 222 Liebeslieder-Walzer

● 417 634-1DM	★ 425 995-2DM	○○ 417 634-4DM
	★ 425 995-2LM	

KF 223 Zum Schluss

● 417 634-1DM	★ 425 995-2DM	○○ 417 634-4DM
	★ 425 995-2LM	

KF 226 Rastlose Liebe

		○○ GL 6318
● REGL 368	★ GL 318	○○ ZCF 368
● Arabesque 8070		○○ Arabesque 9070

KF 227 Wasserfluth

	★ GL 318	○○ GL 6318
● REGL 368	★ CO 3541	○○ ZCF 368
● Arabesque 8070		○○ Arabesque 9070

KF 229 *Grief for sin*

        ◊ CEP 721

○ LW 5083	★ 414 623-2DH	oo 414 623-4DG
● LXT 2757	★ 433 474-2DM	oo 433 474-4DM
● LXT 5382	★ 475 6060 DC10	
● 414 623-1DG	★ GL 307	
○ LD 9096	★ 433 474-2LM	oo 414 623-4LJ
● LLP 688	★ 414 623-2LH	
● 5083	★ 33474	
● 414 623-1LJ		

KF 230 *All is fulfilled*

        ◊ 45-71112
        ◊ CEP 721

	★ RRC1164	
○ LW 5083	★ 414 623-2DH	oo 414 623-4DG
● LXT 2757	★ 433 474-2DM	oo 433 474-4DM
● LXT 5382	★ 475 078-2DX2	
● 414 623-1DG	★ 475 6060 DC10	
○ LD 9096	★ 433 474-2LM	oo 414 623-4LJ
● LLP 688	★ 414 623-2LH	
● 5083	★ 33474	
● 414 623-1LJ		

KF 231 *Qui sedes*

        ◊ 45-71138
        ◊ CEP 722

○ LW5083	★ 414 623-2DH	oo 414623-4DG
● LXT 2757	★ 433 474-2DM	oo 433 474-4DM
● LXT 5382	★ 475 6060 DC10	
● 414 623-1DG	★ RRC1164	
○ LD 9096	★ 433 474-2LM	oo 414 623-4LJ
● LLP 688	★ 414 623-2LH	
● 5083	★ 33474	
● 414 623-1LJ		

KF 232 *Agnus Dei*

        ◊ 45-71138
        ◊ CEP 722

	★ 430 499-2DWO	
	★ 448 055-2DWO	
	★ GL 307	
	★ GFS635	oo 430 499-4DWO
○ LW 5083	★ 414 623-2DH	oo 414 623-4DG
● LXT 2757	★ 433 474-2DM	oo 433 474-4DM
● LXT 5382	★ 475 078-2DX2	oo 448 055-2DWO
● 414 623-1DG	★ 475 6060 DC10	
○ LD 9096	★ 433 474-2LM	oo 414 623-4LJ
● LLP 688	★ 414 623-2LH	
● 5083	★ 33474	
● 414 623-1LJ		

KF 233 *O Thou, that tellest good tidings to Zion*

        ◊ 45-71038
        ◊ CEP 550

	★ 475 6138	
	★ GL 307	
	★ GFS635	
	★ CD AJA 5536	
	★ RRC1164	
○ LW 5076	★ 414 623-2DH	oo 414 623-4DG
● LXT 2757	★ 433 474-2DM	oo 433 474-4DM
● LXT 5382	★ 475 078-2DX2	oo 452 450-4DF2
● 414 623-1DG	★ 475 6060 DC10	
○ LD 9088	★ 433 474-2LM	oo 414 623-4LJ
● LLP 688	★ 414 623-2LH	
● 5083	★ 33474	
● 414 623-1LJ		

KF 234 *Father of Heaven*

			★ 475 6138	
			★ GL 307	
			★ GFS635	
	◇ CEP 723	○ LW 5076	★ 414 623-2DH	oo 414 623-4DG
		● LXT 2757	★ 433 474-2DM	oo 433 474-4DM
		● LXT 5382	★ 475 078-2DX2	
		● 414 623-1DG	★ 475 6060 DC10	
		○ LD 9088	★ 433 474-2LM	oo 414 623-4LJ
		● LLP 688	★ 414 623-2LH	
		● 5083	★ 33474	
		● 414 623-1LJ		

KF 235 *He was despised*

			★ 436 404-2DWO	
			★ 448 055-2DWO	
			★ GFS635	
	◇ CEP 550	○ LW 5076	★ 414 623-2DH	oo KCSP 172
		○ LW 5225	★ 433 474-2DM	oo 414 623-4DG
		● LXT 2757	★ 475 078-2DX2	oo 433 474-4DM
		● LXT 5382	★ 475 6060 DC10	oo 448 055-2DWO
		● PA 172	★ RRC1164	oo 436 404-4DWO
		● 414 623-1DG	★ GL 307	8 ECSP 172
		○ LD 9088	★ 433 474-2LM	oo 414 623-4LJ
		○ LD 9229	★ 414 623-2LH	
		● LLP 688	★ 33474	
		● 5083		
		● 414 623-1LJ		

KF 236 *Return, O God of Hosts*

			★ 444 543-2DF2	
	◇ 45-71038	○ LW 5076	★ 414 623-2DH	oo 414 623-4DG
	◇ CEP 723	● LXT 2757	★ 433 474-2DM	oo 433 474-4DM
		● LXT 5382	★ 475 6060 DC10	
		● 414 623-1DG	★ GL 307	
		○ LD 9088	★ 433 474-2LM	oo 414 623-4LJ
		● LLP 688	★ 414 623-2LH	
		● 5083	★ 33474	
		● 414 623-1LJ		

KF 237 *Grief for sin* (Re-created Stereo)

		● SXL 2234		oo KSDC 286
		● SDD 286		oo KCSP 531
		● AKF 4		oo 160 K2
		● SPA 531	★ 475 6411-9DM	

KF 238 *All is fulfilled* (Re-created Stereo)

		● SXL 2234		oo KSCD 286
		● SDD 286		oo KCSP 531
		● AKF 4		oo 160 K2
		● SPA 531	★ 475 6411-9DM	

KF 239 *Qui sedes* (Re-created Stereo)

		● SXL 2234		oo KSCD 286
		● SDD 286		oo KCSP 531
		● AKF 4		oo 160 K2
		● SPA 531	★ 475 6411-9DM	

KF 240 *Agnus Dei (Re-created Stereo)*

- SXL 2234
- SDD 286
- SPA 322
- AKF 4
- SPA 531   ★ 475 6411-9DM

oo KSDC 286
oo KCSP 322
oo KCSP 531
oo 414 047-4DN
oo 160 K2
8 ECSP 322

KF 241 *O Thou, that tellest good tidings to Zion (Re-created Stereo)*
◇ SEC 5099
- SXL 2234
- SDD 286
- SPA 297
- AKF 4
- SPA 531
- DPA 552   ★ 475 6411-9DM

oo KSDC 286
oo KCSP 297
oo KDPC 552
oo KCSP 531
oo 160 K2

KF 242 *Father of Heaven (Re-created Stereo)*

- SXL 2234
- SDD 286
- AKF 4
- SPA 531
- SDDM 433
- SPA 566   ★ 475 6411-9DM

oo KSDC 286
oo KCSP 566
oo KCSP 531
oo 421 175-4DC
oo 160 K2

KF 243 *He was despised (Re-created Stereo)*
◇ SEC 5099
- SXL 2234
- SDD 286
- AKF 4
- SPA 531
- SPA 448   ★ 475 6411-9DM

oo KSDC 286
oo KCSP 448
oo KCSP 531
oo 411 887-4DN
oo 414 048-4DN
oo 160 K2

KF 244 *Return, O God of Hosts (Re-created Stereo)*

- SXL 2234
- SDD 286
- AKF 4
- SPA 531   ★ 475 6411-9DM

oo KSDC 286
oo KCSP 531
oo 106 K2

KF 246-248
Discovery
Three Songs
Three Psalms
- 6BB 198

★ 475 6060 DC10
★ 430 061-2LM   oo 430 061-4LM
★ 433 472-2DM   oo 433 472-4DM

★ 433 472-2LM
★ 33472

KF 248 *Three Psalms*

★ 470 195-2

235

Selected Bibliography

Books with special references to the commercial recordings and recorded live performances of Kathleen Ferrier:

Blyth, Alan (ed.) (1979) *Opera on Record, Vol. 1,* Hutchinson

Blyth, Alan (ed.) (1983) *Opera on Record, Vol. 2,* Hutchinson

Blyth, Alan (ed.) (1986) *Song on Record, Vol. 1,* Cambridge University Press

Blyth, Alan (ed.) (1988) *Song on Record, Vol. 2,* Cambridge University Press

Blyth, Alan (ed.) (1991) *Choral Music on Record,* Cambridge University Press

Campion, Paul and Runciman, Rosy (1994) *Glyndebourne Recorded,* Julia MacRae

Carpenter, Humphrey (1992) *Benjamin Britten – A biography,* Faber and Faber

Cullingford, Martin (September 2003) *Parting is such sweet sorrow,* article in *Gramophone*

Culshaw, John (1981) *Putting the Record Straight,* Secker and Warburg

Douglas, Nigel (1994) *More Legendary Voices,* André Deutsch

Ferrier, Winifred (1955) *The Life of Kathleen Ferrier,* Hamish Hamilton

Fifield, Christopher (2003) *Klever Kaff – The Letters and Diaries of Kathleen Ferrier,* Boydell and Brewer

Jack, Ian (Winter 2001) *Klever Kaff* in *Granta 76,* pp87-133

Kennedy, Michael (2003) *Barbirolli: Conductor Laureate,* (revised edition) The Barbirolli Society

Leonard, Maurice (1988) *Kathleen,* Hutchinson

Lucas, John (1993) *Reggie – The Life of Reginald Goodall,* Julia MacRae

Mailliet Le Penven, Benoit (1997) *La voix de Kathleen Ferrier,* Balland.

Sanders, Alan (comp.) (1984) *Walter Legge – A Discography,* Greenwood Press

Spycket, Jérôme (1990) *Kathleen Ferrier,* Payot

Spycket, Jérôme (2003) *La vie brève de Kathleen Ferrier,* Fayard

Steane, John (1974) *The Grand Tradition,* Duckworth

Steane, John (1996) *Singers of the Century Vol. 1,* Duckworth

Wake-Walker, Jenni (compiler) (1997) *Time and Concord: Aldeburgh Festival Recollections,* Autograph Books

Indexes
Recordings by Composer

Note: the reference numbers given below are *KF numbers*, as shown in the main text and discography, not page numbers.

General Index

Albert Hall, Manchester, 105, 106, 133; *for Albert Hall, London, see Royal Albert Hall*
Alexander, Sylvia, 194
Alsop, Ada, 70, 71
Anderson, Helen, 193, 196
Andreas, Bengt, 95
Ansermet, Ernest, 32, 35
Anthony, Trevor, 70, 71
Ayars, Ann, 34, 36, 38, 41, 115, 116, 191

Bach, Johann Sebastian, 17, 18, 42, 43, 101, 102, 103, 108, 109, 111, 112, 116, 117, 118, 119, 121, 141, 142, 173, 174, 175, 176, 177, 185, 187, 189
Baillie, Isobel, 4, 5, 11, 12, 13, 14, 57, 58, 80, 104
Baker, Janet, 158, 196
Bannister, Arthur, 103, 104, 105, 188
Barbirolli, Evelyn (Evelyn Rothwell), 106, 146, 194, 196
Barbirolli, John, 46, 68, 97, 105, 106, 128, 132, 133, 134, 145, 146, 147, 156, 157, 158, 169, 176, 177, 181, 188, 193, 195, 196
Barbirolli Society, 145, 147
Bardgett, Herbert, 145, 146
Barker, Tom, 193
Barnes, Maurice, 59
Bates, Cuthbert, 47
Bax, Arnold, 188
BBC Concert Hall, Broadcasting House, London, 106, 108, 141, 153, 154, 167, 168
BBC Maida Vale Studios, London, 14, 15, 55, 59, 60, 65, 66, 69, 70, 108, 151, 155, 172, 173, 181, 183, 184
BBC Studio, Edinburgh, 91, 143
Beard, Paul, 14
Beardsley, Roger, 31, 105
Beecham, Thomas, 36, 46, 57
Beethoven, Ludwig van, 57, 58, 176, 187
Beinum, Eduard van, 85, 86, 169
Benson, Arthur (A C), 145, 147
Berkeley, Freda, 66, 68
Berkeley, Lennox, 66, 67, 68, 69, 96, 105, 155, 156, 189
Berkeley, Michael, 66, 68, 155
Berry, Walter, 116, 118
Bicknell, David, 31, 46

Bing, Rudolf, 26, 31, 32, 38, 39, 51, 63
Bliss, Arthur, 155
Blyth, Alan, 50, 143, 170, 196
Bolton, Edith, 193
Boult, Adrian, 16, 59, 60, 142, 174, 175, 176, 177, 178
Boyce, Bruce, 42, 43, 50, 141, 142
Boyce, William, 188
Brahms, Johannes, 3, 4, 5, 10, 18, 33, 52, 54, 60, 61, 69, 72, 77, 81, 82, 83, 88, 89, 90, 91, 95, 96, 97, 100, 106, 107, 109, 110, 111, 112, 124, 126, 127, 129, 143, 144, 145, 153, 154, 169, 170, 185, 186, 187, 189, 195
Brannigan, Owen, 24, 25, 29, 30
Bridge, Frank, 167, 168
Britten, Benjamin, 16, 20, 23, 24, 25, 26, 27, 28, 29, 31, 85, 86, 87, 100, 114, 151, 152, 153, 168, 185, 186, 187, 188, 193, 194, 196
Broughton, Sarah, 196
Bruck, Charles, 135, 136
Bruckner, Anton, 57
Burnside, Ian, 194
Busch, Fritz, 95, 96
Butt, Clara, 147
Byrd, William, 188

Caniell, Richard, 120, 122
Caplat, Moran, 63
Carey, Henry, 188
Carnegie Hall, New York, 57, 63
Carpenter, Humphrey, 194
CBC Studio, Montreal, 114
Cellini, Renato, 36, 38
Chadwick, Annie, 193, 196
Chausson, Ernest, 114, 132, 133, 134, 157
Christie, George, 196
Christie, John, 35, 40, 51
Christoff, Boris, 122
Clarke, Arthur, 14
Clinton, Gordon, 43, 48, 50
Coates, Albert, 14, 15
Codner, Maurice, 134
Concertgebouw, Amsterdam, 85, 86, 138, 139
Cook, Christopher, 194
Cooper, Stella, 193
Coote, Alice, 194
Cosens, Ian, 134

241